UNCLE SAM
CAN'T COUNT

Burton W. Folsom Jr.

UNCLE SAM CAN'T COUNT

A History of Failed Government Investments,
from Beaver Pelts to Green Energy

BURTON W. FOLSOM JR.
and ANITA FOLSOM

BROADSIDE BOOKS
An Imprint of HarperCollins*Publishers*
www.broadsidebooks.net

HarperCollins books may be purchased for educational, business, or sales promotional use. For information, please e-mail the Special Markets Department at SPsales@harpercollins.com.

Broadside Books™ and the Broadside logo are trademarks of HarperCollins Publishers.

FIRST EDITION

Designed by Sunil Manchikanti

Library of Congress Cataloging-in-Publication Data has been applied for.

ISBN 978-0-06-229269-8

14 15 16 17 18   OV/RRD   10 9 8 7 6 5 4 3 2 1

To Adam,
our favorite entrepreneur

Contents

UNCLE SAM CAN'T COUNT

Introduction

Entrepreneurs are a different breed. They think differently from others. They envision new products not yet invented. They see companies not yet built, providing products that benefit mankind. Society must value its entrepreneurs, or miss the advantages they provide. As Steve Jobs said,

> Here's to the crazy ones—the misfits, the rebels, the troublemakers, the round pegs in the square holes. The ones who see things differently—they're not fond of rules. You can quote them, disagree with them, glorify or vilify them, but the only thing you can't do is ignore them because they change things. They push the human race forward, and while some may see them as the crazy ones, we see them as genius because the ones who are crazy enough to think that they can change the world, are the ones who do.[1]

Steve Jobs and his partner Steve Wozniak believed that they could make a computer small enough, simple enough, and so efficient that every American would want one. What began in the 1970s with a handful of computer geeks working in the Jobs family's garage became the Apple Computer Company—or Apple Computer, Inc—and the world changed.

Other Americans prefer to change the world by using force. While entrepreneurs try to give us what we want—sometimes before we know we want it—other Americans want to force on us what they want, because they believe they know what's best for all. President Obama laid out his plan in his first inaugural address. He wanted government control of three segments of American society: education, health care, and energy production. He has followed that plan. The government now controls student loans to college students. National health care is becoming a reality. And Obama's administration has chosen to subsidize alternative energy sources while limiting drilling in the Gulf of Mexico, halting pipelines across the United States, and refusing to expand refineries.

President Obama has little faith in free enterprise but much confidence in government. "You didn't build that" was his famous statement in a 2012 speech about businessmen, implying that the government had provided the means for their success. To President Obama, the services offered by government are more essential than the work of the individual. "Somebody invested in roads or bridges," President Obama argued. "If you've got a business—*you didn't build that*. Somebody else made that happen." In other words, if government builds the roads, and merchants use them to do business, then government is the real prime mover in economic development.[2]

The contrasting attitudes of Steve Jobs and Barack Obama toward achievement and progress run throughout American history. Steve Jobs, for example, reflects the ideas of many of the Founders. Our Founding Fathers considered the rights of the individual as bedrock to the health of the nation. Personal accountability was the duty of each citizen. And the Founders were determined to set up a society where, in an atmosphere of freedom, those citizens could work, save, provide for their families, and enjoy the fruits of their labors. The Founders had confidence in the individual American.

Faith in the American citizen doesn't mean that such freedom provides a perfect society. What it does provide is freedom of opportunity. Entrepreneurs can develop their new ideas in such an atmosphere, but often there are many bumps along the way. The story of Apple computers and Steve Jobs wasn't always a smooth road. Even after his early success, Jobs continued to use millions of dollars in profits for new designs and concepts. By 1985 he had so angered his board of directors and stockholders that they ousted him from the company. What did he do? He joined the team at Pixar and changed the way animated movies were made. *Toy Story* was Pixar's first success, with Jobs credited as an executive producer. Disney eventually bought Pixar for more than $7 billion, and Steve Jobs became the largest shareholder of Disney stock. But Jobs's work with Apple wasn't finished, either. When Apple ran into problems in the mid-1990s, Jobs was invited back into the company, and the iPod, iPad, and iPhone were the result.[3]

Entrepreneurs succeeded in past generations in the same pattern as shown in the life of Steve Jobs. They took their ideas, and with practical experience and hard work, marketed their new products. They often angered their competitors and even their own investors. Many times they failed. But something inside entrepreneurs always drives them to try again, to succeed, to show the world that their ideas *work*.

We call them *market entrepreneurs*, because they rely on private enterprise and free markets to develop their products and make a profit. Market entrepreneurs realize that they must give others something—a service, a product, a new means of transportation—and in doing that, they succeed and their society improves. American history is full of market entrepreneurs who have changed lives for the better.[4]

President Obama does not believe these entrepreneurs really built America. Government leaders "invested in roads or bridges," and that's where economic development really started. Many Americans share this faith. They believe that spending federal money is the best way to jump-start the economy and spread prosperity. Since the founding of the United States, some Americans have sought and received federal funds to start new enterprises. Many of them have expertly lobbied Congress to get appropriations. We call them *political entrepreneurs*.

From the first days of the Republic, market entrepreneurs have clashed with political entrepreneurs. That battle is virtually unknown, but it was a fight for the heart and soul of America. Its outcome determined the place of the United States in world history.

Two hundred years ago, many Founders, like President Obama today, did not believe entrepreneurs had the capability to "build that" without government to start the process. After the Louisiana Purchase, for example, President Thomas Jefferson supported the first federal road project. Although Jefferson feared big government, even he fell into the trap of believing that government was needed to launch settlement into the new territory west of the Mississippi. In 1806 Congress voted to fund part of what became the National Road, and Jefferson signed the bill. Constitutional arguments were important in this debate. Those who favored the road argued that it was useful for national defense and also as a "post road" for mail delivery, which made funding the project consistent with Article 1, Section 8 of the Constitution.[5]

When construction began, however, the route for the National Road became a political bonanza for enterprising politicians. Eventually it stretched from Cumberland, Maryland, to Vandalia, Illinois, but as it was built, the road began to twist and curve into towns based on political decisions. Congressmen with political pull tried to draw the road to their districts, whether that route made economic sense or not.

From Cumberland, Maryland, to Wheeling, (West) Virginia, for example, the road detoured through Uniontown and Washington, Pennsylvania. Why? Because Jefferson's Treasury secretary, Albert Gallatin, lived in Uniontown, and he persuaded Jefferson to swing the road there. Gallatin also urged Jefferson to run the road on a northern detour into vote-rich Washington County during an election year. "The county of Washington," Gallatin wrote Jefferson, "with which I am well acquainted, having represented it for six years in Congress, gives a uniform majority of about 2000 votes in our favor and that if this be thrown, by reason of this road, in a wrong scale, we will infallibly lose the state of Pennsylvania in the next election." Jefferson responded curtly that "a few towns in that quarter [of Pennsylvania] seem to consider all this expense as undertaken merely for their benefit." But he still sanctioned Gallatin's detours.[6]

Because the road was a government project, no one had an incentive to keep costs down. The National Road was built with stone (crushed and solid), and it became one of the most expensive roads, if not the most expensive, in the United States in the early 1800s. For example, the privately funded Lancaster Turnpike, also built with stone, cost $7,500 per mile—versus $13,000 per mile for the National Road. The builders of the Lancaster Turnpike were spending their own money and had to spend it wisely, or else the tolls wouldn't cover their expenses. Those in charge of the National Road, by contrast, were political appointees, described by one newspaper editor as being "as numerous as the locusts of Egypt." Funded with taxpayer dollars, the National Road never charged tolls and never made a profit.[7]

At the same time, because no one individual owned the National Road, no one had a strong stake in building it well, or preserving it once it was finished. Almost every firsthand account describes the road's shoddy construction. Even in its heyday it was never fully paved; it always had gaps and always needed repairing.[8]

For example, Lieutenant Henry Brewerton of the Corps of Engineers inspected the road in Ohio and found inferior mortar and materials in its construction and tree stumps scattered throughout. Brewerton echoed those who claimed the road fell into disrepair faster than it could be built. Western travelers moaned constantly about the bumpy rides, the steep grades, and the mudslides. David Shriver, the superintendent of the road, complained that travelers stole bridge walls, milestones, and building materials. Lucius Stockton, who traveled the whole of the road and tried to run a passenger service on it, said, "Generally speaking the surface is entirely destroyed, or sunk under the foundation. . . . In one place the foundation itself has been carried away."[9]

R. J. Meigs, the U.S. postmaster general in the 1820s, found the road almost impassable and the mail, therefore, almost undeliverable. Many merchants along the road, in fact, had to hire private couriers to make sure their mail arrived on time.[10]

How ironic! Using the National Road as a federal post road was the key to making it constitutional—yet privatized mail service regularly outperformed the U.S. Post Office. In desperation, the Post Office added "express mail" service to try to compete with private couriers on the road, but even that often proved to be slower and more irregular than the private couriers. Angry residents along the road sent express-mail letters postage-due to congressmen complaining about the poor service. Reeling from an avalanche of hostile letters, the postmaster general instructed all postmasters not to deliver any express mail postage-due to "the President or any head of department."[11]

By the 1830s, therefore, many congressmen were having second thoughts about using federal funds for the National Road. Some of them, like John Campbell of South Carolina, asked, "Who can suppose that the opening of roads by the government is necessary to attract the farmer to the virgin soil of the West?" Other roads, built by the states or by entrepreneurs, also brought immigrants westward. These roads were clearly constitutional and needed no federal tax dollars to operate.[12]

As a solution to the problems it had created, the federal government, in the 1830s, began giving sections of the National Road to the states. Pennsylvania and Maryland, however, refused to accept their roadways even as gifts, until they were repaired and made more usable for travel. By 1840, railroads had emerged, and the National Road, even the serviceable parts, was becoming obsolete. After almost seven hundred miles and $7 million in construction costs, the National Road had done little to encourage settlement. By 1850, it wasn't much used, and soon after that was almost abandoned.[13]

When government "built that," a failed National Road was the result. But what would happen when government controlled and operated a major invention in the public's interest? If government couldn't "build that" or "invent that," perhaps government could at least run a new industry for the good of the nation. The United States tried to do this in the 1840s with the newly invented telegraph, one of the greatest inventions in American history.

With the telegraph, man could at last communicate over long distances at amazing speeds. Gone were the days of messengers only on foot, on horseback, or on ships. The era of instant communication had begun, and the telegraph—just like the Internet today—would change the world. Even with such an amazing leap forward, and with the example of the National Road before them, the children of the Founders in the 1840s still looked to government, rather than American ingenuity, for the capital and brain power to launch this spectacular invention.

The story of the telegraph began in the early 1800s, when many scientists became aware that electrical impulses could be transmitted along miles of metal wire. Samuel F. B. Morse, a painter and college professor, was the first to put that knowledge to use. Morse invented the electromagnetic telegraph by 1837. He could communicate over a wire by a system of dots and dashes he invented and called Morse Code. He patented his invention, but he was no businessman and knew little about how to raise money to put it into operation.[14]

Frustrated, Morse asked for and received thirty thousand dollars from the federal government in 1843 to string forty miles of telegraph wire from Washington, D.C., to Baltimore. At first, Morse tried to lay the wire underground in a protected sheath. When that proved too expensive, Ezra Cornell, his major contractor, began stringing the wire aboveground on wooden poles stuck into the ground.[15]

In Morse's dealings with the government, he quickly became disenchanted. His first problem was Representative Francis Smith (D-Maine), who said he would use his influence against the Morse subsidy unless Morse gave the congressman a one-fourth stake in the company. Morse complied. Then, when Morse received his federal subsidy, some people like Cave Johnson, the postmaster general, argued that the use of the telegraph, "so powerful for good or evil, cannot with safety to the people be left in the hands of private individuals uncontrolled by law." Even Morse agreed: Government should operate the telegraph in "the national interest."[16]

But the government steadily lost money each month it operated the telegraph. During 1845, expenditures for the telegraph exceeded revenue by six-to-one and sometimes by ten-to-one each month. Washington bureaucrats couldn't figure out how to market the new invention and couldn't imagine how it would be used. Therefore, in 1846, Congress officially turned the telegraph business over to private enterprise and invited entrepreneurs to take the risks and figure out how to use this new invention.[17]

The bureaucrats in Washington had scratched their heads over what to do with the telegraph, but the entrepreneurs had dozens of ideas for using Morse's fabulous invention. Telegraph promoters showed the press how it could instantly report stories occurring hundreds of miles away. Bankers and stockbrokers saw how they could live in Philadelphia and invest daily in New York. Steamship companies used the telegraph to report on business and weather conditions long distance. Even policemen used the telegraph to catch escaped criminals. The telegraph business expanded dramatically.[18]

As the quality of service improved, telegraph lines were strung all over the settled portions of the country. Unlike the National Road, which often went where people weren't, the telegraph went where people were. Ezra Cornell helped found Western Union, which became the major telegraph company, and Western Union and other companies increased telegraph miles from 40 in 1846 to 23,000 in 1852. By the 1860s, the United States had a transcontinental telegraph wire—New Yorkers could buy and sell in San Francisco—and by the end of that decade entrepreneurs had strung a telegraph wire across the Atlantic Ocean.[19] Such connections with the outside world must have been even more startling to Americans of the mid-1800s than radio, television, and email were to later generations.

Why couldn't Congress "build that" or even "run that"? Why was Uncle Sam so inept with such a fabulous invention? Part of the answer is that the incentives for bureaucrats differ sharply from those in place for entrepreneurs. When government operated the first telegraph, Washington bureaucrats received no profits from the messages they sent on the wire. And the cash they lost each month was not their own, but merely the money of taxpayers. Therefore, officials had no incentive to improve service on the telegraph, find new customers, or expand it to more cities.

When Congress privatized the telegraph, Ezra Cornell and other market entrepreneurs had strong incentives to find new customers, give them good service, and string wires across the country. The cheaper and better they could do this, the more business they could attract. Just fifteen years after Congress privatized the telegraph, both the costs of construction and the rates for service linking the major cities were as little as one-tenth of the original rates established by Washington.[20] The telegraph only became a reality to Americans because entrepreneurs made it happen.

We can see in the story of the National Road and the telegraph the struggle as Americans discovered the bizarre impact of government subsidies. Is federal aid a curse, not a blessing? That possibility, so strange yet so true, is so unexpected that most historians have missed it. Many of the great industries in U.S. history—from the fur trade to steamships, railroads, chemicals, and airplanes—have started with government subsidies to political entrepreneurs and ended with the triumph of market entrepreneurs. Americans need to know this remarkable story.

If the market meets our needs better, why do political entrepreneurs dominate so much of the discussion today? The answer is Franklin Roosevelt, our thirty-second president. Before FDR, government intervention was infrequent and subsidies uncommon. Private charity cared for the needy. But Roosevelt used the economic problems of the Great Depression to reset the parameters of government. Through his Fireside Chats on radio, he convinced most Americans that government programs were beneficial, "modern," and necessary. The government should care for the poor through social programs. The government should actively direct the American economy. Roosevelt described his plan as "a partnership between Government and farming and industry and transportation, . . . a partnership in planning and partnership to see that the plans are carried out." The government was benevolent, leading its populace to the greater good for all—that was Roosevelt's message.[21]

Roosevelt also declared "war" on businessmen and industrialists. Those "rulers of the exchange of mankind's goods have failed," Roosevelt said, "through their own stubbornness and their own incompetence. . . . Practices of the unscrupulous moneychangers stand indicted in the court of public opinion, rejected by the hearts and minds of men." Only government, not entrepreneurs, could restore prosperity and do so in the public interest. Businessmen,

Roosevelt declared, "know only the rules of a generation of self-seekers. They have no vision."[22]

If not businessmen, then who did have a vision for society? "Government," answered Franklin Roosevelt. FDR portrayed himself as standing up for the common man against the greedy industrialists and bankers—he and his government would protect the public, despite opposition from believers in free enterprise. "Never before in all our history have these forces been so united against one candidate as they stand today," said Roosevelt. "They are unanimous in their hate for me—and I welcome their hatred."[23]

Until FDR's presidency, being successful in business was considered commendable, but something changed during FDR's first two terms. Those who felt a call to succeed in business, to innovate, to be entrepreneurs—their motives were under suspicion. Roosevelt accused them of selfishness, of seeking only what they wanted instead of the good of the entire population. FDR wanted a society where the profits of businesses and individuals went primarily to the government, where government "experts" would disperse these national resources where they chose.

The crisis of World War II finally caused FDR to soften his attack on businessmen, but the war empowered politicians and government bureaucrats to run the economy. Federal subsidies exploded in every sector of society, from transportation to food production to armaments to medicine. The Reconstruction Finance Corporation (RFC), which we discuss in this book, was created under President Herbert Hoover and expanded under Roosevelt to dole out subsidies, independently of Congress, to whatever groups the RFC officials chose. And many ordinary Americans became more comfortable with the new era of big government.[24]

Throughout Roosevelt's administration, the political left applauded the concept of the government as society's economic manager. FDR believed that "experts" could indeed "build that" and run society better than free markets ever could. Many New Deal programs first began in the minds of college professors who had never worked in the private sector but were thrilled at the prospect of being the experts who ran society.[25]

President Obama has moved far beyond FDR. The financial center of the United States is no longer New York City, but Washington, D.C. And K Street, the home of lobbyists, is where government subsidies are divided and disbursed. Obama's cabinet members aren't trained in business, but in academe or government offices. Such a lack of business experience is easy to spot. In 2009, President Obama's $700 billion stimulus package was supposed to promote "shovel-ready jobs" across the country, but that never happened. Instead, states often used the money for their bureaucracies already in place. On energy, President Obama has funded political entrepreneurs who make green energy and stifled market entrepreneurs who drill for oil. But if we look at history, is that the best direction to follow for lifting Americans out of poverty and into prosperity and freedom? When President Jimmy Carter did the same thing in the 1970s, he helped to create the energy crisis.

Market entrepreneurs have clashed head-to-head with political entrepreneurs since the ink dried on the U.S. Constitution in 1787. Looking at the facts of that struggle will give Americans a clear sense of what works and what doesn't. This book is a road map of that story.

1

Beaver Pelts, Big Government, and John Jacob Astor

Beaver pelts were one of the first targets of government subsidies in the United States. Buying and selling furs was a major industry throughout early American society, and the key animal in the fur trade was the beaver. Beaver pelts were in demand for hats that were in style all over Europe in the 1700s. Trading furs was a worldwide enterprise, linking fashionable men and women in Paris to New York exporters who bought pelts from frontier traders who bargained with Indian trappers. The pelts of beavers, muskrats, otters, and minks went one way to become hats, coats, and rugs. Kettles, blankets, axes, and muskets went the other way to pay Indians for their trapping skills.[1]

At first, fur trading in the United States followed established patterns. The French and British had traded with the Indians for centuries, and the Americans simply picked up where they left off. Trapping methods, river routes, and trading posts were all in place.[2]

The man who confounded the normal development of private enterprise in furs was none other than President George Washington. Washington grew up in an era of mercantilism: Governments would freely grant monopolies to gain certain political and economic advantages. Adam Smith, of course, challenged this kind of thinking in 1776 in *The Wealth of Nations*, but ideas take time to percolate. Washington analyzed the British fur trade in the Michigan area (then called the Northwest Territory), and he considered British interference a menace to America's future. British agents might stir up the Indians, win their loyalties, and thwart U.S. expansion.[3]

Private American traders, Washington argued, were too few in number to compete with the larger, more experienced British. The U.S. government itself was needed to build large trading posts, oust the British, "bring in a small profit, . . . and fix them [the Indians] strongly in our Interest." The Indians especially needed to see evidence of American strength, so Washington recommended that the government build and operate a series of fur factories throughout the Northwest Territory (modern-day Ohio, Indiana, Illinois, Michigan, and Wisconsin) and the American South. With Washington's support, Congress appropriated $50,000 for the new factories in 1795, and raised it steadily in later years to $300,000.[4] Such a subsidy was a large expense for a new nation, and one that tested government's ability to succeed in business.

Here is how the factory system worked. The government created a bureaucracy—the Office of Indian Affairs—to conduct the fur trade. It used the $300,000 from Congress to set up trading posts (usually near military forts), stock them with goods, and pay American agents to buy, store, and transfer furs from the trading post to Washington, D.C., where they would be sold at auction. Once the factories were funded, they were supposed to be self-supporting, and perhaps, as Washington said, "bring in a small profit." Agents in the factories would use the first batch of goods to buy furs; then, when the furs were sold, the agents could buy more goods and repeat the cycle.[5]

Almost from the start, however, the factory system struggled. Well into the 1800s, British companies were trading actively throughout the Great Lakes area. So were private American traders. The factories were so poorly run that many Indians held them in contempt and refused to trade there. In 1816, President James Monroe appointed Thomas McKenney, a Washington merchant, to take charge of the Office of Indian Affairs and help the factories expand their business.[6]

Tall, with fiery red hair and a hook nose, McKenney worked hard and took his job seriously. He wrote long letters to Indians, invited them to Washington, and tried to expand his staff so he could deal with them more directly. Indians needed to be assimilated into American life, McKenney argued. Schools and farms, not trapping and hunting, were McKenney's vision for future Indian life. And he believed that an active government was the best way to trade with the Indians and help them assimilate into American culture.[7]

As chief officer of the government fur trade, McKenney put his stamp on the business in many ways. First, he tried to slash costs by limiting credit and gifts—some called them bribes—to the Indians. Giving gifts had long been a custom in the fur trade, and many Indians also requested credit for supplies for trapping. Both trends, to McKenney, were expensive and risky, and he stopped them when he could.

Second, McKenney tried to "buy American" for the factories when possible. Indians, for example, needed muskets. McKenney rejected English imports and gave large contracts to Henry Deringer, which helped Deringer's Pennsylvania gun factory become a major weapons producer.

Third, McKenney so much wanted Indians to become farmers that he stocked the factories with hoes, plows, and other farm equipment. It was part of his campaign to "amend the heads and hearts of the Indian." He urged agents at the factories to have gardens outside their walls to show the Indians what they could grow if they would just exchange their pelts for plows.[8]

McKenney's ideas were a disaster. Indians wanted gifts, needed credit, and shunned plows. But since McKenney was funded regularly each year by government, regardless of his volume of trade, he had no incentive to change his tactics.[9] Private traders, however, had to please Indians or go broke. As private traders grew in numbers and dealt successfully with the Indians, an immigrant named John Jacob Astor joined their ranks, learned the business, and began to prosper.

Astor, the son of a German butcher, came to the United States in 1784 at age twenty to join his brother in selling violins and flutes. Soon, however, he changed his tune. He became fascinated with the fur trade and studied it day and night. He learned prices, markets, and trade routes for all kinds of pelts. The fur territory of New York and Montreal became Astor's initial trading domain. He bought and sold cautiously at first, then with more confidence as the profits rolled in.[10]

He was an odd man to be such a risk taker. Quiet and almost secretive in his business dealings, Astor had a keen mind for enterprise. But he spent years at a time out of the United States, estranged from his wife, and fighting bouts of depression. At the same time, he had a vision of how America would grow, how the fur trade fit into that growth, and how to market furs around the world.[11]

Astor distinguished himself from others through his foresight and perseverance. If the matrons of France wanted beaver hats and otter coats, and if these animals roamed the forests of New York, then that was all most traders cared to know. Astor, however, thought more of world trade. Europeans liked to fight each other; wars disrupted markets; why not expand and sell furs to the Chinese—not for fashion, but for warmth in their unheated houses? Besides, he could bring the tea back from China and profit at both ends.[12]

The large market of the Far East prompted Astor to turn his sights west to Michigan. New York and the Atlantic coast were depleted of furs by the early 1800s. The Great Lakes area—especially the Michigan Territory—then became the heart of the fur trade and pumped out thousands of skins for coats and rugs all over the world. Astor founded the American Fur Company in 1808 and made his move to challenge the government factories.[13]

Under Astor, the American Fur Company resembled a modern corporation with specialists, division of labor, and vertical integration. He ran the company from his headquarters in New York. Mackinac Island, in the Michigan Territory, was the center of the actual trading where most furs were bought, packed on boats, and sent over to the east coast. Astor's agents dotted the rivers throughout the Northwest Territory, and they had log cabins well stocked with goods. They supplied the company's fur traders, who would live with the different Indian tribes and supply them with goods and credit as needed.[14]

In conducting business this way, Astor differed from McKenney and the government factories. McKenney and his predecessors just built trading posts, stocked them with goods, and expected the Indians to come there to trade. Many Indians, however, lived hundreds of miles from a factory and had no supplies for trapping. Even if McKenney had given credit easily and had known whom to trust, the Indians would have been hampered by distances. Under Astor's system, the fur traders lived with the Indians, learned whom to trust, and bought and sold on the spot. If an Ottawa brave capsized his canoe and lost his musket and powder, he could get replacements from Astor's local trader and avoid the ninety-mile walk through swirling snow to see if the government agent in Detroit would give him replacements on credit.[15]

Astor built on this advantage by trading the best supplies he could find at reasonable rates of exchange. Indians wanted guns and blankets, and Astor supplied them at low cost. The best blankets he could find were British-made blue-striped blankets, and Astor bought them at 15 percent less than McKenney paid for lower-quality blankets made in America. Astor bought British-made Tower muskets, the best on the market, for about $10 apiece, but McKenney paid $12.50 each for Henry Deringer's muskets made in Philadelphia.[16]

One reason Astor excelled was that he accepted the Indians as they were, not as he wanted them to be. If they desired axes, kettles, and muskets, he tried to find the best available and sell to them at competitive prices. He respected Indians as shrewd traders and knew he had to have the best goods to get the most business. Mc-Kenney, as we have seen, squandered government resources on hoes and plows that went unsold. He also bought Jew's harps by the gross, and they sat on the shelves gathering dust. One time McKenney splurged and bought a Chinese Mandarin dress, which he sent to the Osage factory along with a note admitting it would be hard to sell.[17]

McKenney was frustrated with Indian culture and wanted to change it. He refused to sell liquor in government factories and urged Indians to be sober, virtuous, and industrious. "The same devotion to the chase, and those irregular habits which have characterized the sons of our forests yet predominate," he lamented.[18]

Liquor was also an item Astor preferred not to supply, even though he knew many Indians wanted it. Not that Astor was a moralist; he was a realist. Drunken trappers gathered no pelts, he discovered. If the factories had been his only competition he probably wouldn't have traded liquor at all. But the traders with Britain's Hudson's Bay Company carried so much liquor they could almost have created another Great Lake. Astor believed that to be competitive he needed to have some liquor available for trade. Ramsay Crooks, Astor's chief administrator, stated company policy this way: "If the Government permit[s] the sale of this pernicious liquid we can have no hesitation in availing ourselves of the privilege, though we are convinced its total prohibition would benefit both the country at large and the natives who are its victims."[19]

Trade was not the only area where Astor outmaneuvered the government factories. Motivating his men was another. He used a merit system to reward his top producers. "As with skins," he said, "for good men we cannot pay too dear & indifferent *ones are at any price too dear.*" Astor paid his chief managers good salaries plus a share of the profits. This guaranteed attention to detail, which Astor needed to stay on top. McKenney and his staff, by contrast, received a standard salary from Congress with no bonuses given in profitable years, and cuts given when trade fell. If McKenney had been on a merit system, he might have been less moved to stock his factories with plows, Jew's harps, and Chinese dresses.[20]

One final area of Astor's genius was his marketing savvy. He sold his furs at auctions all over the world. If he didn't get the prices he wanted in New York, he sent furs to auctions in Montreal, London, Hamburg, St. Petersburg, and Canton. He studied the bidding, searched for trends, and moved quickly when prices changed. Deerskins, Astor once predicted, would go up in price in Hamburg; muskrat would sell higher in St. Petersburg, Philadelphia, and Canton. He acted accordingly and reaped strong profits in each of these cities. Another Astor strategy was this: If he sensed an upward trend in the price of raccoon skins he would alert his agents to collect all they could get. If demand slowed and prices dropped, Astor withdrew his raccoon skins and stored them in New York, Paris, or Canton until prices rose.[21]

McKenney, by contrast, lacked sophistication. He had the furs collected in his factories sent to Washington. Then he sold them at auction in nearby Georgetown for whatever price they would bring. He didn't sell in different cities, nor did he withhold any from the market in bad years. But then again, he had no incentive to study prices, trends, and foreign markets because his salary was constant whether or not he made profits. In any case, even if he had developed insights into markets, Congress might not have approved the risks and costs of storing beaver pelts during depressions, or stockpiling deerskins to send to Hamburg.[22]

Sometime after 1808, John Jacob Astor surpassed the government factories and emerged as the leading exporter of furs in the United States. He widened his lead after the War of 1812. By the 1820s, his American Fur Company employed more than 750 men, not counting the Indians, and collected annual fur harvests of about $500,000, which made it one of the largest companies in America. Many independents also popped up to trade furs. For example, William Ashley in St. Louis, Pierre Menard and Jean-Baptiste Vallé in Illinois, and the Rocky Mountain Fur Company out west all traded furs aggressively. The government system of expecting Indians to come to the factories to trade was proving to be outmoded.[23]

McKenney nervously watched the government's share of the fur trade decline year by year. "Why do the factories lose money?" Congress asked when McKenney came before them each year to renew his subsidy. He was embarrassed by Astor's dominance and perplexed at what to do about it. At one point, he urged his agents, or "factors" as they were called, to stir up Indians against private traders. "[A]ll correct means that may be taken to expel those traders," McKenney wrote, would be "of service to humanity and justice." What these "correct means" were became clearer when he told a factor to impress the Osages "with the belief that such is the design of those traders that [the Indians] must get rid of them; & hope not to be accountable for their own efforts to drive them out." To another factor, he wrote, "I should judge, with your long acquaintance with the Indian tempers, you might upon the most humane and honourable grounds, turn their prejudices against these their enemies [that is, private traders]."[24]

When sabotage failed, McKenney briefly copied Astor's technique of directly trading with the Indians. He sent out "subtraders," people who took government goods from the factories directly to the Indians. He took this step very reluctantly. "It will be necessary for you to use extreme caution in trusting out goods to traders," McKenney wrote one of his factors. "Boats may get upset . . . and even if . . . they should escape being drowned, the tommahawk [*sic*] may put them to rest—and relieve you from the trouble of counting their returns." Nonetheless, he used subtraders in Green Bay and Chicago and reported "an [i]ncrease of factory business." But it didn't last. Astor and the private traders were too shrewd and aggressive for McKenney, and they soon recaptured lost markets.[25]

By 1818, McKenney had reached a dramatic conclusion: The best way to beat Astor was to influence Congress to ban the private fur traders. If this could be done, McKenney could again monopolize the fur trade, sell to the Indians what he wanted them to have, and pursue his dream of amending their heads and hearts. McKenney's chief ally in the House of Representatives was Henry Southard, chairman of the House Committee on Indian Affairs. In a letter to Southard, McKenney argued vigorously for a government monopoly. "I know of no check that could be devised having such a powerful influence as that which this sort of dependence would impose on the Indians," McKenney wrote Southard. "Armies themselves would not be so effectual in regulating the native Inhabitants as would a state of dependence on the Government for their *commercial intercourse*." Sure, McKenney admitted, a monopoly "embraces the idea of compulsion." But "the power over the Indians is covetted [*sic*] only for their good—and also to prevent them from doing harm."[26]

To John C. Calhoun, secretary of war and later vice president, McKenney wrote that the factory system "has its foundation in *benevolence* and *reform*." The private traders, by contrast, wanted only profits. They didn't care about reforming the Indian, McKenney argued, and they even sold him liquor. Calhoun liked McKenney and seems to have been persuaded if not for a monopoly then at least for greater government control. "The trade should," Calhoun wrote, "as far as practicable, be put effectually under the control of the Government, in order that . . . [the Indians] may be protected against the fraud and the violence to which their ignorance and weakness would, without such protection, expose them."[27]

Even with friends in high places, however, McKenney couldn't muster the support in Congress to ban private fur trading. He therefore presented two backup plans. First, the government should increase his subsidy from $300,000 to $500,000. That way he could build eight new factories west of the Mississippi River, which would increase his trade with distant Indians, bring American culture to them, and thereby "serve the great object of humanity."[28]

Second, McKenney wanted to increase the license fees for his competitors. If he couldn't ban private fur traders by law, perhaps he could raise their costs of doing business, and thereby improve the competitive position of the factories. Under existing law, anyone who posted a $1,000 bond could buy a five-dollar license from an Indian agent and trade for two years. McKenney wanted to increase the license fee to $10,000. He argued that hordes of unlicensed traders roamed the West buying furs and selling whiskey. A higher license fee and stiffer penalties, McKenney argued, would slash the number of traders and make them easier to regulate and supervise.[29]

Astor was appalled at McKenney's schemes. Astor was the top fur trader in the country, a man popular with Indians, because he gave them what they wanted, where they wanted it, and when they wanted it. McKenney, by contrast, was failing because he expected Indians to march hundreds of miles to factories to trade for plows they didn't want or muskets they did want but not at McKenney's high prices. Now McKenney was using government to do to his competitors what he could not do to them in the marketplace.[30]

Astor hated to play politics, but he believed he had to be politically shrewd to survive. He wrote to President James Monroe and explained how the American Fur Company helped the U.S. economy. He sent Ramsay Crooks, his chief agent, to Washington to talk with congressmen, and even put some of them on his payroll. Other politicians came to Astor's aid. Governor Ninian Edwards of the Illinois Territory challenged Calhoun: "For my part, I have never been able to discover, and I defy any man to specify, a solitary public advantage that has resulted from it [the factory system] in this country." Governor Lewis Cass of the Michigan Territory told Calhoun that the government factories were "obnoxious and contemptible" to the Indians. "The Government," Cass said, "should never [c]ome into contact with them, but in cases where its [d]ignity, its strength or its liberality will inspire them with respect or fear."[31]

From 1816 to 1822, Congress heard from both sides and had frequent debates on the fur trade. The bill to ban private traders, Astor was pleased to learn, never made it out of the House Committee on Indian Affairs. Neither did the bill to increase McKenney's subsidy to $500,000.[32]

In 1820, however, the Senate passed a bill to force each trader to post a $10,000 bond for the right to trade. The government, through Calhoun and McKenney, would be in charge of issuing licenses, and they had the right to turn down unsuitable applicants. When the bill went to the House, Astor's friends sprang into action. "What is this but giving to the Sec[retar]y at War power to create a Monopoly?" asked William Woodbridge, the Michigan Territory's delegate to Congress. "The plain English is that all our citizens are if possible to be excluded from the Indian trade . . . [and] the . . . Factory Gen[tleme]n are to take it all."[33]

Ramsay Crooks worked overtime in Washington exhorting House members to quash the new license bill. One of the weapons in his arsenal was an eight-page pamphlet he circulated to challenge McKenney's "perversion of facts." The pamphlet excoriated the factory system:

> It never drove a foreign trader from the country; it never ministered
> to the wants, or relieved the necessities of the Indians in the day of

distress; and no instance can be adduced, of its ever composing the differences of contending tribes.[34]

The prospects of another government-licensing bureaucracy must have alarmed Astor. Four years earlier Congress had passed a law requiring all foreigners to be licensed to trade. Before Astor's staff of traders was notified of that law, Major William Puthuff, the federal Indian agent at Mackinac Island, arrested Astor's men as they brought furs to his headquarters on the island. Puthuff used four boats to patrol the island and seized furs from all unlicensed traders—Americans and foreigners alike—throughout the summer in 1816. He further harassed Astor by arbitrarily raising the license fees from five dollars to fifty. Astor finally protested to Calhoun, and Calhoun eventually fired Puthuff. The new licensing bill, like the old one, promised more bureaucrats and fewer traders in the American West.[35]

After a hard-fought debate on licensing, Astor won, and the House refused to act on the Senate's bill. Crooks was ecstatic. "[H]ad Mr. Secretary Calhoun carried his point in getting the proposed law passed," he wrote Astor, "it is no longer concealed that his first step was to license so few traders that the factories were sure of reviving." Without more government help, McKenney was in trouble. His eight factories showed a drop in fur sales from $73,305 in 1816 to $28,482 in 1819. The next year, during the debate on the licensing bill, one of his factors told him that his trade had "almost [e]ntirely ceased."[36]

With McKenney's poor record exposed, Astor took the offensive and urged Congress to abolish the whole factory system. Step one for Astor was to get Congress to see how unpopular the factories were with Indians. Calhoun, McKenney's ally, unwittingly cooperated when, as secretary of war, he helped authorize Jedidiah Morse, a Congregational minister, to go into Indian country and report on the Indian trade. Astor and McKenney had made so many charges and countercharges that Calhoun wanted to get reliable independent information on the issue. He told Morse to "report such facts, as may come within your knowledge, as will go to show the state of the trade with them [the Indians], and the character of the traders, and will suggest such improvements in the present system of trade." Morse was considered a neutral observer and his firsthand report would be the most systematic investigation of the government factories ever done.[37]

Morse visited most of the government factories and interviewed the men who worked in them as well as the private traders nearby. He talked with many tribes of Indians about the fur trade, studied their habits, and recorded their views. He spent almost four months in travel—including twelve days in Detroit and sixteen days on Mackinac Island—and even longer writing up his research.[38]

In his report he came down clearly against the factories. "In the first place," Morse wrote, "I have to observe that the Factory system . . . does not appear to me to be productive of any great advantage, either to the Indians themselves, or to the Government." This conclusion was devastating because it revealed that the factory system had failed to do what Washington had set it up to do—impress the Indians, gain their respect, and challenge the British in the Northwest Territory. Morse further wrote that "the Indians, who are good judges of the quality of the articles they want, are of the opinion that the Factor's goods are not so cheap, taking into consideration their quality, as those of private traders." Even John Johnson, the government's Indian agent at Prairie du Chien, admitted he had received expensive goods from McKenney that were "inferior and unsuitable [in] quality for Indian trade."[39]

Morse was not completely pleased with private traders. They traded too much whiskey, he wrote, and they gave Indians too much on credit, which weakened their work ethic. But he couldn't deny their success, or the "want of confidence in the Government . . . expressed by the Indians in my interviews with them." Abolishing the factories, Morse concluded, was "decidedly the best course, the best adopted to raise and preserve the reputation of the Government in the estimation of Indians, and to secure for it their confidence and respect; the best fitted in all respects to accomplish the great object of imparting to them the blessings of civilization and Christianity."[40]

Armed with the Morse report, Astor's allies in Congress moved to abolish the factories in 1822. Thomas Hart Benton, the new senator from Missouri, had been a lawyer for Astor and knew the fur trade well. On the Senate floor he ridiculed McKenney's purchases, particularly the eight gross (1,152) Jew's harps he had recently sent to the factories. What use, Benton asked, could Indians have for Jew's harps? "I know!" he said sarcastically. "They are part of McKenney's schemes to amend the heads and hearts of the Indians, to improve their moral and intellectual faculties, and to draw them from the savage and hunter state, and induct them into the innocent pursuits of civilized life."[41]

Not surprisingly, Benton urged Congress to end the factory system. "[E]very public consideration," Benton argued, "requires it to be immediately abolished, the accounts of all concerned be settled up and closed, the capital be returned to the public treasury, the salaries of all officers be stopped, and its profit and loss be shown at the next session of Congress." Most congressmen agreed. The Senate voted 17 to 11 to end the factories; the House soon followed; and on May 6, 1822, President Monroe signed Benton's bill.[42]

The closing of the factories was a story in itself. The merchandise inside them was to be collected and sold at auctions around the country. The money received would then be returned to the government to offset the $300,000 federal subsidy. Congress entrusted the Treasury Department, not McKenney, with closing the factories and holding the auctions. In doing their work, the officials in the Treasury were stunned at how unpopular the factory goods were. Lewis Cass, who had a batch sent to him in the Michigan Territory, was appalled at their poor quality. "These goods," Cass said, "were selected I presume, as the worst and most unsaleable in the factories, and certainly they well deserve this character. They are not fit for distribution." Others agreed. The auctions themselves, which became the true test of the market value of the articles in the factories, brought grim news. The government, on its $300,000 investment, received a return of only $56,038.15. As Senator Benton had said, "The factory system grew out of a national calamity, and has been one itself."[43]

Many congressmen were astounded at the waste of government funds revealed by the auctions. If Astor could make millions of dollars trading furs, how could the government lose hundreds of thousands? Critics demanded answers, and Congress formed a committee to investigate why the factories were so unprofitable. Congress sifted through mountains of records and interviewed lines of witnesses. McKenney was on the spot and had to testify, but the committee found no corruption, just "inexplicable" losses. The factory system had simply failed, the committee concluded, but it needed to be studied "not only as a matter of curious history, but for the lesson it teaches to succeeding legislators."[44]

Astor, meanwhile, continued to expand and prosper. New companies entered the fur trade during the 1820s and existing ones continued to challenge Astor. The competition was keen, and Astor's volume of business varied from place to place. In Green Bay, for example, he was a small trader; in Chicago he dominated fur traffic. In the newly settled Great Plains and Rocky Mountains, he often formed partnerships with existing companies. In the Michigan Territory, the Hudson's Bay Company was Astor's ever-present rival. The American Fur Company, however, remained the largest firm in the field after the factories were closed. Astor, better than any American before him, had mastered the complex accounting and organization needed to conduct a worldwide business.[45]

Astor always knew he had to please the Indians to stay on top.

He rarely showed affection for them, but he respected them as suppliers and consumers. Their tastes dictated what he bought; their labor dictated what he sold. Indians were usually shrewd traders, and Astor built his business assuming they would stay that way. Lewis Cass and William Clark, who spent much of their lives working among Indians, made this report to Congress:

> Contrary to the opinion generally entertained, they [the Indians] are good judges of the articles which are offered to them. The trade is not that system of fraud which many suppose. The competition is generally sufficient to reduce the profits to [a] very reasonable amount, and the Indian easily knows the value of the furs in his possession; he knows also the quality of the goods offered to him, and experience has taught him which are best adapted to his wants.[46]

By the late 1820s and into the 1830s, the fur trade began to decline. Astor always knew the trade couldn't flourish forever, because furs were being collected faster than the animals reproduced. More than scarce animals, changing tastes slowed down business. As Astor noted from Paris in 1832, "they make hats of silk in place of Beaver." The Industrial Revolution and the popularity of cheap, mass-produced clothing also shut down markets for furs. "[M]any articles of manufacture which are now very low can be used in place of deer skins & furs," Astor observed in 1823. "[T]hey receive of course the preference."[47]

Just when Astor was wounded by mass production and new fashions, the U.S. government put a tourniquet around his neck. First, to protect the budding American textile industry, Congress passed a tariff on English imports. That meant Astor had to pay more for British woolen blankets, which were prized by the Indians. The Hudson's Bay Company, of course, as a British company, imported the blankets duty-free into Canada and used them in trade against Astor in the Great Lakes area.[48]

Second, Congress shut the faucet on the flow of liquor into Indian territory. Astor would have willingly turned the handle himself if other traders would have agreed to leave it off. But as long as so many Indians wanted whiskey, there would always be American and British traders who would supply it. Astor met with George Simpson from the Hudson's Bay Company to try to work out a mutual agreement to quit trading liquor, but nothing binding was ever worked out.[49]

Third, congressmen evicted his labor supply, or at least rearranged it. In 1830, they voted to remove about one hundred thousand eastern Indians to the Great Plains area. Astor's major depots at Detroit and Mackinac Island lost many of their longtime suppliers as the fur trade moved west.[50]

These three interventions by government badly damaged Astor's fragile position in a competitive market. What must have especially galled him was that a key person behind two of these policies was his old rival, Thomas McKenney. Having been ousted as superintendent of Indian trade in 1822, McKenney resurfaced in government two years later. His old friend John C. Calhoun waited until the furor over the factories died down and then slipped McKenney into the War Department as senior clerk in the bounty land office. Then in March 1824, with congressional approval, Calhoun created the Bureau of Indian Affairs, with almost one hundred employees—agents, interpreters, clerks, and copyists—and Thomas McKenney as superintendent.[51]

As head of the Bureau of Indian Affairs, McKenney continued his program to reform Indian culture. In his letters to the Cherokee, Choctaw, Creek, and others, he often addressed them as "My Children." The government agent was their "Father." McKenney was their "Father in Washington," and the secretary of war was the "Great War Chief." Those who criticized the government were "bad birds." At least one Indian agent complained that these letters weakened his influence. But McKenney believed that "Indians are only children and require to be nursed, and counselled, and directed as such."[52]

McKenney's views of the Indians ran headlong into Astor's plans to employ them in the fur trade. The liquor issue was a major point of dispute. In 1824, Congress passed a law—one McKenney had long advocated—that required government Indian agents, not traders, to choose the places where the fur trade would be conducted. The idea here was that if Indian agents controlled the trading posts they could stop liquor from being traded. McKenney defended the need to keep trade "within the eye of the officers of the Government," but Astor and his staff disagreed. How could they trade furs in the most economical way if government dictated to them where to trade and what not to trade? Robert Stuart, Astor's manager on Mackinac Island, called the law "truly a curiosity unless it originated in the fertile brain of Mr. McKinnie [sic]; but if so, it is perfectly reconcilable with the rest of his blundering absurdities."[53]

The Indian removal plan, which McKenney helped sponsor, was even more damaging to Astor. McKenney argued that new land and a fresh start free of whiskey would help the Indians assimilate into white culture. He called the Indian removal plan "one of the kindest that has ever been perfected." Astor and the Indians dissented; they didn't want to be forced to change their ways of life and business. But McKenney worked hard to help negotiate treaties that sent the Cherokee, Choctaw, and Chippewa, among others, moving westward.[54]

In 1834, three years before Michigan became a state, Astor quit the fur business and sold the American Fur Company. The new silk hats, the factory clothes, and the government restrictions on where he could trade, what he could trade, and where Indians would live all told him it was time to leave. Also, Astor was seventy-one years old and ready for less strenuous work. The same skills that made him America's largest fur trader also made him profits in New York real estate. For many years, he had been buying lots in northern Manhattan, developing the property, and selling it at a profit. This he continued to do. He also invested in the Park Theatre, the Mohawk & Hudson Railroad Company, and the Astor House Hotel. By the time of his death in 1848, he had accumulated America's largest fortune, about $10 million.[55]

The last years of McKenney's life were not so pleasant. President Andrew Jackson fired him as superintendent of Indian affairs, which ended McKenney's career in government. Outside of government, McKenney floundered, and he spent much of the rest of his life trying to get back in. He had no business skills, so he turned to writing and lecturing on American Indians. He published a three-volume *History of the Indian Tribes of North America* and his *Memoirs*, but sold only a few copies. He always had trouble managing money. His wife died; his son became a wastrel; and McKenney lived out of his suitcase, borrowing money and moving from city to city. In 1859 he died, at age seventy-three, destitute, in a Brooklyn boardinghouse.[56]

2

Vanderbilt Goes Upstream
Against the Subsidies

Many children are taught that Robert Fulton was the first American to build and operate a steamboat when his *Clermont* sauntered four miles per hour upstream on the Hudson River in 1807. Fulton, however, was not the first American to put a steam engine on a boat, and when he did succeed, his steamboat was named the *North River*, the nickname that local New Yorkers used for the Hudson River.[1]

The idea of a self-propelled boat going upriver had long fascinated inventors. With the wretched state of roads in all countries of the world, water travel was far easier and often more economical. But how could a boat go upstream? From Leonardo da Vinci to Benjamin Franklin, brilliant thinkers had drawn diagrams and described mechanisms with enough power to fight river currents and free mankind from depending upon the wind or sheer muscle to travel upstream. But no one had been able to build a working motor or engine that would do such a thing. When James Watt set up the first full-sized steam engine in England in 1776, mankind finally had a practical power source that might be harnessed on ships.

Inventors quickly began to adapt steam engines to watercraft, but early steam engines were inefficient and often caused such strong vibrations that boats simply fell apart. The first American to set up an actual steamboat line was John Fitch, described as "a wild-eyed, scruffy genius."[2] Fitch made the unfortunate decision to sail up the Delaware River on a very slow steamboat and try to make a profit at the same time. The banks of the Delaware were flat and the roads along the river good enough that stagecoaches on land actually passed Fitch's boat on its way upstream. Potential passengers also feared explosions of the steam engine itself. Would they be killed or injured if they tried Fitch's wild new invention? Fitch's enterprise soon failed, and he disappeared from history.[3]

Robert Fulton, on the other hand, chose to establish his first steamboat line along the Hudson River. The banks of the Hudson were extremely hilly and almost mountainous north of New York City. Travel by land in that area was difficult at best. The Hudson Valley was also heavily populated, and New Yorkers wanted a convenient method of traveling upstream to Albany, the state capital. And the best reason of all to Fulton, a political entrepreneur, was that his benefactor in New York had great influence in the state legislature.

Fulton had spent almost twenty years in Europe, first in England and then in France. The British had an established tradition of subsidizing all kinds of commercial ventures: shipping, canals, shipbuilding. In England, Fulton tried to get funding from British politicians for his various inventions. Then he moved on to France, where he became an "expert" on the current ideas of how to build a working submarine. He even built an underwater craft, and with two companions, tried to get close enough to British ships in the English Channel to sink one of the vessels and impress French politicians. He lobbied Napoléon Bonaparte for money to develop his submarine and use it against the British navy, but Napoléon declined the offer.[4]

Fulton returned to the United States in December 1806, knowing that Robert Livingston of New York believed in his steamboat project and would back it to the hilt. Livingston was a Founding Father who believed that steamboats would work well on the wide rivers of North America. Livingston and Fulton obtained a monopoly from the New York legislature for the privilege of carrying *all* steamboat traffic in New York for thirty years, if they could produce a working steamboat within two years.[5]

Thus, when Robert Fulton sailed the *North River* up the Hudson River on a hot summer day in August 1807, he had built the first viable steamboat and had just begun the first steamboat line with any measure of success. Fulton opened up new possibilities in transportation, marketing, and city building.

One problem with Fulton's monopoly, however, was that it affected shippers in neighboring states. As steamboats became more common, the Fulton monopoly meant that other companies couldn't sail in New York waters without fear of fines. The monopoly also kept ticket prices high. Finally, in 1817, Thomas Gibbons, a New Jersey steamboat man, tried to crack Fulton's monopoly when he hired young Cornelius Vanderbilt. Gibbons asked Vanderbilt to run steamboats in New York and charge less than the monopoly rates.[6]

Vanderbilt was intrigued by the challenge of breaking the Fulton monopoly. On the mast of Gibbons's ship, Vanderbilt hoisted a flag that read: "New Jersey must be free." For sixty days in 1817, Vanderbilt defied capture as he raced passengers cheaply from Elizabeth, New Jersey, to New York City. He became a popular figure on the Atlantic as he lowered the fares and eluded the law.

Finally, in 1824, in the landmark case of *Gibbons v. Ogden*, the U.S. Supreme Court struck down the Fulton monopoly. Chief Justice John Marshall ruled that only the federal government, not the states, could regulate interstate commerce. This extremely popular decision opened the waters of America to competition. A jubilant Vanderbilt was greeted in New Brunswick, New Jersey, by cannon salutes fired by "citizens desirous of testifying in a public manner their good will." Ecstatic New Yorkers immediately launched two steamboats named for John Marshall. On the Ohio River, steamboat traffic doubled in the first year after *Gibbons v. Ogden* and quadrupled after the second year.[7]

The triumph of free markets in steamboating led to improvements in technology. As one man observed, "The boat builders, freed from the domination of the Fulton-Livingston interests, were quick to develop new ideas that before had no encouragement from capital." These new ideas included tubular boilers to replace the heavy and expensive copper boilers Fulton used. Cordwood for fuel was also a major cost for Fulton, but innovators soon found that anthracite coal worked well under the new tubular boilers, so "the expense of fuel was cut down one-half."[8]

The real value of removing the Fulton monopoly was that the costs of traveling upriver dropped. Passenger traffic, for example, from New York City to Albany immediately dipped from seven to three dollars after *Gibbons v. Ogden*. Fulton's group couldn't meet the new rates and soon went bankrupt. Gibbons and Vanderbilt, meanwhile, adopted the new technology, cut their costs, and earned $40,000 profit each year during the late 1820s.[9]

With such an open environment for market entrepreneurs, Vanderbilt decided to quit his pleasant association with Gibbons, buy two steamboats, and go into business for himself. During the 1830s, Vanderbilt established trade routes all over the Northeast. He offered fast and reliable service at low rates. He first tried the New York to Philadelphia route and forced the "standard" three-dollar fare down to one dollar. On the New Brunswick to New York City run, Vanderbilt charged six cents a trip and provided free meals. As *Niles' Register* said, the "times must be hard indeed when a traveller who wishes to save money cannot afford to walk."[10]

Moving to New York, Vanderbilt decided to compete against the Hudson River Steamboat Association, whose ten ships probably made it the largest steamboat line in America in 1830. It tried to fix prices informally to guarantee regular profits. Vanderbilt challenged it with two boats (which he called the "People's Line") and cut the standard New York to Albany fare from three dollars to one dollar, then to ten cents, and finally to nothing. He figured it cost him two hundred dollars per day to operate his boats; if he could fill them with one hundred passengers, he could take them for free if they would each eat and drink two dollars' worth of food. (Vanderbilt later helped to invent the potato chip.) Even if his passengers didn't eat that much, he was putting enormous pressure on his wealthier competitors.

Finally, the exasperated Steamboat Association literally bought Vanderbilt out: They gave him $100,000 plus $5,000 a year for ten years if he would promise to leave the Hudson River for the next ten years. Vanderbilt accepted, and the association raised the Albany fare back to three dollars. Such bribery may be wrong in theory, but it had little effect in practice. With no barriers to entry, other steamboaters came along and quickly cut the fare. They saw that it could be done for less, and they saw what had happened to Vanderbilt for doing it. So almost immediately Daniel Drew began running steamboats on the Hudson—until the association paid him off, too. At least five other competitors did the same thing until they, too, were bought off. It's hard to figure who got the better deal: those who ran the steamboats and were bought out, or those who traveled the steamboats at the new low rates.[11]

Meanwhile, Vanderbilt took his payoff money and bought bigger and faster ships to trim the fares on New England routes. He started with the New York City to Hartford trip and slashed the five-dollar fare to one dollar. He then knocked the New York City to Providence fare in half from eight to four dollars. When he sliced it to one dollar, the *New York Evening Post* called him "the greatest practical anti-monopolist in the country." In these rate wars, sometimes

Vanderbilt's competitors bought him out, sometimes they went broke, and sometimes they matched his rates and kept going. Some people denounced Vanderbilt for engaging in extortion, blackmail, and cutthroat competition. Today, of course, he would be found "in restraint of trade" by the Sherman Antitrust Act.

Nonetheless, Vanderbilt qualifies as a market entrepreneur: He fought monopolies, he improved steamship technology, and he cut costs. *Harper's Weekly* insisted that Vanderbilt's actions "must be judged by the results; and the results, in every case, of the establishment of opposition lines by Vanderbilt has been the *permanent reduction of fares.*" The editor went on to say, "Wherever [Vanderbilt] 'laid on' an opposition line, the fares were instantly reduced; and however the contest terminated, whether he bought out his opponents, as he often did, or they bought him out, the fares were never again raised to the old standards." Vanderbilt himself later put it bluntly when he said: "If I could not run a steamship alongside of another man and do it as well as he for twenty percent less than it cost him I would leave the ship."[12]

By the 1840s, improving technology changed steamboats into steamships. Larger engines and economies of scale in shipbuilding led to changes in size, speed, and comfort. The new steamers of the midcentury were many times larger and faster than Fulton's *North River.* They were each two decks high with a grand saloon and individual staterooms for first-class passengers. When full, some of these new steamships could hold almost one thousand passengers, and they also had space for mail and freight. These ships were sturdy enough to cross the Atlantic Ocean. The New York to England route was the first to open up the steamship competition; the New York to California line (via Panama) soon followed.[13]

Rapid overseas trade was a new concept, and this reopened the debate for federal aid to eager steamboat operators. Fulton was gone, but others like him argued for government subsidies and contracts.

In 1838, Englishmen were the first to travel the Atlantic Ocean entirely by steam. The open environment was quickly altered when Samuel Cunard, a political entrepreneur, convinced the English government to give him $275,000 a year to run a semi-monthly mail and passenger service across the ocean. Cunard charged $200 per passenger and $.24 a letter; the $.24 for the mail didn't cover the cost of Cunard's shipping, and that's one argument he had for a subsidy. He also contended that subsidized steamships gave England an advantage in world trade and were a readily available merchant marine in case of war. Parliament accepted this argument and increased government aid to the Cunard line throughout the 1840s.[14]

Soon, political entrepreneurs across the ocean began using these same arguments for federal aid to the new American steamship industry. They argued that America needed subsidized steamships to compete with England: first, to show the world American progress and shipbuilding prowess; second, to deliver the mail profitably overseas; and third, to provide a military fleet in case of war.

The man who exploited these three arguments was Edward K. Collins, the operator of the first packet line from New Orleans to New York. For two decades Collins had achieved some success, and this gave him the stature to propose this self-serving plan: If the government would give him $3 million down and $385,000 a year, he would build five ships and outrace the Cunarders from coast to coast. Collins would deliver the mail, too, and Americans would get to "drive the Cunarders off the seas."

Collins appealed to American nationalism, not to economic efficiency: Americans would not be opening up new lines of travel, because the Cunarders had already opened them. Americans would not be delivering mail more often, because the Collins ships, like Cunard's, would sail only every two weeks. Finally, Americans would not be bringing the mail cheaper because the Cunarders could still do it for less.[15]

Once the Senate established the principle of mail subsidy, other political entrepreneurs asked for subsidies to bring the mail to other places. Soon Congress also gave $500,000 a year for two lines to bring mail to California: an Atlantic line to get mail to Panama and a Pacific line to take letters from Panama to California. Cunard, Collins, and the California operators all argued that a generous subsidy now would help them become more efficient and lead to no subsidy later.[16]

Congress gave money to the Collins and California lines in 1847, but the luxurious ships were under construction for years. Collins, especially, had champagne tastes with taxpayers' money. He built four enormous ships (not five smaller ships as he had promised), each with elegant saloons, ladies' drawing rooms, and wedding berths. He covered the ships with plush carpet and brought aboard rose-, satin-, and olive-wood furniture, marble tables, exotic mirrors, flexible barber chairs, and French chefs. The staterooms had painted glass windows and electric bells to call the stewards. Collins stressed luxury, not economy, and his ships used almost twice the coal of the Cunard line. He often beat the Cunarders across the ocean by one day (ten days to eleven), but his costs were high and his economic benefits were nil.[17]

What's more, Collins's four ships were worthless for national defense. The secretary of the navy had an engineer examine Collins's ships, and he found their shape and structure wholly unsuited for war. If the Collins ships were converted for war, the engineer argued, they would be "as disastrous to our national interests as their construction has been to our professional reputation as constructors and engineers."[18]

But with annual government aid, Collins still had no incentive to cut his costs from year to year. To cover his lavish expenses, Collins preferred to compete in the world of politics for more federal aid than in the world of business against price-cutting rivals. So in 1852 he went to Washington and lavishly dined and entertained President Millard Fillmore, his cabinet, and influential congressmen. Collins also hired William W. Corcoran, perhaps the most effective lobbyist—or "borer" as he was then called—in Washington, D.C. Congress eventually voted to increase Collins's subsidy to $858,000 a year (or $33,000 each for twenty-six voyages—which came to $5 per ocean mile) to compete with the Cunarders. Representative John C. Breckinridge of Kentucky said that Collins won the large increase in his subsidy "by the most powerful and determined outside pressure I have ever seen brought to bear upon any legislative body."[19]

Meanwhile, Vanderbilt had been watching this government waste long enough. In 1855 he declared his willingness to deliver the mail for less than Cunard, and for less than half of what Collins was getting. Collins apparently begged Vanderbilt not to go to Congress. He may have offered to help Vanderbilt get an equally large subsidy from Congress—if only he wouldn't compete in the transatlantic steamship trade. But Vanderbilt had told Collins and Congress that he would run an Atlantic ferry for $15,000 per trip, which was cheaper than anyone else's price.[20]

So in 1855, Collins, the subsidized lobbyist, began battle with Vanderbilt, the market entrepreneur. Collins fought the first round in Congress rather than on the sea. Most congressmen, former Whigs especially, backed Collins. To do otherwise would be to admit they had made a mistake in helping him earlier; and this might call into question all federal aid. Other congressmen, especially the New Englanders, had constituents who benefited from Collins's business. Senator William Seward of New York stressed another angle by asking, "Could you accept that proposition of Vanderbilt['s] justly, without, at the same time, taking the Collins steamers and paying for them?" In other words, Seward is saying, "We backed Collins at the start, now we are committed to him, so let's support him no matter what."

Vanderbilt, by contrast, warned that "private enterprise may be driven from any of the legitimate channels of commerce by means of bounties." His point was that it is hard for unsubsidized ships to compete with subsidized ships for mail and passengers. Since the contest is unfair from the start, the subsidized ships have a potential monopoly of all trade. But Collins's lobbying prevailed, so Congress turned Vanderbilt down and kept payments to Collins at $858,000 per year.[21]

President Franklin Pierce, however, dramatically vetoed the Collins subsidy bill on March 3, 1855. He argued that the effect of such a subsidy "would be to deprive commercial enterprise of the benefits of free competition, and to establish a monopoly in violation of the soundest principles of public policy, and of doubtful compatibility with the Constitution." When the president's secretary brought Pierce's veto to Congress, Thomas Hart Benton was elated. Benton had served as the first five-term senator in U.S. history, and had also opposed the government subsidy for the fur trade back in the 1820s. Benton shook the secretary's hand vigorously and said, "Tell the President he has covered himself with glory."[22]

Most congressmen thought otherwise. They attached the full subsidy for Collins to a naval appropriations bill and worked it through Congress that way. "A million dollars a year is a power that will be felt," lamented Senator Robert Toombs of Georgia. "I have seen its influence. I have seen the public treasury plundered by it."[23]

Vanderbilt was so disgusted that he decided to challenge Collins even without a subsidy. "The share of prosperity which has fallen to my lot," said Vanderbilt, "is the direct result of unfettered trade, and unrestrained competition. It is my wish that those who are to come after me shall have that same field open before them." Vanderbilt's strategy against Collins was to charge only $.15 for half-ounce letters and to cut the standard first-class fare $20, to $110. Later he slashed it to $80.

Vanderbilt also introduced a new service: a cheaper third-class fare in steerage. The steerage must have been uncomfortable— people were practically stacked on top of each other—but for seventy-five dollars, and sometimes less, he did get newcomers to travel.[24]

To beat the subsidized Collins, Vanderbilt found creative ways to cut expenses. First, he had little or no insurance on his fleet. He always said that if insurance companies could make money on shipping, so could he. So Vanderbilt built his ships well, hired excellent captains, and saved money on insurance. Second, he spent less than Collins did for repairs and maintenance. Collins's ships cost more than Vanderbilt's, but they were not seaworthy. The engines were too big for the hulls, so the ships vibrated and sometimes leaked. They usually needed days of repairing after each trip. Third, Collins, like Cunard in England, was elitist with his government aid. He cared little for cheap passenger traffic. Vanderbilt, by contrast, hired local "runners," who buttonholed all kinds of people to travel on his ships. These second- and third-class passengers were important because all steamship operators had fixed costs for making each voyage. They had to pay a set amount for coal, crew, maintenance, food, and docking fees. In such a situation, Vanderbilt needed volume business. With third-class fares, Vanderbilt sometimes carried more than five hundred passengers per ship.

Even so, Vanderbilt barely survived the first year competing against Collins. He complained, "It is utterly impossible for a private individual to stand in competition with a line drawing nearly one million dollars per annum from the national treasury, without serious sacrifice." He added that such aid was "inconsistent with the . . . economy and prudence essential to the successful management of any private enterprise."[25]

Vanderbilt met this challenge by spending $600,000 building a new steamship, immodestly named the *Vanderbilt*, "the largest vessel which has ever floated on the Atlantic Ocean." The Commodore built the ship with a beam engine, which was more powerful than Collins's traditional side-lever engines. In a head-to-head race, the *Vanderbilt* beat Collins's ship to England and won the Blue Ribbon, an award given to the one ship owning the fastest time from New York City to Liverpool. By 1856, Collins had two ships—half of his accident-prone fleet—sink (killing almost five hundred passengers). In desperation, he spent more than a million dollars of government money building a gigantic replacement; but he built it so poorly that it could make only two trips and had to be sold at more than a $900,000 loss.[26]

Even Collins's friends in Congress could defend him no longer. Between Collins's obvious mismanagement and Vanderbilt's unsubsidized trips, most congressmen soured on federal subsidies. Senator Judah P. Benjamin of Louisiana said, "I believe [the Collins line] has been most miserably managed." Senator Robert M. T. Hunter of Virginia went further: "The whole system was wrong; . . . it ought to have been left, like any other trade, to competition." Senator John B. Thompson of Kentucky said, "Give neither this line, nor any other line, a subsidy. . . . Let the Collins line die. . . . I want a tabula rasa—the whole thing wiped out, and a new beginning." Congress voted for this "new beginning" in 1858: They revoked Collins's aid and left him to compete with Vanderbilt on an equal basis. The results: Collins quickly went bankrupt, and Vanderbilt became the leading American steamship operator.[27]

And there was yet another twist. When Vanderbilt competed against the English, his major competition did not come from the Cunarders. The new unsubsidized Inman Line was doing to Cunard in England what Vanderbilt had done to Collins in America. The subsidized Cunard had cautiously stuck with traditional technology, while William Inman had gone on to use screw propellers, and iron hulls instead of paddle wheels and wood. It worked, and from 1858 to the Civil War, two market entrepreneurs, Vanderbilt and Inman, led America and England in cheap mail and passenger service.[28]

The mail subsidies, then, actually retarded progress because Cunard and Collins both used their monopolies to stifle innovation and delay technological changes in steamship construction.

Several English steamship companies experimented with iron hulls and screw propellers in the 1840s, but Cunard thwarted this whenever he could. According to twentieth-century economist Royal Meeker,

> The mail payments made it possible for the Cunard company to cling to an out-of-date and uneconomical type of steamer. Both the Admiralty and the Post Office departments refused to permit mail steamers to use the screw propeller until long after other lines had adopted it. . . . Without government aid to inefficiency, the Cunard Company would have been compelled to adopt improvements in order to compete with other and more progressive lines.[29]

Cunard also refused to introduce a third-class rate. So, when William Inman came along in the 1850s with his iron ships and third-class fares, he practically knocked Cunard out of business. After 1850, Inman and other newcomers kept the pressure on Cunard. They experimented with oscillating cabins (to reduce the impact of the swaying of the ship), compound engines (to increase the ship's speed and decrease its fuel consumption), and twin propellers. Cunard's subsidy kept him from having to innovate and protected him from errors of judgment that would have ruined his competitors.[30]

In America, Collins, like Cunard, chose wood and paddle wheels for his ships. Americans were slower to turn to iron ships because their costs of iron construction were higher than those in England. Still, American engineers had been experimenting with iron hulls and screw propellers during the 1840s, partly because iron was more durable in handling the big engines built after 1840. Collins apparently considered using iron, but he was no innovator. So he ended up using wood hulls for his powerful engines, and his ships were not as safe or as seaworthy because of that. With Collins using wood, American steamship operators feared switching to

iron. They had little margin for error because their chief competitor was subsidized. Yet in 1851, Vanderbilt became one of the first
Americans to build and run iron ships (he used them on his California route). But it wasn't until Collins's subsidy expired in 1858 that
Americans began experimenting with iron hulls in a serious way.[31]

Later, this delay in experimenting with iron meant that iron
ships could not be much of a force during the Civil War. John
Ericsson, who in 1862 built the iron-hulled *Monitor,* had been promoting the advantages of iron ships since 1843. But in 1847, when
Collins decided to use wood for his subsidized fleet, only Vanderbilt
dared to risk more experiments with iron hulls. The irony here is
that one of the central arguments for subsidizing Collins was that
his fleet would be usable in case of war. Yet his outmoded wooden
ships—even the ones that didn't sink—would have been helpless
against ironclad opponents. Vanderbilt gave his 5,000-ton ship, the
Vanderbilt, as a permanent gift to the United States during the Civil
War. He even offered to sink the Confederates' *Merrimac,* asking
only that everyone stay "out of the way when I am hunting the
critter." He never got the chance, and, partly because of the Collins
subsidy, the United States never got the chance to blockade Con-
federate ports with an iron fleet. Who knows whether or not that
would have shortened the war? It certainly would have relieved
those who feared that the Confederates would buy iron ships from
England. And it would have relieved Secretary of War Edwin Stan-
ton, who worried that the *Merrimac* would go on a rampage, sail up
the Potomac unmolested, and blow the dome off the Capitol.[32]

In a manner similar to John Jacob Astor's pursuit of new markets, Vanderbilt was always on the hunt for more transportation
routes. While he competed with Collins on the east coast, Vanderbilt also tried to dominate transportation to the west coast. Two
California lines—the U.S. Mail Steamship Company and the Pacific Mail Steamship Company—started mail delivery in 1849 with
$500,000 per year in federal aid. As happened with Collins, these

mail contracts were not opened for bidding; they were a private deal between the Post Office and the two steamship companies.

At first the two lines charged company rates: $600 per passenger from New York to California, via railroad over Panama. As the Gold Rush traffic increased, Vanderbilt became convinced that more gold could be made in steamships than in the hills of California—even without a subsidy. Vanderbilt chose not to challenge the subsidized lines directly through Panama; instead he built a canal through Nicaragua. It took Vanderbilt a year to deepen and clean out the San Juan River in Nicaragua, but it was worth it because the Nicaraguan route was five hundred miles shorter to California. So Vanderbilt agreed to pay the Nicaraguan government $10,000 a year for canal privileges. He then slashed the California fare to $400 and promised all passengers that he would beat the rival steamships to the gold fields. He even offered to carry the mail free. After a year of rate-cutting the fare dropped to $150; yet Vanderbilt and his competitors apparently were still making money.[33]

Such a development says a lot about the subsidy system. The California lines originally got a half million dollars a year from the government; then they charged people $600 to get to California. Yet Vanderbilt, with no outside aid, ran a profitable line to California by charging passengers only $150 and carrying the mail free. He hoped that doing this would expose his subsidized opponents and end their federal aid. But the California lines, like Collins, artfully pleaded with Congress for a subsidy even larger (which they needed to beat Vanderbilt). And they got $900,000 a year to compete with the more efficient Vanderbilt.[34]

In the next stage of the subsidy saga, Vanderbilt had his canal rights revoked by the Nicaraguan government in 1854. Behind this movement was William Walker, an American with a bizarre mission. Walker shipped a small army into Nicaragua, overthrew the existing government, proclaimed himself the president, and revoked Vanderbilt's canal rights. Since Vanderbilt's canal company was chartered in Nicaragua, the American government was technically not obligated to help him. So the enraged Vanderbilt put his ships on the Panama route instead. There he competed head-to-head against the California mail carriers. He then cut the fare to $100 ($30 for third class) and swore he would beat the subsidized California lines and any new line in Nicaragua that Walker might help establish.[35]

The operators of the California lines were typical political entrepreneurs: They didn't want to compete with a market entrepreneur like Vanderbilt. So they bought him out instead by paying him most of their subsidy if he promised not to run any ships to California. Vanderbilt demanded and received $672,000, or 75 percent, of the $900,000 annual subsidy. But more than this, he wanted his Nicaragua canal back. So he dabbled in Central American politics and helped get Walker overthrown. Unfortunately for Vanderbilt, his canal had been permanently destroyed during Walker's coup; but since he had the payoff money from the California lines, he ended up with a profit anyway.[36]

Congress was astonished when it learned what the California lines were doing with their $900,000 subsidy. In 1858 Senator Robert A. Toombs of Georgia said that he admired Vanderbilt: His "superior skills," Toombs said, had exposed the whole subsidy system. "You give $900,000 a year to carry the mails to California; and Vanderbilt compels the contractors to give him $56,000 a month to keep quiet. This is the effect of your subventions. . . . [Vanderbilt] is the king-fish that is robbing these small plunderers that come about the Capitol. He does not come here for that purpose." Toombs's conclusion: End the mail subsidies.[37]

Many people, though, were more critical of Vanderbilt than of the subsidies. They looked at Vanderbilt's tactics, instead of his influence on the market. One court later called Vanderbilt's actions "immoral and in restraint of trade." The New York Times compared Vanderbilt to "those old German barons who, from their eyries along the Rhine, swooped down upon the commerce of the noble river, and wrung tribute from every passenger that floated by."[38] From Vanderbilt's standpoint, the California lines were the ones "in restraint of trade." Their subsidies gave them an unfair advantage over all competition, and they used this advantage to charge monopoly rates to passengers. As for the "swooping" metaphor, Vanderbilt had "swooped down" and "wrung tribute" from the subsidized lines, not from "every passenger." Passengers paid lower fares to California because Vanderbilt's competition had slashed the fares permanently.[39] And, of course, if there had been no government subsidy, there would have been no Vanderbilt payoff. Vanderbilt ran his California lines as a personal investment and charged passengers less than one-fourth the fare that the subsidized lines had been charging. Congress, however, had committed its support for political entrepreneurs. And the annual $900,000 subsidy proved to be so large that the California lines could give three-fourths of it to Vanderbilt and still make money. Without Vanderbilt, this political entrepreneurship might have gone on much longer.

This clash between market and political entrepreneurs changed the competitive environment of American steamboating. Between 1848 and 1858, the American government paid the two California lines and Edward Collins more than $11 million to build ships and carry mail. Vanderbilt, by contrast, engaged these men in head-to-head competition free of charge. Largely because of Vanderbilt, Congress in 1858 ended all mail subsidies. Afterward, Vanderbilt and others carried the mail only for the postage; and the passenger rates after 1858 were still competitive: only $200 to California, far below the original monopoly rate of $600.[40]

Vanderbilt's victory marked the end of political entrepreneurship in the American steamship business. America didn't end up with perfect free trade, but it was closer to it than ever before. In this environment, Americans found railroads to be more profitable investments than steamships. So, after the Civil War, Vanderbilt and others sold their fleets and spent their money building railroads. The percentage of American exports carried on American ships dropped from 67 down to 9 percent from 1860 to 1915, but that was no problem. England's comparative advantage in shipping lowered America's cost for freight, mail, and passenger service throughout these years. And since the English were anxious to buy America's grain, Vanderbilt took his steamship profits and built his New York Central Railroad over one thousand miles out to Chicago and other midwestern cities. When Vanderbilt shipped midwestern grain to New York and had it loaded on English ships to be sold in Liverpool, both countries were finally doing what they could do best. By Vanderbilt's death in 1877, he had been a central figure in America's industrial revolution, both in steam and in rails. He also was worth almost $100 million, which made him the richest man in America.[41]

This study of American steamboating focuses on the market and the impact different entrepreneurs had on the market. The political entrepreneurs—Robert Fulton, Edward Collins, and Samuel Cunard—cannot be lumped with Thomas Gibbons, Cornelius Vanderbilt, and William Inman, the market entrepreneurs, because of their differing attitudes toward innovation, technology, price-cutting, monopolies, and federal aid. In the steamship industry, political entrepreneurship often led to price-fixing, technological stagnation, and the bribing of competitors and politicians. The market entrepreneurs were the innovators and rate-cutters, which was necessary in order to survive against subsidized opponents. Some of them were personally repugnant—Vanderbilt disinherited his son and placed his own wife in an asylum, while Gibbons tried to horsewhip one of his rivals. But they advanced their industry and cut passenger fares permanently. Since Vanderbilt ended up as the richest man in America during his lifetime, perhaps he was blessed to have received no federal aid. Collins, like Thomas McKenney in the earlier fur trade, seemed to have more problems than blessings from all the subsidies he took from the federal government.

3

The Boy Governor
Endorses State Subsidies

On July 12, 1831, President Andrew Jackson, who was no prankster, did something that made many people laugh, some curse, and others rub their eyes in disbelief. He appointed nineteen-year-old Stevens T. Mason to serve as secretary and acting governor of the Michigan Territory.[1]

Surely, the critics wondered, this was the worst case of political patronage ever seen! But during the next ten years, the youthful Mason often vindicated Jackson's judgment, becoming so popular that he went from acting governor to elected governor. He had been a child prodigy, a boy genius, and he became a shrewd politician. He plotted the strategy that brought Michigan into the Union; he made deals that defined Michigan's boundaries on two peninsulas; and he was the mastermind who directed Michigan's massive canal and railroad building in the 1830s.[2]

The career of Stevens T. Mason helps answer the question, "Can a state-directed program of internal improvements succeed if it is run by the smartest and most popular man available?"

The Mason story begins in Virginia, on the plantations of a great colonial dynasty. During the 1600s and 1700s, generation after generation of Masons led America from the battlefields of war to the halls of Congress. John T. Mason, the father of Stevens, hobnobbed with senators and even presidents on or near his thousand-acre estate in Loudoun County. The birth of his son Stevens T. Mason III in 1811 on the family plantation seemed to cement the Mason clan to Virginia.[3]

But John Mason had an adventurous spirit, a desire to move west and make his own success. In 1812, he packed up his family, crossed the Cumberland Gap, and traveled to Lexington, Kentucky. There he practiced law and joined his brother-in-law, William T. Barry, on the board of the Lexington branch of the Bank of the United States.

In this setting, young Stevens Thomson Mason—who was called Tom—was discovered to be a child prodigy. He absorbed knowledge like a sponge and could repeat verbatim highly detailed information months later. Tom breezed through the lesson "A is for apple" and moved into the declension of Latin nouns. Soon he could trace Caesar's battle routes and recount the history of Virginia. By age seven, he could debate the merits of the Second Bank of the United States with his father's guests. By age eight, young Tom had completed most of the entrance requirements to enter Transylvania University in Lexington. That year, 1819, General Andrew Jackson passed through Kentucky and visited the Mason family. Tom, who already knew the Battle of New Orleans intimately, astounded Jackson with his depth of knowledge.

Tom avoided the common trap of child prodigies: a haughty spirit and poor social skills. He was shy but also congenial and empathetic. He could listen as well as talk. Everyone—neighbors, family, and slaves—seemed to like him. He spent a year at a private school, and eventually a year at Transylvania University, and this helped him mix with others and set goals. He would be a governor someday, he was told, so he must train to be a leader of men, not just a master of facts.[4]

As Tom grew older, his father had some business mishaps and sought refuge in politics. John's brother-in-law, William T. Barry, led the Democratic Party in Kentucky and helped Andrew Jackson carry the state and nation in the hotly contested presidential election of 1828. With Jackson in power, Barry was brought into the cabinet as postmaster general. He used his clout with Jackson to get John Mason appointed to a patronage job, the secretary of the Michigan Territory. Mason, of course, knew nothing about Michigan, but that was fine. He could learn from Lewis Cass, the territorial governor and a strong Jackson supporter.[5]

John Mason worked at the territorial capital, which was then in Detroit, and Tom, now eighteen, tagged along with his father to help. John was no politician and soon grew bored with his job. Tom, however, flourished. He ran errands, greeted visitors, and copied letters. Governor Cass marveled at Tom's amazing retentive skills and efficient office work.[6]

After a year in Michigan, John was restless again and wanted to move to Texas, where he had inherited some land. In July 1831, President Jackson rearranged his cabinet and came up with a stunning solution: Cass would come to Washington as secretary of war; John Mason would go to Texas and seek his fortune; and Tom Mason—age nineteen years, eight months, and twenty-eight days— would be the new territorial secretary and acting governor! Young Tom was clearly overwhelmed, but he went to Washington to meet with the president. Jackson spent several days with him, doting on him, and treating him like a son. "Now Tom write to me," urged the president. "I'll back you to the limit, boy. Assert your authority and if you get into trouble, *notify me!*"[7]

When Mason arrived in Detroit, he was tactful. Yes, he told the prominent citizens, the president knew that he was only nineteen, but had confidence that Mason could do the job. Moreover, the Constitution of the United States, which allows the president to appoint territorial officers, gave Jackson authority to choose Mason as governor.[8]

Having answered the legal arguments, Mason asked for advice and guidance. Would wise men help him to lead Michigan? He put this question one-on-one to influential people throughout the territory. For example, he traveled on horseback to Mount Clemens to ask Judge Christian Clemens, a key leader, for his help. Judge Clemens said, "Go to it, boy. Do what is right. Up here, we'll back you." And so did many others across the state. "Youth yields to advice," Mason wrote to the Detroit Free Press, "age seldom or never." The "Boy Governor," as he later came to be called, thus turned his age to his advantage. He spent many evenings during the next few years in the fashionable bar at Uncle Ben Woodworth's Steamboat Hotel, listening to Detroit's politicians.[9]

Seven generations of Masons in America had produced four major generals, three ambassadors, five U.S. senators, three governors—and now one acting governor. But Michigan would soon learn that Mason had been studying government and the history of civilization since he was six years old. In fact, his family had contributed greatly to the debate in America about individual liberty and limited government. His great-granduncle, George Mason, wrote the Virginia Declaration of Rights, which became the basis for the Bill of Rights in the U.S. Constitution. The proper sphere of government, as expressed in the Constitution, was to provide for the national defense and to promote law and order. When young Tom Mason applied these family principles to Michigan, he governed well.[10]

His first crisis was one of national defense—the Black Hawk War. Chief Black Hawk, leader of the Sauk, urged Indians in Michigan to join him on raids against the white settlers. Mason called out the territorial militia, and three hundred men volunteered and marched toward Chicago, where Black Hawk was ultimately captured. The Boy Governor won praise for decisive action to protect his citizens.[11]

Mason's second crisis was one of law and order: the cholera outbreak of 1832. As a major port, Detroit was vulnerable to epidemics. No one knew much about disease control, and open sewers flowed through the city. During 1832, a cholera plague blighted Detroit and claimed the lives of 10 percent of its residents. With death and disease everywhere, Mason took swift action. First, he offered the top floor of the capitol building as a hospital. Then he worked day and night to keep the roads to and from Detroit open so that medicine, food, and supplies could reach the ravaged city. When, for example, the town of Pontiac blocked its road to Detroit, Mason ordered the barriers removed. Then Mason galloped into towns throughout the territory opening roads, tending the sick, and securing medicine for Detroit. When winter came and the plague subsided, Michiganians praised the Boy Governor for risking his life to restore order in the territory.[12]

Mason's daring leadership in the cholera scare was good preparation as he guided Michigan into statehood. The Northwest Ordinance of 1787 had set up the procedure for the territory, so he ordered a population count. Then he surveyed the boundaries and directed the writing of the state constitution. In the quest for statehood, Mason had to overcome border disputes in which Ohio won control of Toledo, but Michigan gained its upper peninsula from Wisconsin. Finally, in 1835, the Michigan Territory held its first election under its new constitution.[13]

Mason won the contest for governor, and used his skills and the power of his office to negotiate the best deal for Michigan that he could. The sooner Michigan became a state, the sooner it could receive a share of the surplus that the federal Treasury had remarkably amassed back in the 1830s.[14]

With his encyclopedic mind, Mason no doubt knew about the government debacle in fur and carefully considered its implications for his administration. Would Mason, as governor, stick to enforcing the laws, or would he move the government into economic development? The event that would shape Mason's thinking on this subject—and that of millions of other Americans as well—was the digging of a long ditch in western New York.[15]

In 1825, the Erie Canal opened navigation between Lake Erie on the west and the Hudson River on the east, which flowed into New York City. An astonishing achievement in engineering, the new canal had an enormous impact on American thinking: a channel 363 miles long connected the Great Lakes with the Atlantic coast—and suddenly New York City could easily trade with farms and cities throughout the Midwest. Profits from tolls along the canal flowed into New York's treasury, and the whole Great Lakes region boomed. And the Erie Canal was funded neither by private entrepreneurs nor by the federal government, but by the state of New York.[16]

The building of the Erie Canal, and the politics surrounding it, became a landmark event in American economic history. On the subject of transportation, almost all Americans wanted better roads and new canals—"internal improvements" as they were called. Better rivers and roads brought goods to market quicker and cheaper. Trade expanded, cities grew, land values skyrocketed, and prosperity occurred. All of this especially applied to New York's Erie Canal, which would bring to New York the commerce along the Great Lakes. Building the Erie Canal was a splendid idea. The only question was how to fund it: with federal spending, state spending, or by entrepreneurs?[17]

New Yorkers had wanted their canal finished as quickly as possible, and in 1811 Congressman Peter Porter from New York argued before Congress for federal spending. The Erie Canal, he insisted, would have national benefits and tie much of the country together in a prosperous enterprise. The Constitution, however, did not empower the federal government to tax all people for a road that mainly benefited one state. Porter's canal bill failed. But after the War of 1812, New Yorkers brought the bill back, and Congress barely passed it in 1817.[18]

President James Madison, on March 3, 1817, his next to last day in office, vetoed the Erie Canal bill. "I am constrained by the insuperable difficulty I feel in reconciling the bill with the Constitution of the United States," Madison wrote. Then he expanded his argument by making two points.

First, "to refer the power in question to the clause 'to provide for the common defense and general welfare' would be contrary to the established and consistent rules of interpretation." He added, "Such a view of the Constitution would have the effect of giving to Congress a general power of legislation instead of the defined and limited one hitherto understood to belong them, the terms 'common defense and general welfare' embracing every object and act within the purview of a legislative trust." Madison, of course, was a leader at the Constitutional Convention, so he knew how restricted the general welfare clause was intended to be.

Second, Madison endorsed internal improvements, but suggested they be undertaken by the states or by private citizens. "I am not unaware of the great importance of roads and canals and the improved navigation of water courses, and that a power in the National Legislature to provide for them might be exercised with signal advantage to the general prosperity." But because the Constitution does not allow such an expansion of the federal government, "I have no option but to withhold my signature from it, and to cherishing the hope that its beneficial objects may be attained" by other means. Madison wanted the Erie Canal, but not with federal funding.[19]

After the veto, New Yorkers immediately sprang into action. J. Rutsen Van Rensselaer, a large landowner, suggested private funding to get the canal going, but DeWitt Clinton urged the state legislature to fund the canal immediately through taxes and bonds. Clinton was mayor of New York City and soon to be governor of New York; as a lifelong politician he was prone to seeking political solutions to economic problems. Some New Yorkers, however, balked at the taxes and at the possibility that such a large economic undertaking might fail. State senator Martin Van Buren, Clinton's chief political rival, decided to back the state funding scheme and swung the state senate behind Governor Clinton. The House approved as well, and in 1817, the state of New York began building the Erie Canal.[20]

The results were spectacular. The tolls on the increasing traffic on the 363-mile canal paid for its $8.4 million cost of construction, and it was profitable even before it was finished in 1825. According to Cadwallader D. Colden, one of the canal's promoters, "We see [in 1825] with astonishment, the progress already made in populating regions which only yesterday, it may be said, were uninhabited. Already the whole Canal line is occupied. Almost at every turn in its course the traveler will find a village presented to his view, about which everything indicates, by the newness of its appearance, that it is but the growth of a few months." As for New York City, it surged into first place as the largest city in the United States. As one observer noted, "If the canal is to be a shower of gold, it will fall upon New York; if a river of gold, it will flow into her lap." Of the Erie Canal, one of DeWitt Clinton's friends wrote, "Next to the establishment of American Independence, it is the greatest achievement of the age."[21]

After 1825, thousands of New Yorkers filtered into Michigan via the Erie Canal. Governor Mason himself eagerly used the Erie Canal when he had to go to and from Washington to see President Jackson. Almost everyone in Michigan gushed with praise for this new water route, which brought immigrants to their state and took their exports to markets on the east coast. The message seemed obvious: States that wanted to get ahead needed active governments to tax their citizens to build a transportation network.[22]

To compete with New York, for example, Pennsylvania spent $14.6 million on its Main Line Canal from Philadelphia to Pittsburgh. Maryland and Massachusetts joined in the rush with a variety of state-supported projects. Ohio and Indiana began elaborate canal networks in 1837, just when Michigan entered the Union. Railroads were being built, too, and some states laid tracks and bought locomotives.[23]

To Governor Mason this was all exhilarating. Maybe the traditional theory of limited government was wrong! Maybe states could be creators, at least in the area of transportation. And after all, it was state governments, not the one in Washington, that were building these canals.[24]

Even as territorial governor, Mason urged Michigan to lay the foundation for the state to build internal improvements. When delegates met in 1835 to write the Michigan constitution, they—with Mason's encouragement—wrote the following into law:

> Internal improvements shall be encouraged by the government of this state; and it shall be the duty of the legislature, as soon as may be, to make provisions by law for ascertaining the proper objects of improvement, in relation to [roads], Canals, and navigable waters.[25]

That's the way Mason wanted it: The new constitution almost required the state to fund internal improvements. "The spirit and enterprise which has arisen among our citizens, if fostered and encouraged by the State, cannot fail to lead to lasting prosperity," Mason said. By 1837, three weeks before Michigan entered the Union, Mason was more urgent: "The period has arrived when Michigan can no longer, without detriment to her standing and importance as a state, delay the action necessary for the development of her vast resources and wealth." He was also optimistic: "[W]e

cannot fail soon to reach that high destiny which awaits us. I . . .
demand immediate legislative action."[26]

Mason wanted to proceed wisely. Therefore, he urged the state
legislature to create a Board of Internal Improvements, just as New
York had done, to survey routes and choose locations. He believed
that such a board of experts would avoid "extravagant, unprofitable,
and useless expenditures."[27]

With Mason leading the cheers, the legislature met and almost
unanimously passed an elaborate internal improvements bill. Democrats and Whigs supported it. When the alternate strategy of private ownership came up, Mason recommended that the canals and
railroads "should never be beyond at least the partial control of the
state." "Extortion from the public" was what Mason called one bill
to charter a private railroad. Most Michiganians seemed to agree.
As the *Detroit Daily Advertiser* noted, "DeWitt Clinton . . . built the
[Erie] Canal with the funds of the state. What would be thought of
the policy of surrendering that great work to the control of a private
corporation[?]"[28]

The politicians of Michigan, and in many other states as well,
could not even imagine building a canal or railroad without "the
funds of the state." The example of the Erie Canal had become the
ace that trumped all opposing arguments.[29]

In following the lead of New York, Governor Mason and many
others believed New York was typical. They overlooked the fact
that the Erie Canal was a special case: New York had unique advantages for canal building. Granted, the Erie Canal was an engineering marvel, but it was dug across relatively flat terrain; also,
the canal connected many strategically located lakes, all of which
made the building easier and not so costly. And the route of the Erie
Canal had only five hundred vertical feet separating its high and
low points. When other states tried to build canals over much hill-
ier terrain, the costs of construction and maintenance skyrocketed.[30]

Another advantage for New York was the remarkably large population groups connected by the Erie Canal. New York City, the eastern port for the canal, already had strong commercial ties throughout the world and was a funnel for immigration. Lake Erie, the western terminus, had outstanding access to the interior of the nation. The potential was high for large profits from huge amounts of trade along this route.[31]

The leaders of Michigan, and other states, saw only the profits from the Erie Canal, not its unique advantages. Michigan eagerly copied New York's example, and if one state subsidy was good, two must be better, and three better yet. Michiganians were so confident their state projects would flourish that they promised to build two railroads from Lake Erie to Lake Michigan, along with a couple of major canals.

Mason calculated that Michigan should spend $5 million to build these projects. At a time when a dollar a day was excellent family income, $5 million was huge. But Governor Mason did not worry. As soon as the anticipated tolls started pouring in—as happened with the Erie Canal—the state could then build even more. The legislature approved the $5 million that Mason suggested, and gave him authority to negotiate a $5 million loan with the lender of his choice under the best terms he could get, as long as he didn't exceed interest payments of 5.25 percent. The state, in this arrangement, would issue bonds for the $5 million and pay them back as tolls came in from the railroads and canals.[32]

Bad luck was the first problem to strike. The national economy went into a tailspin—the Panic of 1837—and capital was hard to borrow. Then came distractions. Mason talked with investors and studied the bond market in New York. During his discussions, he became sidetracked in New York City by Julia Phelps, the daughter of a wealthy leather merchant, Thaddeus Phelps. Mason courted and married her in 1838.[33]

Then came bad judgment. Businesses were failing because of the panic, and most sound investors wanted more than 5.25 per-

cent for their money. Mason finally persuaded the officers of the
Morris Canal & Banking Company, a reputable firm, to buy the
Michigan bonds. They promised to pay him the $5 million in reg-
ular $250,000 installments over several years. Mason gave them the
bonds and went back to Michigan with their promise. The Morris
Company then turned most of the bonds over to the Pennsylvania
Bank of the United States, which then sent them to Europe as col-
lateral for its own investments. Within three years, both the Morris
Company and the Pennsylvania Bank went broke, which left Michigan with a $5 million debt scattered among European investors.[34]

An even greater disaster loomed as construction on the actual
projects began. First, builders began a canal in Clinton Township
near Detroit and planned to extend the waterway 216 miles west to
Kalamazoo. Governor Mason broke ground in Mount Clemens in
1838 to celebrate the Clinton-Kalamazoo Canal. Bands, parades,
speeches, and a thirteen-gun salute commemorated the occasion.
Then came reality. The Board of Internal Improvements, which
Mason appointed to supervise the projects, hired different contractors for each mile of the canal, and these contractors each had different ideas on how to build it. One thing they all did wrong was
to make the canal only twenty feet wide and four feet deep—too
shallow for heavy freight and too narrow for easy passing.[35]

After seven years, and only sixteen miles of digging, the ledger
for the unfinished canal read: "Expenses $350,000, Toll Receipts
$90.32." With funding scarce, the board decided sometime around
1843 to cut its losses, abandon the canal, and focus on the two railroads. When construction on the canal stopped, some workers went
unpaid, and they stole materials from the three locks on the canal.
Soon even the completed parts of the canal were ruined.[36]

The two railroads also had problems. The Michigan Central was
to go from Detroit west through Ann Arbor, then on to Jackson,
Kalamazoo, and St. Joseph on Lake Michigan. Boats at St. Joseph
could then take freight or passengers to and from Chicago. The

route went through prosperous wheat farms and the state's larger cities, but the Central was built with only strap-iron rails, which consisted of thin strips of iron strapped onto wooden rails. These rails were too fragile to carry heavy loads. Rather than switch to the more expensive and durable T-rails, the Board of Internal Improvements chose to run regular heavy shipments over the existing tracks and repair them frequently. Not only was this practice dangerous but it was also more costly to the state in the long run.[37]

Robert Parks, who wrote a detailed book on Michigan's railroads, found a deplorable situation on the Central:

[O]verloaded locomotives were run at twice the recommended safe speed. Under the strain of continuous operation and jarring impact of high speed on strap-iron rails, locomotives and cars were shaken to pieces, and the cost of operation mounted dramatically. Rails were broken and timbers crushed under the heavy loads bouncing over their surface.

By 1846, the Central had been extended only to Kalamazoo. It was in financial trouble and did not earn enough to pay for needed repairs or new rails.[38]

The second railroad, the Michigan Southern, was to parallel the Central in southern Michigan from the town of Monroe to New Buffalo. Financially, the Southern was a stunning failure. It had the same problem as the Central with heavy loads on strap-iron rails. What's worse, the Southern was poorly built. The roadbed was shaky and the curves too sharp for locomotives.

The port at Monroe, Michigan, on Lake Erie, proved to be too shallow for heavy freight to enter or exit. Also, the small towns west of Monroe sent little traffic on the Southern. By 1846, the tracks had only reached Hillsdale, about halfway across the state, costing more than $1.2 million to build with very small earnings. The railroad did little to move goods or people across the state;

instead, it drained capital that could have been used more wisely.[39]

Michigan spent almost $4 million on the Clinton-Kalamazoo Canal, the Michigan Central, and the Michigan Southern. In addition, the state spent about $70,000 surveying the Michigan Northern Railroad, from Port Huron to Lake Michigan, before abandoning it. The state also spent $47,000 clearing the route for a canal and turnpike near Saginaw. Officials soon quit the project and the materials "either rotted or were expropriated by local residents."[40]

Many of these problems occurred after Mason was governor, but he received most of the blame because he had touted the projects and signed the loan. In 1837, he narrowly won reelection as governor, but in 1839 his Whig critics were loud and brutal. Mason chose not to seek a third term. By that year he had begun to consider that the problems with the projects were more than just bad luck or poor management. Maybe the state should never have drifted into economic development. In Mason's final address as governor, he said:

> [T]he error, if error there is, was the emanation of that false spirit of the age, which forced states, as well as individuals, to over-action and extended projects. If Michigan has overtasked her energies and resources, she stands not alone, but has fallen into that fatal policy, which has involved in almost unparalleled embarrassments so many of her sister states. Now, however, the period has arrived, when a corrective should be applied to the dangers which seem to surround her.[41]

But in a state-supported system, as Mason had begun to realize, this result would have been hard to avoid. The "false spirit of the age" had done its damage. The funding must come through the legislature, and the legislators naturally wanted projects in their districts. Jobs and markets were at stake. Some historians have suggested that if the Michigan Central had been the only project built, the strategy of state funding might have worked. But this was politically impossible. The legislators in the towns along the Central—

Detroit, Ann Arbor, and Kalamazoo—needed votes elsewhere to have their railroad built. And the price for these votes was a commitment to build canals in Mount Clemens and Saginaw and a second railroad in Monroe and Hillsdale.[42]

Mason, being very intelligent, saw this problem early and tried to stop it by centralizing power in a Board of Internal Improvements. That would allow experts, not politicians, to plan the routes, buy the materials, and build the roads. The board's decisions, however, proved to be just as politically motivated as the legislature's actions. First, many legislators pressured (and possibly bribed) those on the board. Second, some of the board members secretly made money building the projects.[43]

The story of Levi Humphrey is a case in point. Mason appointed Humphrey, a seemingly trustworthy Democrat, to the Board of Internal Improvements. However, when Humphrey took bids for constructing the Michigan Southern, he rigged the results to ensure that his friends in the firm of Cole & Clark won the contracts. Cole & Clark then charged three to four times the market price for supplies. When protests reached the legislature, Cole & Clark used some of their profits to bribe witnesses. The Whigs complained loudly, but when they won the governorship in 1839, they did not do much better. In 1840, the board overspent its budget and covered it up by falsifying its records.[44]

Much of the problem with the board and the politicians points to a distinct tendency of human nature: People do not spend government funds as wisely as they spend their own. If Governor Mason, for example, had been a wealthy industrialist, would he have invested $5 million of his own money with bankers he hardly knew during a national depression? Would any of the legislators have done so?

The spending policies of the board raise similar questions. In 1838, for example, the board had a bridge built over the Rouge River. The problem was that the bridge they decided to build could not carry heavy freight. The Central Railroad, not the builders, lost almost ten thousand dollars that year hauling passengers and freight around the bridge. Since no individual or private company owned the bridge, no one had a direct financial stake in building it well—or even protecting it. The next year an arsonist destroyed the bridge.[45]

In another example, the board ordered iron spikes for the Michigan Southern in 1841. The contractors, however, only put one spike in every other hole along the track. They stole the rest of the spikes and, when questioned, persuaded the board that the unused spikes were defective. The board simply believed the contractors and left the track partly unspiked.[46]

The Boy Governor, no longer a boy, left office in 1840 at age twenty-eight. He had served almost nine years as secretary, acting governor, or elected governor. During this time, he had focused so intently on administration that he left office almost penniless.

Mason decided to leave Michigan for New York City, his wife's home, and seek his fortune there in law and business. As he entered Buffalo, and made his way across the Erie Canal to New York City, he may have wondered why the experiment with an active government worked so much better in New York than in Michigan.

During the next two years, however, if Mason studied local politics, he saw New York repeat Michigan's experience. New Yorkers were in such euphoria over internal improvements that they committed their state to widening and deepening the canal. Then, under pressure from other parts of the state, New York pledged to build eight branch canals that would feed into the Erie.[47]

New Yorkers, under the direction of Whig governor William Seward, voted to fund the new canals and the expansion of the Erie by state debt, not by tolls or taxes. Seward argued, in effect, that if we build it, they will come—that the canals will generate settlement, prosperity, and profits wherever they are built. Seward's economic advisors predicted that revenues would quickly exceed expenses. Mason arrived in New York in 1840, just in time to see Governor Seward struggle with a rise in debt, not revenues. In 1840, New York's projected $2 million surplus became a $15 million debt instead.[48]

The branch canals, for example, were a disaster. The state projects in New York, like those in Michigan, had become "the false spirit of the age." Some of them, like the Black River Canal from Rome to Boonville, were doomed from the start. The Black River Canal was only thirty-five miles, but it ran through the Adirondack Mountains. Engineers had to build 109 expensive locks (the whole Erie Canal had only 83) to get boats and barges up and down the channel, and the costs of construction and upkeep were huge. In a similar way, the Chenango & Binghamton Canal cost three times more to build than it took in from revenues. The Genesee Canal was worse—it ran south to Olean to connect with the Allegheny River, but the costs of construction were seven times what was earned in tolls. The eight branch canals cost New York $9.4 million, and all of them drained more cash than they took in.[49]

Governor Seward, like Governor Mason, left office under a wave of criticism. New Yorkers were so upset that many wanted to stop construction entirely; others wanted to sell the canals, if buyers could be found, to private investors. Eight banks, which held investments in the canals, had closed, and new taxes had to be imposed. In 1846, the state of New York elected delegates to a state convention that quickly pledged New York would take on no new debt, and would try to retire existing debt as soon as possible. Horatio Seymour, who followed Seward as governor, was so restrained, and even appalled by New York's financial mess, that he delivered a warning to the nation not to let any federal money be spent for "extravagant systems of internal improvement."[50]

Governor Mason must have been amazed at how New York had followed Michigan's failure. In 1843, five days after Seward left office in disgrace, Mason died in New York City from cholera.

Both were casualties of the "false spirit of the age," but Seward reinvented himself on the slavery issue five years later and won a Senate seat in New York. In 1861, he became secretary of state under President Abraham Lincoln.

Many states other than Michigan joined New York in the canal craze, and all suffered from imitating the example of the Erie Canal. Pennsylvanians, for example, borrowed $14.6 million, almost twice what New York had spent, on a risky Main Line Canal from Philadelphia to Pittsburgh. The expense was greater because the rugged terrain between these two cities was much harder to penetrate than the flatter route between New York City and Buffalo. Furthermore, Pennsylvania also built six expensive canals throughout the state that would connect with the Main Line Canal. The large losses on these projects each year forced the state into default on its bonds, which also damaged American credit abroad. Since Pennsylvania made no effort to connect its canals with the Erie system in New York, a private company built the eighteen-mile Junction Canal to tie the two states together. Finally, in 1857, Pennsylvania sold all of its canals to private ownership for about one-third of what it cost to build them.[51]

After the canals were sold, the privately owned Pennsylvania Railroad began to return the prosperity to Pennsylvania that was taken away by the Main Line Canal. Philadelphia, which had been the largest city in the nation before the Erie Canal, was about half the size of New York (including Brooklyn) by 1860. Some Pennsylvanians, pondering the failed canals, noticed that the terrain in their state was steeper and more rugged than in New York. Building the Erie Canal on relatively flat land in an area with many lakes had been easier and cheaper than building in Pennsylvania's somewhat mountainous terrain.[52]

The Ohio legislature, in 1825, voted funding for two statewide canals that would link their state with Lake Erie. Like Pennsylvania, Ohio also funded other canals throughout the state, many of which, like the Walhonding Canal, were built only as political patronage. The Ohio projects lost so much money that Ohio held a constitutional convention in 1850 to stop the red ink. State funding came to a halt, and Ohioans earnestly sought to turn their projects over to private enterprise. In 1861, the state finally leased their canals to private operators. "Everyone who observes," one newspaper editor said, "must have learned that private enterprise will execute a work with profit, when a government would sink dollars by the thousand."[53]

Indiana had a strategy very similar to Michigan's. In 1836, Indiana committed to building $10 million in canals, railroads, and turnpikes. By 1840, the state was deep in debt, and the projects were generating much expense and little income. By 1846, Indiana had abandoned its canal system except for the Whitewater and the Wabash & Erie canals, which were finally completed—like those in Michigan—by a private corporation.[54]

Maryland racked up $15 million in debts by 1840 in funding canals and railroads. The tolls and revenue from these state investments were so small that Maryland didn't even make annual interest payments for eight years to its foreign creditors, the Baring brothers in London. The Baring brothers, frustrated with Maryland, decided to manipulate Maryland politics to get their money back. They hired American influence peddlers to campaign for the election of candidates for governor and the state legislature in Maryland who favored repayment of the state's debt. Such political lobbying seems to have helped, and Maryland paid off its debt from internal improvements in the 1850s.[55]

The story of state government failure goes on and on. In 1837, Illinois voted $10.2 million for various canals, railroads, and state projects—but the only results from these expenses were a massive state debt and twenty-six miles of railroad. In the state legislature, Abraham Lincoln was one of the misguided promoters. In Missouri, voters were so dismayed by their failed state-supported railroads that they passed a constitutional amendment forbidding their state from loaning money for future enterprises.[56]

By the mid-1840s, Mason had left Michigan, but his "false spirit of the age" speech had reopened the debate on the role of Michigan's state government in economic development. William Woodbridge, the governor who followed Mason, suggested selling the railroads to entrepreneurs and getting government out of the internal improvements business. At first, many resisted privatization.[57]

As the number of blunders on the projects began to multiply, however, more pressure came for the state to privatize. John Barry, who was elected governor after Woodbridge, echoed Mason and talked about "the spirit of the times unfortunately [becoming] the governing policy of states." Barry argued that "in extraordinary cases only . . . should a state undertake the construction of public works." He continued: "Seeing now the errors of our policy and the evils resulting from a departure from correct principle, let us with the least possible delay correct the one by a return to the other."[58]

Thomas Cooley, Michigan's most prominent lawyer in the 1800s, observed firsthand the way his state ran its railroads. "Doubts were arising in the minds of the people," Cooley wrote, "whether the state had been wise in undertaking the construction and management" of internal improvements. "These doubts soon matured into a settled conviction that the management of railroads was in its nature essentially a private business, and ought to be in the hands of individuals. By common consent it came to be considered that the state in entering upon these works had made a serious mistake."[59]

By 1846, Governor Alpheus Felch, who had followed Governor Barry, carried the day for privatization. "The business of transporting passengers and freight by railroad is clearly not within the ordinary design of state government," Felch observed. The legislature finally agreed and voted to sell the state's public works in 1846. The state took bids and sold the Central for $2 million and the Southern for $500,000. As a result, Michigan recovered 90 percent of its investment in the Central and 44 percent in the Southern. If the losses on the canals and other projects are included, the state—through this sale—recaptured about 55 percent of its total investment in internal improvements.[60]

As a condition of the sale, the new railroad owners had to agree to rebuild both lines with quality rails and extend them to Lake Michigan within three years. It had taken the state nine years to move the lines not much more than halfway across the state; the new entrepreneurs had to rebuild that part and complete the rest in just three years. When they did so, and kept rates competitive, too, Michiganians showed they could learn from history.[61]

In 1850, Michigan held a state convention to replace the 1835 constitution, which had mandated government support for internal improvements. Instead, the new constitution stated, "The State shall not subscribe to or be interested in the stock of any company, association, or corporation." Further, "the state shall not be a party to or interested in any work of internal improvement, nor engaged in carrying on any such work" except for the donation of land.[62]

The public debate that followed showed overwhelming support for the new constitution. "Looking at it as a whole," said the *Grand Rapids Enquirer*, "we honestly believe that if it had been adopted at the organization of our [s]tate [g]overnment, our [s]tate would now be out of debt, prosperous, and flourishing." In November 1850, the voters of Michigan overwhelmingly accepted the new constitution. Michigan, like its neighboring states of Ohio, Pennsylvania, and New York, had learned from its history.[63]

The story of the Erie Canal and its impact on the nation reveals the dynamics of large government projects.

First, when the state of New York built the Erie Canal, it was a landmark event in American thought. Many citizens believed the state should be active in promoting internal improvements, and perhaps most economic development. The Erie Canal seemed to be proof of the blessings of such government action. It made profits on tolls even before it was completed, and along the Erie line, towns flourished, real estate values skyrocketed, and the prices of goods dropped. New York City became the commercial center of the entire nation.

Second, in analyzing the dramatic success of the Erie Canal, most Americans overlooked New York's natural advantages. The topography and relatively flat terrain gave New York good options, and by using the Hudson River and the Finger Lakes as part of the route, construction costs were manageable. And the terminus at Buffalo allowed New York to connect the Great Lakes with the Atlantic Ocean, which guaranteed a burgeoning trade with a huge population.

Third, many other states, especially those near the Erie Canal, focused more on New York's state activism than on New York's excellent topography. Michigan, Pennsylvania, Maryland, Ohio, Indiana, and Illinois all launched elaborate internal improvement projects at state expense. Politicians asked, "Wouldn't simply building the canal, or railroad, cause prosperity and settlement to spring forth?" Even Governor Mason, with his brilliant mind, believed that he and his Board of Internal Improvements could plan routes, buy materials, and profitably build two railroads and two canals across Michigan.

Fourth, the government projects in all of these states were massive failures. Even New York, because of its unprofitable branch canals, eventually lost money on its canal system. Governor Mason, when he saw what happened, dubbed the idea of making profits from state-built internal improvements as the "false spirit of the age."

The reasons for failure were similar in every state. Politicians needed votes in the legislature to pass bills to build these large projects, and only by steering canals and railroads into many districts could those votes be secured. Entrepreneurs, by contrast, have to choose the best routes and build wisely to make a profit. Entrepreneurs try to cut operating expenses and make profits; the state governments, by contrast, created large canal bureaucracies staffed with political appointees, and the higher operating costs from state control were passed on to taxpayers. Incentives matter. Since no private individual or company owned the canals or railroads, no one was fully accountable for mistakes in construction, or even for guarding the projects to prevent theft.

Many economists and historians have tried to defend the Erie Canal and other state projects by stressing their high "social rate of return," that is, the ratio of costs to the overall benefit to society. For example, canals cut the costs of shipping from 20 cents per ton-mile to less than 3 cents per ton-mile. Those huge savings, many economists argue, cancel out the taxes, corruption, and inefficiencies of state-built projects. And didn't villages spring up all along the Erie Canal?[64]

True, the building of internal improvements often sparked trade, cut costs, and helped to settle the country. They could be a wonderful blessing. But they didn't have to be built by state governments. If they had been built privately by entrepreneurs right from the start, the economic advantages of canals and railroads would still be present, and without the high costs to taxpayers. Sure, the canals would have been built more slowly, but routes could have been straighter and more profitable. In Michigan, for example, the social rate of return on the Michigan Central Railroad was small until 1846, when it was sold to entrepreneurs, who rebuilt it and extended it across the state. In New York and Pennsylvania, the social rate of return on their canal systems sharply increased when a private company built the Junction Canal, which tied the two state systems together.

To summarize, the "false spirit of the age" had initially lured most Americans into believing that state funding was the best method for internal improvements. In the 1830s, voters eagerly endorsed state constitutions that mandated such government action.

But by the late 1840s, the American public had experienced a large dose of reality. The state-run projects were costly failures that left the state governments in debt, which then had to be paid for by the taxpayers. However, the social rate of return on *privately* built internal improvements seems to have greatly exceeded the return from state projects. At least, that is what most Americans thought by the 1850s. Voters responded as state after state sold railroads and canals to private companies, with much better results for the states' residents.

As the 1840s gave way to the 1850s, hadn't the American public learned its lesson about government intervention? Certainly, intervention by state governments for internal improvements had not worked well. But what about the federal government? Would federally operated projects succeed?

4

James J. Hill vs.
Subsidized Railroads

"Dodge, what's the best route for a Pacific railroad to the West?"
Abraham Lincoln, candidate for president, posed that question in
1859 to Grenville Dodge, possibly the best railroad man in the
West. The dream of a transcontinental railroad had excited promoters and patriots ever since the Mexican War and the acquisition
of California. Congress spent $150,000 during the 1850s surveying
three possible routes from the Mississippi River to the west coast.
William Seward, who would become Lincoln's secretary of state,
spoke as highly of the Pacific Railroad as he did earlier about the
Erie Canal. They were federal and state dollars well spent. Most
historians agree. "Unless the government had been willing to build
the transcontinental lines itself," historian John Garraty typically
asserted, "some system of subsidy was essential."[1]

When Lincoln became president, he moved to have the federal
government subsidize the building of the transcontinental railroad.

In 1862, with the southern Democrats out of the union, Congress hastily passed the Pacific Railroad Act. This act created the Union Pacific (UP), which would lay rails west from Omaha, Nebraska, and the Central Pacific (CP), which would start in Sacramento, California, and build east. Since congressmen wanted the road built quickly, they did two key things. First, they gave each line twenty alternate sections of land (at 640 acres per section) for each mile of track completed. Second, they gave loans: $16,000 for each mile of track of flat prairie land, $32,000 per mile for hilly terrain, and $48,000 per mile in the mountains.[2]

President Lincoln was brilliant in his understanding of natural rights, but less perceptive on economics. He had confidence that federal dollars used to build the railroad would be well spent. "If the subsidies provided are not enough to build the road," Lincoln told Representative Oakes Ames (D-Mass.), "ask double, and you shall have it." The UP and CP, then, would compete for government largesse. The line that built the most miles would get the most cash and land, which, of course, could be sold. In this arrangement, the incentive was for speed, not efficiency. The two lines spent little time choosing routes; they just laid track and cashed in.[3]

The subsidies shaped the UP builders' strategy in the following ways. They moved west from Omaha in 1865 along the Platte River. Since they were being paid by the mile, they sometimes built winding, circuitous tracks to collect for more mileage. For construction the UP used cheap, light wrought-iron rails, soon to be outmoded by Bessemer rails. And Thomas Durant, vice president and general manager, stressed speed, not workmanship. "You are doing too much in masonry this year," Durant told a staff member, "substitute tressel [sic] and wooden culverts for masonry wherever you can for the present."

Also, since trees were scarce on the plains, Durant and Grenville Dodge, who became chief engineer, were hard-pressed to make railroad ties, 2,300 of which were needed to finish each mile of track. Sometimes they shipped in wood; other times they used the fragile cottonwood found in the Platte River valley; often, though, they artfully solved their problem by passing it on to others. The UP simply paid top wages to tie-cutters, and daily bonuses for ties received. Hordes of tie-cutters, therefore, invaded Nebraska, cut trees wherever they were found, and delivered freshly cut ties right up to the UP line. The UP leaders conveniently argued that, since most of Nebraska was unsurveyed, farmers in the way were therefore squatters and held no right to any trees on this "public land." Some farmers used rifles to defend their land; in the wake of violence, even Durant discovered "that it was not good policy to take all the timber."[4]

The rush for subsidies caused other building problems, too. Nebraska winters were long and hard, but, since Dodge was in a hurry, he laid track on the ice and snow anyway. Naturally the line had to be rebuilt in the spring. What was worse, unanticipated spring flooding along the Loup fork of the Platte River washed out rails, bridges, and telephone poles, doing at least $50,000 in damage the first year. No wonder some observers estimated the actual building cost almost three times what it should have.[5]

By pushing rail lines through unsettled land, the transcontinentals invited Indian attacks, which caused the loss of hundreds of lives and further ran up the cost of building. The Cheyenne and Sioux harassed the road throughout Nebraska and Wyoming; they stole horses, damaged track, and scalped workmen along the way. The government paid the costs of sending extra troops along the line to protect it. But when they left, the graders, tie-setters, tracklayers, and bolters often had to work in teams with half of them standing guard and the other half working. In some cases, such as the Plum Creek Massacre in Nebraska, the UP attorney admitted his line was negligent when it sent workingmen into areas known to be frequented by hostile Indians.[6]

As the UP and CP entered Utah in 1869, the competition

became fiercer and more costly. Both sides graded lines that paralleled each other, and both claimed subsidies for this mileage. As they approached each other the workers on the UP, mostly Irish, assaulted those on the CP, mostly Chinese. In a series of attacks and counterattacks, using boulders and gunpowder, many lives were lost and much track was destroyed. Both sides involved Presidents Andrew Johnson and Ulysses Grant in the feuding. With the threat of a federal investigation looming, the two lines finally agreed to meet at Promontory Point. There they joined tracks on May 10, with hoopla, speeches, and the veneer of unity. After the celebration, however, both of the shoddily constructed lines had to be rebuilt and sometimes relocated, a task that the UP didn't finish until five years later. As Dodge said one week before the historic meeting, "I never saw so much needless waste in building railroads. Our own construction department has been inefficient."[7]

After the construction was completed, many were astonished at its costs. The UP and CP, even with 44 million acres of free land and more than $61 million in cash loans, were almost bankrupt. Two other circumstances helped to keep costs high. First, the costs of building were high after the Civil War. Capital and labor were scarce; also, even without the harsh winters and the Indians, it was costly to feed thousands of workmen who were sometimes hundreds of miles from a nearby town. Second, the officers of the Union Pacific and Central Pacific created their own supply companies and bought materials for their roads from these companies. The UP, for example, needed coal, so six of its officers created the Wyoming Coal & Mining Company. They mined coal for $2 per ton (later reduced to $1.10) and sold it to the UP for as high as $6 a ton. Even more significant, the Crédit Mobilier, which was also run by UP officials, supplied iron and other materials to the UP at exorbitant prices.[8]

Many people then and now have pointed accusing fingers at the UP with its Crédit Mobilier and its wasteful building. But this misdirects the problem. The subsidies themselves dictated the building strategy and dramatically shaped the outcome. Granted, the leaders of the UP were greedy and showed poor judgment. But the presence of free land and cash tempted them to rush west and then made them dependent on federal aid to survive.

No wonder the UP courted politicians so carefully! In this arrangement, politicians were more precious than freight or passengers. In 1866, Thomas Durant wined and dined 150 "prominent citizens" (including senators, an ambassador, and government bureaucrats) along a completed section of the railroad. He hired an orchestra, a caterer, six cooks, a magician (to pull subsidies out of a hat?), and a photographer. For those with ecumenical palates, he served Chinese duck and Roman goose; the more adventurous were offered roast ox and antelope. All could have expensive wine and, for dessert, strawberries, peaches, and cherries. After dinner some of the men hunted buffalo from their coaches. Durant hoped that all would go back to Washington inclined to repay the UP for its hospitality. If not, the UP could appeal to a man's wallet as well as his stomach. In Congress and in state legislatures, free railroad passes were distributed like confetti. For a more personal touch, the UP let General William T. Sherman buy a section of its land near Omaha for $2.50 an acre when the going rate was $8. Also, Oakes Ames, president of the UP, handed out Crédit Mobilier stock to congressmen at a discount "where it would do the most good." It was for this act, not for selling the UP overpriced goods, that Congress censured Oakes Ames and then investigated the UP line.[9]

The airing of the Crédit Mobilier scandal—just four years after the celebrating at Promontory Point—soured many voters on the UP. Others were annoyed because the UP was so inefficient that it couldn't pay back any of its borrowed money. Just as the UP was birthed and nurtured on federal aid, though, so it would have to mature on federal supervision and regulation.

In 1874, Congress passed the Thurman Law, which forced the

UP to pay 25 percent of its net earnings each year into a sinking fund to retire its federal debt. Because the line was so badly put together, it competed poorly and needed the sinking fund money to stay afloat. Building branch lines to get rural traffic would have helped the UP, but the government often wouldn't give them permission. President Sidney Dillon called his line "an apple tree without a limb," and concluded, "unless we have branches there will be no fruit." Congress further squashed any trace of ingenuity or independence by passing a law creating a Bureau of Railroad Accounts to investigate the UP books regularly. Of these federal restrictions, Charles Francis Adams Jr., a later UP president, complained: "We cannot lease; we cannot guarantee, and we cannot make new loans on business principles, for we cannot mortgage or pledge; we cannot build extensions, we cannot contract loans as other people contract them. All these things are [prohibited] to us; yet all these things are habitually done by our competitors." The power to subsidize, Adams discovered, was the power to destroy.

John M. Thurston, the UP's solicitor general, saw this connection between government aid and government control. The UP, he said, was "perhaps more at the mercy of adverse legislation than any other corporation in the United States, by reason of its Congressional charter and its indebtedness to the government and the power of Congress over it."[10]

When Jay Gould took control of the UP in 1874, his solution was to use and create monopoly advantages to raise prices, fatten profits, and cancel debts. For example, he paid the Pacific Mail Steamship Company not to compete with the UP along the west coast. Then he raised rates 40 to 100 percent and, a few weeks later, hiked them another 20 to 33 percent. This allowed him to pay off some debts and even declare a rare stock dividend; but it soon brought more consumer wrath, and this translated into more government regulation and, eventually, helped lead to the Interstate Commerce Commission, which outlawed rate discrimination.[11]

The history of the UP's struggle for survival and collapse into bankruptcy is sad. Yet it's hard to see how its history could have taken any other direction, given the presence of such lavish government aid. The aid bred inefficiency; the inefficiency created consumer wrath; the consumer wrath led to government regulation; and the regulation closed the UP's options and helped lead to bankruptcy.

The Central Pacific did better, but only because its circumstances were different. Its leaders—Leland Stanford, Collis Huntington, Charles Crocker, and Mark Hopkins—were united on narrow goals and worked together effectively to achieve them. These men, the "Big Four," focused mainly on one state, California, and used their wealth and political pull to dominate (and sometimes bribe) California legislators. Stanford, who was elected governor and U.S. senator, controlled politics for the Big Four and prevented any competing railroad from entering California. Profits from the resulting monopoly rates were added to windfall gains from their Contract & Finance Company, which was the counterpart of the Crédit Mobilier. Unlike the UP leaders in the Crédit Mobilier scandal, the Big Four escaped jail because the records of the Contract & Finance Company were "accidentally" destroyed. Without records, it was left to Frank Norris to tell the story of the CP monopoly in his novel *The Octopus*. Privately funded railroads didn't appear in California until almost 1900, when they mustered the financial strength and the political muscle to take on the entrenched CP (renamed the Southern Pacific) in California politics.[12]

In case Congress needed another lesson, the story of the Northern Pacific again featured government subsidies. Congressmen chartered the Northern Pacific in 1864 as a transcontinental running through the Northwest. The NP received no loans, but did get forty sections of land per mile, which was twice what the UP received. Various owners floundered and even bankrupted the NP, until Henry Villard took control in 1881.

Villard had come to America at age eighteen from Bavaria in 1853. Shortly after he arrived, he showed a flair for journalism and wrote compelling accounts of events for his readers, including the Civil War. Villard developed his ability to persuade people to follow him, and he used this talent as a railroad tycoon. He first became interested in the Northwest in 1874, when he was hired as an agent for German bondholders in America and went to Oregon to analyze their investments. He liked what he saw and began to have grandiose visions about a transportation empire in the Northwest. Soon he began buying NP stock and took charge of the stagnant railroad in 1881.[13]

Villard had many of the traits of his fellow transcontinental operators. First, like Jay Gould, he manipulated stock; in fact, he bought his NP shares on margin and used overcapitalized stock as collateral for his margin account. Second, like the Big Four on the CP, Villard liked monopolies. He even bought railroads and steamships along the Pacific coast, not for their value, but to remove them as competitors. Finally, like the leaders of the UP, Villard eagerly sought the 44 million acres the government had promised him for building a railroad. He would have agreed with Governor Newton Booth of California, who said, "It is easier, more delightful, and more profitable to build with other people's money than our own."[14]

Villard's strategy, then, resembled that of the other builders. He had an added plus, though, in his skills in promoting and coaxing funds from wealthy investors. "I feel absolutely confident," he wrote, "that we shall be able to work results . . . that will astonish every participant." Hundreds of German investors, and others too, heeded the call for funds and sent Villard $8 million to bring the NP to the west coast. Businessmen everywhere were amazed at Villard's persuasive ways. "This is the greatest feat of strategy I ever performed," Villard proclaimed, "and I am constantly being congratulated . . . upon . . . the achievement." So with his friends' $8 million, and with the government's free land, Villard pushed the NP westward and arrived in Seattle, Washington, in 1883. His celebration, however, was short-lived because that same year the NP almost declared bankruptcy, and Villard was ousted.[15]

Why had he failed? First, like the other transcontinental builders, he rushed into the wilderness to collect his subsidies. Villard knew that the absence of settlement meant the absence of traffic, but his solution was to promote tourism as well as immigration. He thought tourists would pay to enjoy the beauty of the Northwest, so he built some of the line along a scenic route. This hiked Villard's costs because he had to increase the grade, the curvature, and the length of the railroad to accommodate the Rocky Mountain view. Villard also built expensive health spas around the hot springs at Bozeman and in Broadwater County, Montana. He put glass domes around the hot springs and built plush hotels near them to accommodate the throngs of tourists he predicted would come. Despite lavish advertising in the East, though, the tourists went elsewhere and Villard went broke.[16]

The federal aid and the foreign investors had given Villard some room for error. But he made other mistakes, too. He was so anxious to rush to the coast that he built when construction costs were high. They were much lower three years before and three years after he built. High costs meant high rates, and this deterred freight and immigrants from traveling along the NP. Villard could have cut some of these costs, but as historian Julius Grodinsky has observed of Villard, "What was asked, he paid." He didn't bother to learn much about railroads; in fact, during 1883 he seems to have been more interested in leveling six houses in New York City to build a glamorous mansion in which to entertain the city's elite. He thought he could promote immigration, tourism, scenic routes, and health spas, and use the free land and foreign cash to cover the costs of building the NP.

When his bubble burst, the NP went bankrupt and the German

investors were ruined. But not so Villard—from his mansion in New York City, he raised more money and took control of the NP again five years later. The smooth-talking Villard, however, still could not overcome his earlier errors. The poorly constructed Northern Pacific was so inefficient that even the Villard charm could not make it turn a profit. In 1893, the NP went bankrupt again; the Villard era was over.[17]

Granted, the American Northwest had a sparse population and a rugged terrain. But one man did build a transcontinental through the Northwest. In fact, he built it north of the NP, almost touching the Canadian border. And he did it with no federal aid. That man was James J. Hill, and his story tells us a lot about the larger problem of federal aid to railroads.

Hill, like Astor and Vanderbilt, came from a poor background. He was born in a log cabin in Ontario, Canada, in 1838. His father died when the boy was young, and he supported his mother by working in a grocery for four dollars per month. He lost use of his right eye in an accident, so his opportunities seemed limited. But Hill was a risk taker and a doer. At age seventeen he aimed for adventure in the Orient, but settled for a steamer to St. Paul, Minnesota. There he clerked for a shipping company and learned the transportation business. He was good at it, and he became intrigued with the future of the Northwest.[18]

The American Northwest was America's last frontier. The states from Minnesota to Washington made up one-sixth of the nation but remained undeveloped for years. The climate was harsh and the terrain imposing. There were obvious possibilities with the trees, coal, and copper in the region, but crossing it and connecting it with the rest of the nation was formidable. The Rocky Mountains divided the area into distinct parts: to the east were Montana, North Dakota, and Minnesota, which were dry, cold, flat, and, predictably, empty. It was part of what pioneers called "the Great American Desert."

Once the Rockies were crossed, the land in Idaho and Washington turned green with forests and plentiful rain. But the road to the coast was broken by almost uncrossable canyons and the jagged peaks of the Cascade Mountains. Since the Northwest was fragmented in geography, remote in location, and harsh in climate, most settlers stopped in the lower Great Plains or went on to California.

To most, the Northwest was, in the words of General William T. Sherman, "as bad [a piece of land] as God ever made." To others, like Villard, the Northwest was a chance to grab some subsidies and create a railroad monopoly. But to Hill the Northwest was an opportunity to develop America's last frontier. Where some saw deserts and mountains, Hill had a vision of farms and cities. Villard might build a few swanky hotels and health spas, but Hill wanted to settle the land and develop the resources. Villard preferred to approach the Northwest from his mansion in New York City. Hill learned the Northwest firsthand, working on the docks in St. Paul, piloting a steamboat on the Red River, and traveling on snowshoes in North Dakota. Villard was attracted to the Northern Pacific because of its monopoly potential; Hill wanted to build a railroad to develop the region, and then to prosper with it.[19]

Hill's years of maturing in St. Paul followed a logical course: From investing in shipping, he switched to steamships, and then to railroads. In 1878, he and a group of Canadian friends bought the bankrupt St. Paul & Pacific Railroad from a group of Dutch bondholders. The St. Paul & Pacific story was eerily similar to that of the transcontinentals: federal subsidies, stock manipulation, profit-taking on construction, and bankruptcy. Along one ten-mile section of track were fifteen separate patterns of iron. Bridge material, ties, and equipment were scattered along the right-of-way. When Hill and his friends bought this railroad and announced their intention to complete it, critics dubbed it "Hill's Folly." Yet he did complete it, ran it profitably, and soon decided to expand it into

North Dakota. It was not yet a transcontinental, but it was in the process of becoming one.[20]

As Hill built his railroad across the Northwest, he followed a consistent strategy. First, he always built slowly and developed the export of the area before he moved farther west. In the Great Plains this export was wheat, and Hill promoted dry farming to increase wheat yields. He advocated diversifying crops and imported seven thousand cattle from England and elsewhere, handing them over free of charge to settlers near his line. Hill was a pump primer. He knew that if farmers prospered, their freight would give him steady returns every year. The key was to get people to come to the Northwest. To attract immigrants, Hill offered to bring them out to the Northwest for a mere ten dollars each if they would farm near his railroad. "You are now our children," Hill would tell immigrants, "but we are in the same boat with you, and we have got to prosper with you or we have got to be poor with you." To make sure they prospered, he even set up his own experimental farms to test new seed, livestock, and equipment. He promoted crop rotation, mixed farming, and the use of fertilizers. Finally, he sponsored contests and awarded prizes to those who raised meaty livestock or grew abundant wheat.[21]

Unlike Villard, Hill built his railroad for efficiency, not for scenery. "What we want," Hill said, "is the best possible line, shortest distance, lowest grades and least curvature that we can build. We do not care enough for Rocky Mountain scenery to spend a large sum of money developing it." That meant that Hill personally supervised the surveying and the construction. "I find that it pays to be where the money is being spent," noted Hill, but he didn't skimp on quality materials. He believed that building a functional and durable product saved money in the long run. For example, he usually imported high-quality Bessemer rails, even though they cost more than those made in America. He was thinking about the future, and quality building materials cut costs in the long run. When Hill constructed the solid granite Stone Arch Bridge—2,100 feet long, 28 feet wide, and 82 feet high—across the Mississippi River, it became a Minneapolis landmark for decades.[22]

Hill's quest for short routes, low grades, and few curvatures was an obsession. In 1889, Hill conquered the Rocky Mountains by finding the legendary Marias Pass. Lewis and Clark had described a low pass through the Rockies back in 1805, but later no one seemed to know whether it really existed or where it was. Hill wanted the best gradient so much that he hired a man to spend months searching western Montana for this legendary pass. He did in fact find it, and the ecstatic Hill shortened his route by almost one hundred miles.[23]

As Hill pushed westward, slowly but surely, the Northern Pacific was there to challenge him. Villard had first choice of routes, lavish financing from Germany, and 44 million acres of free federal land. Yet it was Hill who was producing the superior product at a competitive cost. His investments in quality rails, low gradients, and short routes saved him costs in repairs and fuel on every trip across the Northwest. Hill, for example, was able to outrun the Northern Pacific from coast to coast at least partly because his Great Northern line was 115 miles shorter than Villard's NP.

More than this, though, Hill bested Villard in the day-to-day matters of running a railroad. For example, Villard got his coal from Indiana, but Hill bought coal from Iowa and saved two dollars per ton. In the volatile leasing game, Hill outmaneuvered Villard and got a lower cost to the Chicago market. As Hill said, "A railroad is successful in the proportion that its affairs are vigilantly looked after."[24]

Villard may have realized he was outclassed, so he countered with obstructionism, not improved efficiency. One of Hill's partners alerted him to Villard's "egotistic stamp" and concluded that "Villard's vanity will be apt to lead him to reject any treaty of peace that does not seem to gratify his vain desire to obtain a triumph." Before Hill could build his railroad farther west from Minnesota, for example, the NP refused him permission to cross its line at Moorhead, along the Minnesota–North Dakota border. Local citizens apparently wanted Hill's line, and he wrote, "I had a letter from a leading Moorhead merchant today offering 500 good citizen tracklayers to help us at the crossing." Each move west that Hill made threatened Villard's monopoly. Ironically, Hill sometimes had to use the NP to deliver rails; when he did, Villard sometimes raised rates so high that Hill used the Canadian Pacific when he could.

Villard found that manipulating politics was the best way to thwart Hill. For example, the gaining of right-of-way through Indian reservations was a thorny political issue. Legally, no railroad had the right to pass through Indian land. The NP, as a federally funded transcontinental, had a special dispensation. Hill, however, didn't, so the NP and UP tried to block Congress from granting Hill right-of-way through four Indian reservations in North Dakota and Montana. Hill gladly offered to pay the willing Indians fair market value for their land, but Congress stalled, and Hill said, "All our contracts [are] in abeyance until [this] question can be settled." Hill had to fight the NP and UP several times on this issue before getting Congress to grant him his right-of-way. "It really seems hard," Hill later wrote, "when we look back at what we have done in opening the country and carrying at the lowest rates, that we should be compelled to fight political adventurers who have never done anything but pose and draw a salary."

In the depression year of 1893, all the transcontinental owners but Hill were lobbying in Congress for more government loans. To one of them Hill wrote, "The government should not furnish capital to these companies, in addition to their enormous land subsidies, to enable them to conduct their business in competition with enterprises that have received no aid from the public treasury." He proudly concluded, "Our own line in the North . . . was built without any government aid, even the right of way, through hundreds of miles of public lands, being paid for in cash."

Shortly after Hill wrote this, the Union Pacific, the Northern Pacific, and the Santa Fe, another line, all went bankrupt and had to be reorganized. This didn't surprise Hill. He gloated, "You will recall how often it has been said that when the Nor Pac, Union Pac and other competitors failed, our company would not be able to stand. . . . Now we have them all in bankruptcy . . . while we have gone along and met their competition." In fact, the efficient Hill cut his costs 13 percent from 1894 to 1895.

Hill criticized the grab for subsidies, and here is the irony: Those who got federal aid ended up being hung by the strings that were attached to it. In other words, there is cause and effect between Hill's company having no subsidy and prospering, while the other transcontinentals received aid and went bankrupt. First, the subsidies, whether in loans or land, were always given on the basis of each mile completed, placing the incentive on building quickly. This resulted not only in poorly built lines but in poorly surveyed lines as well. Steep gradients meant increased fuel costs; poor building meant costly repairs and accidents along the line. Hill had no subsidy, so he built slowly and methodically. "During the past two years," Hill said in 1884, "we have spent a great deal of money for steel rails, ballasting track, transfer yards, terminal facilities, new equipment, new shops, and in fact we have put the road in better condition than any railway similarly situated that I know of." Hill, then, had lower fixed costs than did his subsidized competitors.

By building the Great Northern without government interference, Hill enjoyed other advantages. He could build his line as he saw fit. Until Andrew Carnegie's triumph in the 1890s, American rails were inferior to some foreign rails, so Hill bought English and German rails for the Great Northern. The subsidized transcontinentals were required in their charters to buy American-made steel, so they were stuck with the lesser product. Their charters also required them to carry government mail at a discount, and this cut into their earnings. Finally, without congressional approval, the subsidized railroads could not build spur lines off the main line. Hill's Great Northern, in contrast, looked like an octopus, and he credited spur lines as being critical to his success.

In debating the Pacific Railway Bill in the 1860s, some congressmen argued that even if the federally funded transcontinentals proved to be inefficient, they should still be aided because they would increase the social rate of return to the United States. Some historians and economists, led by Robert Fogel, winner of a Nobel Prize, have picked up this argument, and it goes like this: The UP made little profit and was poorly built, but it increased the value of the land along the road and promoted farms and cities in areas that could not have supported them without cheap transportation. Fogel claimed that the value of land along a forty-mile strip on each side of the UP was worth $4.3 million in 1860 and $158.5 million by 1880. Without the UP, this land would have remained unsettled and the United States would not have had the national benefits of productive farms, new industries, and growing cities in the West. To the nation, then, the high social rate of return justified the building of the UP, CP, NP, and Santa Fe railroads.[25]

What this argument overlooks is the *negative* social, economic, and political return to the United States that came with using federal subsidies to build railroads. The gain in social return that Fogel described is only temporary. If the government had not subsidized a transcontinental, then more private investors like Hill would have built them. Subsidy promoters tried to deny this argument at the time, but Hill's achievement shows that it would have been done, only at a slower (but more efficient) pace. Hill's success refutes the following statement in Congress by Representative James H. Campbell of Pennsylvania: "This [Union Pacific] road never could be constructed on terms applicable to ordinary roads. . . . It is to be constructed through almost impassable mountains, deep ravines, canyons, gorges, and over arid and sandy plains. The Government must come forward with a liberal hand, or the enterprise must be abandoned forever."[26]

Here is a key point: The gain in social return was only temporary, but the loss of shipping with an inefficient railroad was permanent. The UP and NP were inefficient in gradients, curvature,
length, quality of construction, repair costs, and use of fuel. This
meant permanently high fixed costs for all passengers and freight
using the subsidized transcontinentals.

The subsidizing of railroads cost the nation in other ways, too.
First, the land that was given to the railroads could not be sold for
revenue. Second, the giving of subsidies to one was a precedent for
giving subsidies to many. When the government gave 20 million
acres to the UP, the NP and others clamored for aid; the result
was the giving of 131 million acres of land to various railroads.
Third, the granting of all this land and money, too, made for shady
business ethics and political corruption. The Crédit Mobilier is an
example of poor business ethics, and the CP's tight control over
California politics is a sample of political corruption. Part of this
corruption is reflected in the automatic monopolies that subsidized
transcontinentals had. When Jay Gould doubled rates along parts
of the UP, not much could be done. It took time to build privately
financed lines, and, when they were finished, they had to compete
with a railroad that had, thanks to the government, millions of
acres of free land and large cash reserves.

A final hidden cost of subsidizing railroads is seen in the mass of
lawmaking, much of it harmful, all of it time-consuming, by state
legislatures, Congress, and the Supreme Court after watching the
UP, CP, and NP in action. The publicizing of shoddy construction,
the Crédit Mobilier scandal, rate manipulation, and bankrupt health
spas angered consumers; and angry consumers pestered their congressmen to regulate the railroads. Much of the regulation, however, had unintended consequences and made the situation worse.

For example, when voters learned of the corruption in building
the UP, public outrage led to a congressional investigation. The UP
had made no payment on its government loans, so Congress passed the

Thurman Law, which forced the UP to pay 25 percent of its annual earnings toward retiring its debt to the government. The problem here is that the shoddy construction of the UP made for high fixed costs, and the lack of spur lines limited its chances for profits. This meant that the UP had to raise rates for passengers and freight to pay back its loans. The rate hikes, though, caused even more public outcry. Many noticed, for example, that the UP and NP were charging more than Hill's Great Northern, and this led to demands for rate regulation. Congress obliged and, in 1887, created the Interstate Commerce Commission (ICC) to investigate and abolish rate discrimination. Two new problems emerged: First, it was now illegal to give discounts. Hill argued that rate cutting had led to lower rates over the years and that this allowed the United States to capture a larger share of overseas trade. Hill insisted that the ICC law, if enforced (which it eventually was), would hurt railroads in domestic and overseas trade. Second, the ICC law funded thousands of federally funded bureaucrats, who listened to shippers all over the nation and snooped into the detailed records of almost every railroad in the country.[27]

The issue of foreign trade is important and was hotly disputed during Congress's debates on the transcontinentals. Advocates of federal aid strongly argued that subsidized railroads would capture foreign trade and increase national wealth. "Commerce is power and empire," said Senator William M. Gwin of California. "Give us, as this [Union Pacific] Railroad would, the permanent control of the commerce and exchanges of the world, and in the progress of time and the advance of civilization, we would command the institutions of the world." Yet the UP and NP were so inefficient, they couldn't even capture or develop the trade of their own regions, least of all the world. If Hill hadn't built the Great Northern, the United States wouldn't have captured many Oriental markets.[28]

In order to compete in the Orient, Hill had studied the opportunities for trade there and marveled at its potential. "If the people of a single province of China should consume [instead of rice] an ounce a day of our flour," Hill wistfully said, "they would need 50,000,000 bushels of wheat per annum, or twice the Western surplus." The key, Hill believed, was "low freight rates," and these he intended to supply. In 1900, he plowed $6 million into his Great Northern Steamship Company and shuttled two steamships back and forth from Seattle to Yokohama and Hong Kong. Selling wheat was only one of Hill's ideas. He tried cotton, too. Ever the pump primer, Hill told a group of Japanese industrialists he would send them cheap southern cotton, and deliver it free, if they would use it along with the short-staple variety they got from India. If they didn't like it, they could have a refund and keep the cotton. This technique worked, and Hill filled many boxcars and steamships with southern cotton destined for Japan. Hill's railroads and steamships also carried New England textiles to China. In 1896, American exports to Japan were only $7.7 million; but nine years later, with Hill in command, this figure had jumped to $51.7 million.[29]

An even greater coup may have been Hill's capturing of the Japanese rail market. Around 1900, Japan began a railroad boom, and England and Belgium made bids to supply the rails. In this case, the Japanese may have underestimated Hill: It didn't seem likely that he could be competitive if he had to buy rails in Pittsburgh, ship them to the Great Northern, carry them by rail to Seattle, then by steamship to Yokohama. Hill was so efficient, though, and so eager for trade in Asia, that he underbid the English and the Belgians by $1.50 per ton and captured the order for 15,000 tons of rails. Hill was spearheading American dominance in the Orient.[30]

Hill worked diligently to market the Northwest's exports: wheat from the plains, copper from Montana, and apples from Washington. Without Hill's low freight rates and aggressive marketing, some of these Northwest products might never have been competitive exports. Washington and Oregon, for example, were covered with western pine and Douglas fir trees. But it was southern pine that had dominated much of the American lumber market. Hill could provide the lowest freight rates, but he needed someone to risk harvesting the western lumber. He found Frederick Weyerhaeuser, his next-door neighbor, and sold him 900,000 acres of western timberland at six dollars an acre. Then Hill cut freight costs from ninety to forty cents per hundred pounds, and the two of them captured some of the midwestern lumber market and prospered together.[31]

Hill became America's greatest railroad builder, he believed, because he followed a consistent philosophy of business. First, build the best line possible. Second, use this efficient line to promote the exports of the region—in other words, Hill helped others to prosper, and at the same time Hill flourished. Third, do not overextend; expand only as profits allow. Hill would probably have agreed with Thomas Edison that genius is 1 percent inspiration and 99 percent perspiration. Few people were willing to exert the perspiration necessary to learn the railroad business and apply these principles. Hill criticized the failure of his competitor: "If the Northern Pacific could be handled as we handle our property, it could be made [a] great property . . . but it has not been run as a railway for years, but as a device for creating bonds to be sold."

The only thing that Hill did seem to fear was the potential for damage when the federal government stepped in to direct the economy. He understood why this happened—why people pressured Congress to involve itself in economic matters. California, isolated on the Pacific coast, wanted the cheap goods that a railroad would bring. So Senator Gwin of California lobbied in Congress for transcontinental subsidies. American steel producers wanted to sell more steel, so they pushed Congress to put a tariff on imported steel. Hill's problem was that when his rivals were subsidized, and when tariffs forced him to pay 50 percent more for English steel, he had to be twice as good to survive. One way out, which Hill took, was to support those politicians in the Northwest who would fight subsidies and high tariffs, and who would urge Congress to give him the right-of-way through Indian land.[32]

What Hill ultimately deplored more than tariffs and subsidies were the ICC and the Sherman Antitrust Act. Congress passed these vague laws to protest rate hikes and monopolies. They were passed to satisfy public clamor (which was often directed at wrongdoing committed by Hill's subsidized rivals). Vaguely written, these laws were harmless until Congress and the Supreme Court began to give them specific meaning. And here came the irony: Laws that were passed to thwart monopolists were applied to thwart Hill.

The ICC, for example, was created in 1887 to ban rate discrimination. The Hepburn Act, passed in 1906, made it illegal for railroads to charge different rates to different customers. This law was partly aimed at rate manipulators like Jay Gould. But it ended up striking Hill, who now could not offer rate discounts on exports traveling on the Great Northern en route to the Orient. Hill had given the Japanese and Chinese special rates on American cotton, wheat, and rails to lure them to American exports. But if the Hepburn Act passed, Hill said, U.S. trade with the Orient would suffer. Hill testified vigorously during the Senate hearings that preceded the Hepburn Act, but was ignored. When the act became law he was furious that he had to publish his rates and give all shippers anywhere the special discount he was giving the Asians to capture their business. Since he couldn't do this and survive, he eventually sold his ships and almost completely abandoned the Asian trade. Thus, American exports to Japan and China dropped 40 percent ($41 million) between 1905 and 1907.[33]

Hill may have lost his battle with politicians on the Hepburn Act, but he won his point with them on federal subsidies. All major politicians of the 1860s had argued vehemently that no transcontinental railroad could ever be built without huge amounts of federal aid. Not only did Hill prove them wrong, but he had also made the case that no transcontinental could be profitable, well built, and responsive to customers unless it was built privately and with no federal aid.

5

Herbert Dow Changed
the World

The failures of the Union Pacific and Central Pacific railroads actually led to new insights for many Americans: Why should government subsidize any business? Such subsidies increased graft and
waste, and in the long run, the firms that received the subsidies
either went bankrupt or had to be rebuilt.

Thus, during the three decades following the 1869 comple-
tion of the Union Pacific–Central Pacific rail line, most U.S.
politicians abandoned talk of federal aid for business (other than
occasional tariffs). This atmosphere of freedom ignited a burst
of industrial production and invention that had never been seen
before, and a new term for the late 1800s gained popularity: the
Gilded Age.

Of course not all politicians during the Gilded Age resisted the
temptations of voting for lucrative subsidies for companies in their
home states. But if they tried to do so, they were stopped by consti-

tutional presidents like Grover Cleveland, who vetoed 414 pieces of legislation from Congress during his first term alone.

With the failure of subsidized canals, steamships, and railroads, American leaders finally became serious about limiting government and cutting expenditures. After 1865, the United States had twenty-eight straight years of federal budget surpluses, and cut two-thirds of its entire national debt.[1]

The most prominent industrialists of the Gilded Age were John D. Rockefeller and Andrew Carnegie. Rockefeller founded Standard Oil to set the "standard" with his cheap and dependable oil. By the 1890s, Standard Oil had a 60 percent share of the world's kerosene market; better still, homeowners could burn kerosene lamps in their homes for only one cent per hour, and the former need for whale oil for lighting was swept away. Rockefeller's cheap kerosene may have saved more whales than any other strategy to date, even while he made the United States so dominant in the petroleum industry. Meanwhile, Andrew Carnegie cut the price of steel rails from $56 to $11.50 per ton, which made the United States the world leader in steel production. The United States entered the twentieth century with superior oil and steel industries.[2]

Ironically, both Rockefeller and Carnegie won their international competition in part by defeating foreign cartels, which were aided by foreign governments. While the United States followed the path of free enterprise in the late 1800s, other countries began regulating and subsidizing business in a big way. By 1900, for example, 275 cartels in Germany produced coal, iron, steel, and chemicals, and other products. In addition, Russia became a major oil producer, and its government regulated that industry and slapped a high tariff on American oil in order to hinder Rockefeller from selling Standard Oil products there, as did the Austro-Hungarian Empire.[3]

As a result of these trends, any American business trying to enter the chemical industry in the late 1800s also faced large and well-financed international cartels. Herbert Henry Dow, born in 1866 and a child of the Gilded Age, grew up in an era of innovations, but he would still have to be a tough competitor to beat the cartels and succeed in the American chemical business.

Dow had the advantage of learning from a skilled father who encouraged him to believe in himself and try new ideas. The senior Dow developed equipment for the U.S. Navy, so Herbert grew up eager to learn new scientific methods.[4]

During his senior year of high school, Dow watched the drilling of an oil well outside Cleveland, Ohio. At the well site, he noticed that brine had come to the surface. The oil men considered the oozing brine not as a by-product to be developed but as a nuisance. One of the well drillers took some brine to Dow and asked him to taste it. "Bitter, isn't it?" the driller noted. "It certainly is," Dow added. "Now why would that brine be so bitter?" the driller asked. "I don't know," Dow said, "but I'd like to find out."[5]

He took a sample of the brine to his lab, tested it, and found lithium in the brine, which helped explain the bitterness, and also bromine. Bromine was used both as a sedative and also in photography to develop film. Dow wondered if bromine could be extracted profitably from the abundant brine in the Cleveland area. Others had extracted salt (sodium chloride), but perhaps he could do the same thing with bromine and sell it commercially.

The key to selling bromine was finding a way to separate it cheaply from brine. The traditional method was to heat a ton of brine, remove the crystallized salt, treat the remaining mixture with chemicals, salvage only two or three pounds of bromine, and dump the rest. Dow thought this method was expensive and inefficient. Why did the salt—which was often unmarketable—have to be removed? Was the use of heat—which was very expensive to apply—really necessary to separate the bromine? And why throw the rest of the brine away? Were there economical methods of removing the chlorine and magnesium also found in brine?[6]

After graduating in 1888 from Case Western Reserve, Dow took a job as a chemistry professor at the Huron Street Hospital College in Cleveland. There he had his own lab and an assistant. During the next year, he developed two processes—electrolysis and "blowing-out." In electrolysis he used an electric current to help free bromine from the brine; in blowing-out, he used a steady flow of air through the solution to separate the bromine. Once Dow showed he could use his two methods to make small amounts of bromine, he assumed he could produce enough bromine to market it worldwide.[7]

Next, young Herbert Dow founded the Canton Chemical Company. With grand aspirations but no experience, he persuaded three partners in Ohio to invest in his blowing-out process. The bad news was that his cheap ramshackle equipment turned out only small amounts of bromine. His company was cash poor, and he went broke in less than a year. The good news was that Dow never saw failure as permanent, but only as a path to later success. He had proved he could make bromine, and if he had a better source of brine he just knew he would thrive.

Before starting another business, Dow scoured the Ohio-Michigan area for brine with high bromine content. His journey ended in the small town of Midland, Michigan, 125 miles northwest of Detroit. After testing the brine in Midland, Dow approached J. H. Osborn and several Cleveland-area businessmen. If they would supply him with the starting capital, he would repay them with profits from the sale of his bromine. Together they launched the Midland Chemical Company in 1890.[8]

But again Dow struggled. He never had enough money because nothing ever worked as expected. Electrolysis was new and untested. His brine cells were too small, and the current he passed through the brine was too weak to free all the bromine. When he strengthened the current, he freed all the bromine, but some chlorine seeped in, too. Instead of being frustrated, Dow would later go into the chlorine business as well. Meanwhile, the chlorine and bromine were corroding his equipment and causing breakdowns. He needed better carbon electrodes, a larger generator, and loyal workers.[9]

Dow found himself working eighteen-hour days and sleeping at the factory. Sure, he was making bromine with his new methods, but it wasn't yet pure enough to market effectively. That made the Cleveland investors nervous, and they balked at sending Dow more cash. He went weeks with delayed pay, or none at all. When unpaid coworkers wanted their cash, Dow had to promise bonuses, and that led to more haggling with his investors.[10]

Dow economized to survive. He built his factory in Midland with cheap local pine and used nails sparingly. He saved twenty-nine cents buying a padlock in Midland instead of Saginaw. "Crazy Dow" is what the Midland people called him when he rode his dilapidated bike into town to fetch supplies. Laughs, not dollars, were what most townsfolk contributed to his visionary plans.[11]

Dow needed three years before he sold bromine at a profit. His investors finally relaxed, but Dow agonized about pouring the unused residue from the brine down the sewer. If he could use electrolysis to separate the bromine, why not try to separate the chlorine as well? So while his investors moaned, Dow began making the wood and tar cells that would help him produce chlorine from brine.[12]

Dow's struggle to develop new products is common to many entrepreneurs. In Dow's first experiment with chlorine, he blew up his building and destroyed the equipment. His investors were furious and demanded that Dow make bromine and forget the chlorine, which was more than Dow would agree to do. He left the Midland Chemical Company and returned to Ohio.

For Dow, the return to Ohio meant that he could work on his ideas to produce chlorine. In the town of Navarre, he worked in privacy with a small staff trying to produce chlorine safely by electrolysis. New investors took notice of this, and some of the old ones also became interested. By 1897, Dow was back in Midland as head of the new Dow Chemical Company.[13]

For Dow's company to become a major corporation, it faced some giant hurdles. First was the European challenge. Germany in particular dominated world chemical markets in the 1800s. The Germans, and to a lesser extent the English, had experience and access to top-flight scientists and used them to monopolize world markets and control prices. The American chemical industry was almost nonexistent in the 1800s; whatever the Europeans charged, the Americans paid.

Dow's first battle with the Europeans was in chlorine, a traditional disinfectant. But chlorine's market as a bleach expanded in the 1890s because of newspapers. The inventing of the Linotype machine and the rotary press created a new demand for wood pulp as paper. The dozens of new companies making wood pulp needed tons of bleach each day to change the pulp from wood color to white.

More than forty companies throughout Great Britain began selling bleach to most of the world. They formed a cartel, or combine, called the United Alkali Company, which controlled the output of its members and set the price of bleach throughout the world. The members of the United Alkali Company controlled the huge potash deposits in Britain, from which they made their bleach. They were so dominant that Dow could only sell competitively in the Great Lakes states, where lower shipping costs and a protective tariff worked to his advantage.[14]

The optimistic Dow always believed he could match the United Alkali cartel in the price and quality of his bleach. What he didn't foresee was the predatory price cutting they used to try to knock him out of business. Each December, United Alkali announced a price for bleach for the following year. Before Dow entered the picture, the standard price was $3.50 a hundredweight, a high figure that reflected United Alkali's near monopoly of the world market.

Just when Dow came on the scene in the mid-1890s, the British cut their price almost in half, from $3.50 to $1.87. But Dow had improved his efficiency enough to match that price. When the British saw this, they cut the price again to $1.65. As Dow later said,

> The reasoning that governed these prices is apparent; namely the United Alkali Company fixed the price in the United States at the highest figure they thought they could secure without bringing about competition. When they found competition was starting they realized their American price ($3.50) was too high and they lowered it (to $1.87 and then to $1.65).[15]

Even after this last cut, Dow increased his bleach production from 9 to 72 tons per day from 1897 to 1902. His electrolysis method of producing chlorine was efficient enough to match the British price. Other American firms were selling bleach, too, but the British went in for the kill. They decided to sell at a loss temporarily; this, they reasoned, would oust the Americans from the market. Then the British could hike prices when Dow and the others were gone.

Late in 1902, United Alkali announced another drop in bleach prices—from $1.65 to $1.25 (which included a twenty-cent tariff, plus freight charges). The other American companies shut down, and Dow must have been tempted to join them. But if he did he would lose not only a large part of his business; he would also lose the chance to improve his manufacturing process as he increased his output. Dow believed he was the most efficient producer; and besides, he hated giving in to a cartel.

When Dow agreed to match the British price, they slashed it again to $1.04. Dow barely survived during 1903, so the cartel announced it would sell bleach in 1904 for a large loss at only 88.5 cents a hundredweight. Dow countered by signing contracts for his entire 1904 output at 86 cents. That decision meant a $90,000

loss for his company. After he did this, United Alkali cleverly announced it was raising bleach prices to $1.25.

Even so, Dow still honored his 86-cent contracts. This was hard
to do because the company was teetering on the edge of bankruptcy. Even before United Alkali's last price cut, Dow's company
was $225,000 in debt and $92,000 overdrawn at a Cleveland bank.
In fact, for Dow to get another loan to survive, each of the directors
of the company had to endorse the notes. "It seems too bad," Dow
wrote a stockholder, "that we have to bear the entire cost of bringing the United Alkali Company to its knees."[16] But by matching the
low British price and honoring his contracts, he earned respect. The
British gave up trying to oust Dow from the chlorine business and
kept the price steady at $1.25.

No sooner had the bleach war ended than Dow stumbled into a
bromine war with Germany. In other words, his major chemicals—
chlorine and bromine—were both under attack in the early 1900s.
The Germans had been the dominant supplier of bromine since it
first was mass-marketed in the mid-1800s. The vast potash deposits
near Stassfurt supplied bromine to the Germans as a by-product.
Only the United States emerged as a competitor to Germany in the
bromine market, and then only as a minor player. Some small firms
along the Ohio River sold bromine, but only within the country.[17]

Americans did not compete with the Germans because of
threatened predatory price cutting. About thirty German firms
combined to form a cartel, Die Deutsche Bromkonvention, which
fixed the world price for bromine at a lucrative 49 cents a pound.
Customers either paid the 49 cents or they went without. Dow and
other American companies sold bromine inside the United States
for 36 cents. The Bromkonvention made it clear that if the Americans tried to sell elsewhere, the Germans would flood the American
market with cheap bromine and drive them all out of business. The
Bromkonvention law was, "The U.S. for the U.S. and Germany for
the world."[18]

Herbert Dow entered bromine production with these unwritten rules in effect. And he followed them for a while. The bleach war, however, put him so deeply in debt that he decided to break the unwritten rules, challenge the Germans, and sell bromine in Europe to recover his losses.

Dow easily beat the cartel's 49 cent price and courageously sold America's first bromine in England. He hoped that the Germans, if they found out what he was doing, would ignore it. In fact, throughout 1904 he merrily bid on bromine contracts throughout the world.

After a few months of this, Dow encountered an angry visitor in his office from Germany—Hermann Jacobsohn of the Bromkonvention. Jacobsohn announced he had "positive evidence that [Dow] had exported bromides." "What of it?" Dow replied. "Don't you know that you can't sell bromides abroad?" Jacobsohn asked. "I know nothing of the kind," Dow retorted. Jacobsohn was indignant. He said that if Dow persisted, the Bromkonvention members would run him out of business whatever the cost. Then Jacobsohn left in a huff.[19]

Dow's philosophy of business differed sharply from that of the Germans. He was both a scientist and an entrepreneur: He wanted to learn how the chemical world worked, and then he wanted to improve lives by making the best product at the lowest price. The Germans, by contrast, wanted to discover chemicals in order to monopolize them and extort high prices for their discoveries. Those like Dow who tried to compete with the cartel learned quickly what "predatory price cutting" meant. The Bromkonvention, like other German cartels, had a "yellow dog fund," which was money set aside to use to flood other countries with low-cost chemicals to drive out competitors.[20]

Dow, however, was determined to compete with the Bromkonvention. He needed the sales, and he believed his electrolysis produced bromine cheaper than the German cartel could do. Also,

Dow was stubborn and hated being bluffed by a bully. When Jacob-sohn stormed out of his office, Dow continued to sell bromine to countries from England to Japan.

Before long, in early 1905, the Bromkonvention went on a rampage: It poured bromides into America at 15 cents a pound, well below its fixed price of 49 cents, and also below Dow's 36-cent price. Jacobsohn arranged a special meeting with Dow in St. Louis and demanded that he quit exporting bromides or else the Germans would flood the American market indefinitely. The Bromkonvention had the money and the backing of its government, Jacobsohn reminded Dow, and could long continue to sell in the United States below the cost of production. Dow was not intimidated; he was angry and told Jacobsohn he would sell to whoever would buy from him. Then Dow left the meeting with Jacobsohn screaming threats behind him. As Dow boarded the train from St. Louis he knew the future of his company—if it had a future—depended on how he handled the German cartel.[21]

On that train, Herbert Dow worked out a daring strategy. First, Dow Chemical would sell a token amount of bromine in the United States at 12 cents a pound to persuade the Germans that they had a fight on their hands. Second, Dow told his agent in New York to buy hundreds of thousands of pounds of German bromine at their 15-cent price, without letting the cartel know who was receiving the bromine. Third, Dow repackaged the German bromine and sold it in Europe—including Germany!—at 27 cents a pound. "When this 15-cent price was made over here," Dow said, "instead of meeting it, we pulled out of the American market altogether and used all our production to supply the foreign demand. This, as we afterward learned, was not what they anticipated we would do."[22]

Dow had secretly hired British and German agents to market his repackaged bromine in their countries. They had no trouble doing so because the Bromkonvention had left the world price above 30 cents a pound. The Germans were selling in the United States at far below the cost of production, and they hoped to offset their U.S. losses with a high world price. Dow courageously repackaged and recycled their bromine and still made a profit. A. E. Convers, the worried president of Dow Chemical, backed Dow's plan. "It seems as though the only way to bring Jacobso[h]n to terms will be to demoralize his market if possible at the point where he is getting his profit."[23]

Meanwhile, the Germans were befuddled. They expected to run Dow out of business, and this they thought they were doing. But why was U.S. demand for bromine so high? And where was this flow of cheap bromine into Europe coming from? Was one of the Bromkonvention members cheating and selling bromine in Europe below the fixed price? The tension in the Bromkonvention was dramatic. According to Dow, "The German producers got into trouble among themselves as to who was to supply the goods for the American market, and the American agent [for the Germans] became embarrassed by reason of his inability to get goods that he had contracted to supply and asked us if we would take his [15-cent] contracts. This, of course, we refused to do."[24]

The confused Germans kept cutting U.S. prices—first to 12 cents and then to 10.5 cents a pound. Dow meanwhile kept buying the cartel's cheap bromine and reselling it in Europe for 27 cents. These sales forced the Bromkonvention to drop its high world price to match Dow and that further depleted the Bromkonvention's resources. Dow, by contrast, improved his foreign sales force, often ran his bromine plants at top capacity, and gained business at the expense of the Bromkonvention and all other American producers, most of whom had shut down after the price cutting.

Even when the German cartel finally caught on to what Dow was doing, it wasn't sure how to respond. As Dow said, "We are absolute dictators of the situation." He also wrote, "One result of this fight has been to give us a standing all over the world. . . . We are . . . in a much stronger position than we ever were." He also added that "the profits are not so great" because his plants had trouble matching the new 27-cent world price. He needed to buy the cheap German bromides to stay ahead, and this was harder to do once the Germans discovered and exposed his repackaging scheme.[25]

The bromine war lasted four years (1904–1908), when finally the Bromkonvention invited Dow to come to Germany and work out an agreement. Since they couldn't crush Dow, they decided to at least work out some deal where they could make profits again. The terms were as follows: The cartel agreed to quit selling bromine in the United States, and Dow agreed to quit selling in Germany. The rest of the world was open to free competition. The bromine war was over, but low-priced bromine was now a fact of life.

While Dow was in Germany, he saw the bromine factories there and later the bleach plants in England. He concluded that his methods and factories for making both bromine and chlorine were the best in the world. "[W]e are therefore in a much stronger position than we ever were before," Dow concluded, "by reason of the Germans having respect for us, which is a very hard thing to obtain."[26]

Dow talked tough, but he knew he had to improve to survive. He constantly worked at finding new products and new markets for his chlorine and bromine. One of the first uses for his bromine was in making mining salts for separating gold from inferior ores. These mining salts became a major Dow export and were used in the gold rushes in Australia and South Africa. He also expanded into the bromine market in pharmaceuticals and photography. In 1908 Dow won Eastman Kodak's business and personally serviced their large account for the rest of his life.[27]

As early as 1900, Dow also sold chlorine as sulfur chloride, used in the production of rubber. When sales to rubber producers dropped, Dow used his sulfur chloride to make chloroform, which became an important Dow product. Another use of chlorine was to make carbon tetrachloride, which is nonflammable and therefore used in fire extinguishers.

Selling these new bromine and chlorine products was crucial. Early on, Dow established his own sales department to push Dow products at home and abroad. The profits from these sales helped him survive the bleach and bromine wars. He promoted iron chloride for engraving work and zinc chloride as a soldering flux. Insecticides came next as the Dow product line expanded.

Jesse B. Fay, the company's patent lawyer and a major stockholder, helped Dow patent dozens of his discoveries, and watched him turn a flow of chemicals into a mountain of cash. "So far as I am able to judge," Fay told Dow,

> your mind does not work according to any normal law. Logic seems superseded by inspiration. . . . Things that to the ordinary mind appear to be fixed facts and axioms, to you appear faulty and capable of being changed for the better in many ways. You start with one idea and before you can put it into words new avenues of thought open up to you that divert you from the original idea. . . . You should . . . not use up your energy in doing something that another man could do as well as you.[28]

Dow took Fay's advice and delegated authority whenever possible. One thing that helped was that he hired the best scientists he could find and turned them loose to innovate. W. R. Veazey, one of his top scientists, later recalled, "He encouraged everybody to find out things in their own way. It was not uncommon for him to put several people or a group of people to work on the same problem at the same time and run the whole show like a horse race to see which one would come up first with the answer."[29]

The better scientists imitated Dow's creativity. Charles Strosacker, for example, was often the opportunist, taking abandoned materials and making a marketable product from them. Mark Putnam was the perfectionist, figuring out how to make products as pure as possible. Ed Barstow was the innovator, mixing new concoctions. Barstow worked out a way to treat chlorine with toluene to make benzoic acid, which could be converted into a popular preservative. Barstow also invented a complicated process that could separate calcium and magnesium from Michigan brine. That later allowed Dow to produce ammonia, Epsom salts, and calcium chloride, which was used for settling dust in mines and unpaved roads. When Dow pumped brine into his vats in Midland, more and more went into chemicals for market and less and less went into sewers as waste.[30]

Dow was a hands-on boss. Rarely was he in his office working. Usually he was in the labs talking shop or out on the floor giving advice. There was Dow, a shovel in hand, showing a man how to spread coal evenly over a fire. There was Dow, hands in the air, encouraging his chemists and arguing with them so vehemently that others all over the building could hear him. When problems were debated and resolved, however, Dow and his men were a united front.

Dow respected his employees, especially those loyal to him in the early and precarious years. In fact, one of the reasons Midlanders called him "Crazy Dow" was that he paid high local wages to get the best workers he could. Early in the company's history, Dow started a plan to share 2 percent of the company's profits with all employees each year. Dow knew this plan would make his workers more loyal and more eager to do their jobs well.

Money to Dow was a means to an end, not the end itself, which it was for the German cartels. Dow once said, "I'd rather work for myself for $3,000 a year than to work for someone else and make $10,000."[31] At Dow Chemical, he tried to create an environment where talented chemists would have satisfying lives helping him unlock the secrets of Michigan's brine and making cheap products from it to sell to the world.

Even after Dow's success in the bromine war, the dye business remained almost exclusively a German preserve. Ever since synthetic dyes had been produced from coal tars in 1856, German chemists put energy, capital, and manpower into producing and nearly monopolizing the world's dyes. The German dye trust, like the Bromkonvention, shared secrets, fixed prices, and divided the world markets among its members. When rivals in other countries dared to compete, the dye trust cut prices and tried to knock them out of business. Those who bought dyes from rivals had to face an angry and vindictive dye trust—all of which helped keep prices high and the Germans on top.[32]

Herbert Dow had planned to attack the German dye trust for many years. He reasoned logically: Bromine was a major by-product of his brine; bromine was a key ingredient in the making of indigo; indigo was "the most important of all the dyes," the favorite of most textile makers and the heart of German dominance. Therefore, Dow should hire organic chemists, give them space, and turn them loose to figure out how to make indigo, and make it cheaply. When Dow tried to do this in 1906—in the middle of the bromine war—his directors flatly refused to risk the capital or irritate the powerful German dye trust.

In 1914, the outbreak of World War I reopened the dye issue. With Europe at war, England used its navy to try to starve the Germans into surrendering. That meant blockading German ports, and that act was quickly felt in the United States. American textile manufacturers relied on the German dye trust; a blockade of Germany meant shortages, and shortages meant high prices for scarce dyes, even though the United States was still neutral.

At one point, Germany tantalized its American customers by exporting dyes to Baltimore in submarines. Usually, however, the Germans artfully manipulated the dye shortages to coax the United States into pressuring England to lift its blockade. Count Johann Heinrich von Bernstorff, the German ambassador in Washington, cabled his leaders "that the stock of dyes in this country is so small that by a German embargo about 4,000,000 American workmen might be thrown out of employment."[33]

What a paradox this was! Before the war, the German dye trust threatened to ruin any American firm that bought dye from Dow or anyone else. Now Germany, through its manipulations, forced American textile men to rush to Dow and urge him to figure out how to make dyes as quickly as possible. As prices skyrocketed, newspapers echoed the cry, "Why haven't our chemical companies experimented sufficiently to produce synthetic dyes, pharmaceutical products, essential oils, and synthetic perfumes, in the production of which Germany seems to have almost a monopoly?"[34]

With prices high, pseudo-chemists throughout the country went to work trying to make yellow dyes out of banana peels and green dyes out of grass. Dow was more realistic. With prices high and the dye trust on the sidelines, here was his chance to break into the indigo market.

In 1915, almost a year after Germany went to war, Dow made his move. He hired a top organic chemist from the University of Michigan and then exhorted him, and others on his staff, to unlock the chemical secrets for synthesizing indigo. The investment Dow made in cash, equipment, and manpower shocked some of his directors—who found out only after the fact what Dow was doing. They were horrified and raised the following objections.

First, the German cartel had taken many years of teamwork to figure out how to make indigo. Dow's team would have to produce this same indigo more quickly with fewer scientists and less capital. If they were too slow, the war would end (which, of course, could happen anytime), and the dye trust would quickly recapture lost markets.

Second, Dow, by betting the company's future on indigo, was bypassing the chance to invest in profitable but less complicated chemicals. Dr. Albert W. Smith, a chemist and a member of Dow's board of directors, found this point to be compelling. "The indigo proposition," he wrote Dow, "really seems the most difficult of many that might be tried. For that reason possibly the time and energy spent on that could be more profitably spent in making some of the other numerous organic chemicals that are very high-priced and whose manufacture would be decidedly simpler."[35]

Third, even if Dow's chemists could produce indigo in large and profitable quantities—which were two major assumptions—he would still have to fight the dye trust after the war and maybe during the war for every indigo buyer in the world. Even Dow admitted this to be true. "It will require . . . a very large investment to complete an indigo plant," Dow told the Federal Trade Commission in 1915. "[T]he question will then arise as to whether the price will immediately be reduced the minute we start to manufacture."[36] Nobody doubted for a minute that the Germans would resume their customary price cutting in the dye industry, just as they had done with bromine ten years earlier.

With confidence and cunning, Dow believed he would discover how to make indigo and then sell it competitively after the war. In December 1916, eighteen months after Dow Chemical began work on indigo, the company shipped the first batch off to market at $1.50 per pound. At last, America was in the dye business to stay. When the Germans came back into the world market, Dow was ready for them. Through improvements in manufacturing, the price dropped to $.75 per pound a year after the war and was only 14 cents a pound by 1925, which was less than the Germans had charged. As Mark Putnam, a vice president at Dow Chemical, wrote years later, "This accomplishment, while important from an economic standpoint, was even more important from a moral standpoint because it tended to remove the heretofore strong doubts as to whether America could produce a self-contained and vigorous dye and organic chemical industry."[37]

Dow's massive and effective war production helped the United

States win World War I and also helped to win the peace afterward. Many of the war chemicals Dow produced had peacetime uses as well. Phenol, for example, became a major ingredient in dozens of products, from aspirin to plastics. Acetic anhydride was also a key ingredient in aspirin, but that pain reliever had been a German monopoly before the war, with the Germans charging $8.50 per pound for it. During the war, Dow began shifting some of his acetic anhydride into the making of aspirin for the soldiers. Afterward, Dow had his costs of producing aspirin down to 60 cents a pound; he was ready to supply America's needs and also to challenge the Germans for aspirin markets all over the world.

The Novocain story is yet another example of German inventiveness coupled with a tendency to monopolize and overcharge. Novocain was first synthesized by the Germans and sold as an anesthetic. They reaped monopoly profits and charged $1,600 per pound for Novocain before the war. But after the war, the defeated Germans had to turn many of their patents over to the Alien Property custodian. Dow applied for the patent for Novocain, learned how to make it efficiently, and quickly slashed its price to $30 per pound. As a result, dentists and doctors around the world could use Novocain to deaden pain.[38]

Dow's last major battle was not with the Germans, but with the British. The two chemicals at stake were bromine and iodine, and the issue was usable gasoline for cars. The problem was that the low-octane gasoline of the early 1900s caused engines in cars to "knock," which happened when the gasoline exploded unevenly in the cylinders. Scientists at General Motors had found that adding iodine to the gasoline eliminated the knock, but iodine was tightly controlled by a British-Chilean cartel that charged $4.50 per pound.

Dow's scientists, working with those at General Motors, produced ethylene dibromide, which when added to tetraethyl lead, would stop the knock in engines. And it was about seven times cheaper than iodine. What was needed now was a cheap and plentiful source of bromine, which spurred Dow to mine bromine from the ocean by using his blowing-out technique to separate bromine from seawater.[39]

Mining bromine from the ocean was risky: Even if it could be done, it might be too expensive. Dow, therefore, hedged his bets with a two-pronged assault on the iodine cartel. One of his scientists, Coulter W. Jones, used Dow's blowing-out process to separate iodine from oil field brine in Louisiana. When Dow died suddenly in 1930, his successor and son Willard helped Jones build an iodine plant in McDade, Louisiana. In the next few years, Jones was able to produce iodine so cheaply that they broke the iodine cartel and slashed the world market price from $4.50 to 81 cents per pound. Dow Chemical now had two products—iodine and eth-ylene dibromide—that removed the knock from gasoline engines, and this gave the company a solid stake in the booming auto indus-try. As for Britain, Chile, and Germany, they had done no better with their cartels than McKenney, Collins, and Dodge had done with their federal subsidies.

In 1866, when Herbert Dow was born, two major assump-tions dominated the thinking of businessmen and politicians in the United States and abroad. First, that government assistance made good companies better. Second, that big cartels and oligopo-lies, with their near monopoly power, could not be beaten by any smaller, renegade entrepreneur. Herbert Dow's astonishing career in the chemical industry refuted both of these assumptions again and again. "Your mind does not work according to any normal law," Dow's lawyer told him. Maybe not. But the legacy from Dow's genius was wonderfully cheap products ranging from aspirin to gas-oline, readily available to Americans and to the world.

6

The Wright Brothers
Conquer the Air

Alexander Graham Bell sat calmly in his rowboat, camera in hand. He hoped to get a photo of major historical importance. The great scientist Samuel Langley was on the shore holding a stopwatch, about to launch his miniature "aerodrome." Suddenly, Langley signaled, and his flying machine took off from the nearby houseboat into the air. After a wobbly start, the two wings steadied, the small engine buzzed, and the unmanned plane soared over the Potomac River in a circular path. Bell was so excited he almost forgot to snap the picture.

Langley clocked the flight at ninety seconds, and computed the distance at a half mile. "Like a living thing," he wrote, it "swept continuously through the air." He added, "As I heard the cheering of the few spectators, I felt that something had been accomplished at last."[1]

Langley's triumph on May 6, 1896, made him the favorite to

fulfill man's dream of flying. Sure, most people still doubted that humans would ever fly, but here was the intrepid Langley, age sixty-two, leading the way to invent the airplane. Engineers in England, France, and Germany had all started aeronautical societies, and they recorded their progress in new academic journals.[2] But it was an American, Samuel Langley, head of the Smithsonian Institution and author of *Experiments in Aerodynamics*, who had launched a minia-ture craft that seemed to fly. After this, the world would praise him as the undisputed global leader in the quest to invent the airplane.[3]

Langley inhaled the accolades of his peers and the "cheering of the . . . spectators." As one of his employees once noted, Lang-ley was a "born aristocrat." He exuded authority, confidence, and strength. Growing up in Boston, he excelled in mathematics, me-chanics, and astronomy. He became a Renaissance man as he also mastered literature and history. Later he built his own telescope and invented the bolometer, which measured energy and heat given off by the sun.[4]

As Langley moved from academic posts in astronomy at Har-vard, the U.S. Naval Academy, and the University of Pittsburgh, he easily rubbed elbows with the rich and famous along the way. Perhaps his best friend was fellow inventor Alexander Graham Bell, who foresaw that air travel would benefit mankind even more than his own invention of the telephone twenty years earlier. Bell wanted to be present at Langley's demonstrations, even as a mere photog-rapher. Langley also dazzled scientists and intellectuals around the world. He traveled to Europe frequently and cultivated the friend-ship of great English thinkers, such as historian Thomas Carlyle, who called Langley "the most sensible American he had ever met." He attended parties at the estates of the English elites, and Oxford University awarded him a doctorate of civil law.[5]

Langley was honored at home as well. American historians, in-cluding Henry Adams, and university presidents, such as Andrew Dickson White of Cornell, cultivated Langley's advice and even wrote articles about him. The prestigious American Association for the Advancement of Science elected Langley—author of more than two hundred scholarly publications—as its president. In 1887, when the Smithsonian Institution in Washington, D.C., was seeking a president, Langley was the logical choice, and Professor Asa Gray of Harvard eagerly recommended him for the job. Some observers thought Langley was America's greatest scientist, and the experiments he began at the Smithsonian to unravel the mysteries of flight earned respect around the world.[6]

After Langley completed a second test of his miniature flying machine in November 1896, he pondered his next step: building a larger version of his "aerodrome," as he called it, powerful enough to carry a passenger. "I believe," Langley wrote, "that the results already accomplished on May 6/96, and Nov 18/96, make it as nearly certain as any untried thing can be, that with a larger machine of the same model, to carry a man, or men . . . flight could be maintained for at least some hours."[7]

The problem for Langley was finding the cash to build his larger plane. He wasn't independently wealthy, and he preferred to spend what he earned on travel and fine living. Thus, he sought a philanthropist to fund his aerodrome. For example, Langley wrote Octave Chanute, a Chicago engineer and flight enthusiast, "If anyone were to put at my disposal the considerable amount—fifty thousand dollars or more—for . . . an aerodrome carrying a man or men, with a capacity for some hours of flight, I feel that I could build it and should enjoy the task." But Langley made it clear to Chanute and others that advancing science, not making a profit, was his motive. He shunned "commercial strife," and asked Chanute if he knew "anyone who is disposed to give the means to such an unselfish end." Chanute replied, "I know of nobody who is disposed to give the means for a purely scientific experiment"—and indeed no one came forward to fund Langley's Great Aerodrome, as some called it.[8]

So Langley pursued another angle. On February 15, 1898, the

Maine blew up in Havana harbor, and the United States and Spain lurched toward war. Congress appropriated $50 million for defense, so Langley developed an argument about the military value of flight. Five weeks after the sinking of the *Maine*, Langley exploited his connection with Charles Walcott, head of the U.S. Geological Survey, who had access to President William McKinley. Langley told Walcott of his ability to build "a man-carrying aerodrome as a possible engine of war for the government."[9] Would Walcott meet with McKinley and help secure the funds?[10]

Walcott did even more. He showed McKinley the photo that Bell had taken of Langley's earlier unmanned flight, and then sold the president on the project, and key cabinet members as well. Teddy Roosevelt, assistant secretary of war, was especially exuberant: "The machine has worked. It seems to me worthwhile for this government to try whether it will not work on a large enough scale to be of use in the event of war."[11]

Roosevelt's endorsement was important because the subsidy disasters with the Union Pacific Railroad and the Collins steamship line had, for the past generation, knocked the government out of economic planning. Many politicians doubted the government's ability to pick winners and losers through federal aid. But Langley and his Great Aerodrome seemed to be different, and worthy of political support. First, Langley was a seasoned and preeminent scientist who was leading the international race to invent the airplane. Second, he had already shown he could "fly" miniature planes. Why not fund him for a bigger model? Third, Langley had friends in high places. As one employee at the Smithsonian observed, "[Langley] was invited to dine at the White House, he was on familiar terms with the Chief Justice of the United States. . . . Members of the House of Representatives and sometimes senators waited in his anteroom."[12]

Perhaps this was the moment in history when a strategic federal gift would foster the invention to vault the United States into military dominance in the world. Langley found himself before key political and military leaders with the chance to state his case.

First, he pitched his proposal to a special committee of key officers from the army and navy, and then to the Department of War, through its Board of Ordnance and Fortification (BOF).[13] Of his flying machine, Langley tantalized these military men with the prospect of using it as "an engine of war." These army and navy men salivated at the thought "of dropping from a great height high explosives into a camp of fortification." With the prospect of a government subsidy, Langley was deferential to the BOF, but firm. "Concerning the use of the aerodrome in war, it is hardly for me, a civilian, to insist upon its utility to a board of military men. But I think I might be justified in saying that anything which, like this, would enable one party to look into the enemy's tactics and movements . . . would tend to modify the present art of war, much as the game of whist might be modified if a player were allowed to look into his opponent's hand."[14]

The BOF peppered Langley with questions, and he answered them readily. He expected his aerodrome to fly for hours at a time, perhaps at a speed of 25 to 30 miles per hour. He added that "the machine will be completely built and ready for trial within a year," but might take longer to test and modify for use in war. He exuded confidence. The BOF members were impressed. They concluded that Langley's proposed aircraft gave "promise of great military value," and they authorized a fifty-thousand-dollar subsidy for his aerodrome.[15]

With federal cash flowing, Langley began his work. First, he hired engineer Charles Manly, a recent Cornell University graduate, as pilot and supervisor for construction of the aerodrome. Langley also hired engineers, carpenters, machinists, and mechanics. Manly came to Washington, and the Smithsonian bustled with activity. It became the international clearinghouse for knowledge and research on flight.[16]

With all of Langley's duties and his regular trips abroad, he couldn't answer incoming mail. One of his clerks responded to a May 5, 1899, query from a thirty-two-year-old bicycle mechanic—a man who had lost several teeth as well as the chance to go to college because he had been ill for many years. This bicycle mechanic requested materials on the subject of flight, a topic he said interested him. "I wish to avail myself of all that is already known," he said. The clerk at the Smithsonian dutifully mailed Langley's short bibliography on flight to the modest home of the mechanic in Dayton, Ohio. His name was Wilbur Wright.[17]

To the casual observer, Wilbur Wright, or Will as he was called, had no training and no aptitude that would ever enable him to advance the science of aerodynamics. He was the third son of a minister, and seemed least likely to succeed even within his own family. Unlike his parents, his two older brothers, and his sister, Will never went to college. He was smart, well read, and athletic, but he seemed to be perpetually ill. It started when he had several teeth smashed out in a hockey game at age nineteen. After that, he became bedridden by various ailments and stomachaches. He rarely left home, which, during his twenties, kept him idle rather than making his place in the world. True, he cared for his invalid mother and helped his father with ministry business. But he became quiet, pensive, and more of a loner. "What does Will do?" wrote his older brother from Kansas. "He ought to be doing something. Is he still cook and chambermaid?" As Will regained his health, he helped his younger brother Orville set up a print shop to publish their church's theological materials and also a local newspaper. Then Wilbur and Orville opened a bicycle shop, where they built and repaired bicycles together.[18]

Will's life revolved around family activities, but he also read widely, reasoned impeccably, and thought deeply about many things. "The strongest impression one gets of Wilbur Wright," a friend observed, "is of a man who lives largely in a world of his own." Printing newspapers and fixing bicycles gave him time to think and dream about what he might yet accomplish in life. "My imagination," Will told his sister Kate, "pictures things more vividly than my eyes."[19]

The subject of flight entered Will's imagination in 1894, when he read an article in *McClure's* about Otto Lilienthal, the German engineer who had built wings and experimented with hang gliding. At first, Lilienthal explained, he merely hopped off a hill and let the wind under his wings take him a short distance. With practice, he tried bigger hills and soon was in the air for five and sometimes ten seconds. His article in *McClure's* had a picture of him in flight, and Will and Orville both studied the photo and marveled at the idea of airborne travel. But Lilienthal died during one of his flights in 1896, the same year that Langley flew his model plane over the Potomac, so attention now focused more on Langley. Three years later, with Langley's aerodrome in the news, Will composed his letter to the Smithsonian.[20]

After reading the items on Langley's list, Will was most impressed with the German and French contributions. In particular, Lilienthal, a German, and Louis Mouillard, a Frenchman, stressed the mastery of gliding as a prerequisite to mechanical flight. Both men watched birds carefully and noticed how they artfully used wind against their wings and even coasted through the sky. Lilienthal had stressed "continual practice," trial and error, and step-by-step improvement to master the art of gliding. Octave Chanute, Langley's friend, wrote *Progress in Flying Machines*, and Will learned from that book, too. Chanute described the importance of stability and balance, which had to be achieved in the midst of varying wind patterns.[21]

Then there was Samuel Langley, the leader in the race to fly. Unlike Lilienthal and Chanute, Langley stressed engine power more than gliders and wind control. After all, Langley's unmanned aerodrome had soared across the Potomac on a calm day with a capable engine and not much attention to wings and balance. That time, it worked. What he needed next, he argued, was another calm day and a bigger aerodrome with a lightweight gas engine that could propel it, and the pilot, through the air. Langley dismissed his critics, who pointed out that some of the test models for his aerodrome had simply dropped into the river. Was the one success that had sailed half a mile just a lucky fluke? The skeptics compared that "flight" to a kite being caught on a strong breeze.

Langley liked to make an analogy between flight and ice-skating. A skater can sometimes skate effectively on thin ice until he stops—at which point the full weight of the skater breaks the ice. As long as the skater is moving, he can pass over ice that is not able to bear his full weight. In the case of flight, Langley argued, a powerful engine moves the plane rapidly through air, which normally would bear no weight. But with the powerful engine propelling the plane, the air allows the plane to pass through smoothly.[22]

Thus, Langley made his top priority the building of an engine, light in weight and strong in power. Once he had his federal aid, he hired Stephen Balzer, an expert engineer who had already designed the first automobile to run in New York. Langley called Balzer "the only competent [engine] builder in the United States," which gave Langley confidence he could produce his Great Aerodrome in 1899, as he had promised the BOF.[23]

Wilbur Wright disagreed. He concluded, after studying Langley and his work carefully, that stressing engine power over glider maneuvering was wrong. Will wanted to build a new type of glider that could harness the wind, but he wanted to balance and steer with his hands while lying prone on the glider, not dangling beneath it as Lilienthal and Chanute had done. Only when Will had learned and mastered the art of gliding would he build the engine. If he could learn to control a glider, he believed, the engine would take care of itself. With both Lilienthal and Mouillard dead, and with Langley headed down a different path, Will wrote to Octave

Chanute, explained his ideas, and the two men gradually formed a friendship.[24]

When asked later about Langley's strategy of engine first, then wind control later, Will responded, "Unfortunately, the wind usually blows." That statement spoke volumes about the practical and financial side of Will's thinking. He wanted to invent the airplane, in part, to make a profit. But Will knew that to make a plane that people would want to buy, or to fly in, he would have to invent one that could fly safely in all kinds of weather. What good was a plane that could be used to drop bombs, deliver mail, or carry passengers if it was regularly grounded by even light winds? Langley, by contrast, wanted fame but not profits. His Great Aerodrome, funded by taxpayers, would be his gift to the nation, and his legacy to science. If it had the potential to make money, that task would be left to others.[25]

As Langley, with federal subsidy in hand, was testing his theory of flight, Will prepared for his own tests. He searched for a climate warmer than Dayton's, and for an area with hills, wind, and privacy, where he could build his glider and test it. He would use his own money to pay the bills, so the tests had to be as cheap as possible. Chanute recommended the Atlantic coast, leading Will to write to weather stations near the ocean. Finally he settled on the windy and remote village of Kitty Hawk, North Carolina.[26]

Will needed a talented confidant and for that he had his younger brother Orville at hand. Orville soon captured the vision and became a full partner in flight, just as he was in bicycles. The two brothers were inseparable and each influenced the other. "From the time we were little children," Will said, "my brother Orville and myself lived together, played together, and worked together and, in fact, thought together." But they also loved to argue with each other. "Orv is such a good scrapper," Will once said, but he liked that. "Honest argument," he insisted, "is merely a process of mutually picking the beams and motes out of each other's eyes so both can see clearly." And Will wanted to see as clearly as possible when he built his first glider in a spare room in their bicycle shop.[27]

In building their glider, the Wright brothers had to construct a device that could control the energy of the wind. In doing so, they used existing knowledge and then modified or advanced it. For example, the principles of lift and drag were widely understood: Lift is the force of the wind pushing a wing upward, and a curved surface, like that of birds' wings, captures that force better than a flat one. Drag is the force that slows the wing's forward motion. Knowing this, Will invented wing warping, by which he curved the wing's surface to capture more energy from the wind. He decided that double-decker wings, recommended by Chanute, were best both for wing warping and efficient, steady gliding. The Wrights also needed to turn their glider in the air, so they added a rear rudder. To control up and down movements, they added a horizontal rudder. They installed wires to control the horizontal rudder and raise and lower the wings. The pilot, lying prone in the middle of the bottom wing, used his hands and feet to pull these wires to guide the glider through the air.[28]

Much of this process evolved through trial and error. Winter was the off season for bicycle work in Dayton, so the Wright brothers descended on Kitty Hawk for five weeks in late 1900 for the first of four annual visits. Before leaving Dayton, Will wrote his father, "While I am taking up the investigation [of flight] for pleasure rather than profit, I think there is a slight possibility of achieving fame and fortune from it." But not that winter. In their first visit to Kitty Hawk, they set up their tent near the hills outside of town, made the acquaintance of the few locals, and drafted (and paid) some of them to help them with their homemade glider. While one of the Wright brothers manned the glider, the other brother and a local would do the running launch from a hill. They also measured wind patterns and the distances of their flights.[29]

Over time, the Wrights became familiar figures to the residents of Kitty Hawk, even though their glider seemed to be an odd contraption. "They were two of the workingest boys I ever saw," said John Daniels, "and when they worked they *worked*. I never saw men so wrapped up in their work in my life. They had their whole heart and soul in what they were doing." But Daniels and other locals liked the Wrights; they were "good with the children" and "courteous to everyone." Ever the minister's sons, the Wrights didn't drink or smoke, and they always rested on Sundays. When they conducted their flights, they wore white shirts with stiff collars and ties.[30]

From 1900 to 1903, Orville and Wilbur spent spring and summer in Dayton at the cycle shop, and parts of the fall or winter in Kitty Hawk. They funded their flight experiments from profits in their shop, so they were frugal and used time wisely. Each year, during downtime in Dayton, the brothers used part of their shop to build new and bigger gliders with improvements to the wings, the wiring, and the rudders. They speeded up their progress by building a six-foot wind tunnel with a glass top and a powerful fan on the side. Next they built miniature wings of different sizes from scrap metal. By using the fan to produce a strong wind in the tunnel, the brothers tested different curvatures for the wings and used the results to improve their designs. "Wilbur and I could hardly wait for morning to come," Orville said, "to get at something that interested us. *That's* happiness."[31]

For the tests at Kitty Hawk, the brothers brought their tools and equipment to make adjustments on the spot. One year, for example, they improved their glider by adding a movable tail to the wing-warping wires. Sometimes, however, they were delayed by crashes, by wind gusts that would blow down their tent, and by pesky mosquitoes, which, according to Orville, "chewed us clear through our underwear and socks. Lumps began swelling up all over my body like hen's eggs."[32]

Octave Chanute began to respect the unknown Wright broth-

ers, and he read Will's letters with interest. He even visited the
Wrights at both Dayton and Kitty Hawk. He watched their remarkable progress first hand. "You have done a great work," Chanute told them, "and have advanced knowledge greatly." Perhaps
thinking of the subsidized Langley, Chanute asked the Wrights if
"some rich man should give you $10,000 a year to go on, to con-
nect his name with progress, would you do so? I happen to know
Carnegie. Would you like for me to write him?"[33]

Will considered his words carefully. "I do not think it would
be wise for me to accept help in carrying our present investigations
further," he said. He added, "I would not think it wise to make
outside work [on the flying machine] too pronounced a feature of
business life." Orville reached the same conclusion in a different
way. He later said, "Unfortunately, unlike many who use other
people's money in their experiments, and therefore must keep records to make a showing of their work, we were working for ourselves, and just for the fun of it."[34]

In October 1902, Chanute wrote a letter to Langley warning
him that the Wrights were no mere tinkerers; they were "very inge-
nious mechanics and men of high character and integrity." Langley
wondered what he could learn from the Wrights. He sent a telegram to Kitty Hawk and asked the Wrights if he might visit them,
but Will declined politely and said they would soon be returning to
Dayton. The Wrights later refused to travel to Washington to meet
with Langley at his expense.[35]

Langley probably thought little of the upstart Wright brothers
at the time. He had enough problems of his own trying to complete his Great Aerodrome. When he wrote to the Wrights, he was
already three years overdue with the Department of War, and had
to explain his many delays. One problem was the engine, which
was, of course, the key to his theory of flying. Stephen Balzer, the
builder of his engine, was having problems creating the powerful
lightweight engine he had promised. Langley wanted at least ten

horsepower to fly his plane, but Balzer struggled to get that power without adding too much weight. He also wrestled with overheating, breakdowns, and malfunctioning parts. Langley was regularly sending Balzer cash from the subsidy, and when two of Balzer's machinists quit, Langley even sent him two machinists from the Smithsonian.[36]

At one point, Langley and his pilot Charles Manly went to Europe in search of a workable engine, or for someone who could make one. He visited Sir Hiram Stevens Maxim, the English expert who had tried to build a flying machine in 1894. Langley was pleased when Maxim insisted, "Without doubt, the motor is the chief thing to be considered," but Maxim had no engine to offer. Langley next went to Paris to plead for help from the renowned Comte Albert de Dion, who had built superb gas-powered engines for cars. But the Frenchman had no help for Langley, either. In a similar way, Manly traveled to Germany and Belgium, searching in vain for something to power the aerodrome. Finally, Langley and Manly came home empty-handed, and thus Manly himself designed the engine that would ultimately launch the Great Aerodrome.[37]

Even with Manly's diligent work, Langley was frantic. Problems with the engine, with the construction of the aerodrome, with getting work out of his carpenters and machinists, with the persistent questions from the War Department—all this delayed him. His government subsidy was gone, and he raided a reserve fund at the Smithsonian for another twenty thousand dollars. He simply had to get his aerodrome in shape to fly. If that could be done, Manly argued, "the funds for the further prosecution of the work would be readily forthcoming."[38]

Before launching the Great Aerodrome, Langley and Manly tested a miniature model of their plane. They shot it upward from their catapult on their houseboat on the Potomac on August 8, 1903. Reporters flocked to the site and watched it soar gracefully over the Potomac for a minute, and then flutter into the river. Success! Manly was invigorated as he described its "strange, uncanny beauty"; to him it "seemed visibly and gloriously alive."[39]

The "entirely successful" launch of the unmanned version set expectations high for the real thing. Langley's confidence knew no bounds, as he told Manly not to fly more than ten or twelve minutes at most. Manly, meanwhile, became "thoroughly familiar with this portion of the [Potomac] river, so that I can recognize all the landmarks while flying through the air."[40]

Two months later, on October 7, 1903, Manly's staff hoisted the Great Aerodrome onto the houseboat and prepared for the launch. Manly stepped into the cockpit at 12:20 p.m. and signaled an assistant to fire two rockets into the air to announce the big event. From the houseboat, another assistant released the lever on the catapult, and the aerodrome surged down the sixty-foot track. For an instant it was airborne, and Manly had "an indescribable sensation of being free in the air." Soon, however, the sensation became more describable as the aerodrome plunged nose first into the Potomac. Manly frantically struggled to eject himself from the submerging machine and groped upward for air. He reached the surface without injuries.[41]

The reporters present were very critical. The *Washington Post* writer, for example, called the crash "a crushing blow to [Langley's] theory." The editorial writer at the *Post* said, "any stout boy of fifteen . . . could have skimmed an oyster shell much farther, and that without months of expensive preparation or . . . government fleets, appliances and retinues." Langley, however, rationalized the result by insisting that success "is in no way affected by this accident, which is one of the large chapters of accidents that beset the initial stages of experiments so novel as the present ones."[42]

Meanwhile, the engine was fully salvaged, and so were other parts of the aerodrome. While Langley desperately scoured the Smithsonian for cash, Manly quickly began repairs for one final trial. To get further federal funds, they had to score a success and do so quickly. On a cold and windy December 8, with chunks of ice floating in the Potomac, Langley and Manly prepared the Great Aerodrome for another launch. "It seemed almost disastrous to attempt an experiment," Manly admitted. But "it was practically a case of 'now or never.' "[43]

Manly, wearing a cork-lined jacket, climbed onto the houseboat and into the cockpit, while Langley watched hopefully from a tugboat nearby. No rockets were fired this time to advertise the event. The engine whirred smoothly and an assistant triggered the catapult. Suddenly Manly felt "an extreme swaying motion immediately followed by a tremendous jerk which caused the machine to quiver all over." Then, according to one witness, "the whole rear of the wings and rudder [were] completely destroyed" in midair. The gigantic wings tore apart at the rapid speed of the aerodrome hurtling off the catapult. Manly, after some "intense moments," struggled under water to climb out and get to the surface once more. He "uttered a voluble series of blasphemies" after being fished out of the water. He would not be the first pilot to fly after all.[44]

Reports of the event varied from mirth at the pretentious disaster to irritation at the wasted federal funds. The *Boston Herald* urged Langley to abandon flying machines and focus instead on submarines. The *New York Times* had already concluded that a flying machine might yet be built, but only if mathematicians and engineers worked hard at it for the next million or so years.[45]

The *San Francisco Chronicle* put Langley's "disastrous" effort in economic perspective: "The destruction of Langley's machine should put an end to Congressional appropriations of any kind in every field of experiments which properly belongs to private enterprise." The editor concluded, "The reward which will surely follow the production of a practical airship is a sufficient stimulus in itself to private competition."[46]

During 1903, the Wright brothers, working in obscurity, had also been preparing for motorized flight. On their gliders, they had mastered the hand controls to bend the wings and harness the wind. To go from a glider to an airplane they needed sturdier wings to hold the added weight, two propellers for thrust, and, of course, a lightweight engine to power the flight.

On the subject of the engine, they happily knew little of Langley's travails. Will naively wrote to several manufacturers and asked if they could provide an eight-horsepower gas engine that weighed less than two hundred pounds. Everyone said no. So Will next asked Charlie Taylor, a mechanic in their cycle shop, if he could do the job. He studied the matter, gathered parts locally, and made some tests. "We didn't make any drawings," Taylor said later. But in six weeks he had built a superb twelve-horsepower engine that weighed only 179 pounds. What took Langley four years and an international search took the Wright brothers six weeks, using only labor and materials found in Dayton, Ohio.[47]

Making propellers that worked well was much more complicated. The Wrights filled five notebooks with formulas, tests, and computations that showed how forward thrust could be created by the rotating of specially curved propeller blades. "Isn't it astonishing," Orville wrote, "that all these secrets have been preserved for so many years just so that we could discover them?" By the fall of 1903 they were ready to load up the parts of their plane, return to Kitty Hawk, and piece them together for a test flight.[48]

Oddly, the Wrights hardly took notice of Langley's highly publicized attempts to fly. They assumed their theory of flight was the right one, and so they pursued it where it logically led. After Langley's first crash, Will said, "I see that Langley has had his fling, and failed. It seems to be our turn to throw now."[49]

Back in Kitty Hawk, the Wrights assembled their plane and built a movable starting track from which to launch it. The track was a long wooden path, which they could strategically assemble and place on a downward slope; the plane sat atop landing skids on a two-wheeled dolly that would roll slowly down the track. The brothers flipped a coin to see who would try first. Wilbur won, but his maiden effort on December 14 crashed into the sand, which forced a minor delay. Nonetheless, Will telegrammed his father these words: "Success Assured Keep Quiet."[50]

Orville's turn came next. On a cold and windy December 17, the brothers, aided by a stray teenage boy and five men from a nearby lifesaving station, slowly moved their seven-hundred-pound plane toward the hill to position it on their wooden runway. At 10:35 a.m., Orville crawled onto the bottom wing, assumed a prone position, and grabbed the controls. As he later said, "The [weather] conditions were very unfavorable." Will, noting that fact, clapped, cheered him on, and urged the others to do so. They started the engine and let it warm up. Then they let the plane go, but strong 27 mile-per-hour winds made the trip down the runway slow. Soon the plane lifted from the ground. Orville was in the air. "The course of the flight up and down was exceedingly erratic," he said later, "partly due to the irregularity of the air, and partly to [my] lack of experience in handling this machine." This first motorized flight through the air lasted twelve seconds and covered 120 feet. The brothers tried three more flights that day with Will setting the record by staying aloft for fifty-nine seconds and traveling 852 feet before a hard landing finished their flights for the day. Their victory telegram to their father opened with the key word, "Success."[51]

December 17, 1903, became a landmark date in U.S. history, but almost no one knew it at the time. The men helping to push the plane up the hill for each of the launches realized that they had seen something remarkable. One of them, Johnny Moore, was so excited that he ran toward Kitty Hawk to spread the news. He told the first person he met, "They done it! They done it! Damn'd if they ain't flew!" But no newspaper reporters had been present. The *Dayton Daily News* was one of the few papers to report the event, and in the following months the story became garbled in those newspapers that did report it. Even enthusiasts in the aeronautics community didn't fully grasp what had happened. When Octave Chanute, for example, heard from the Wrights, he told them he was "immensely pleased at your success." But then he wrote the skeptical Langley, "As you surmise, the Wrights have not performed what the pesky newspapers credit them with."[52]

The confusion over the Wrights' flight on December 17 opened the door for Langley, who was trying to overcome his mechanical disasters. He and Manly now insisted that their aerodrome had always been perfectly sound, and that their two flight attempts were thwarted by a malfunctioning pin in the launch mechanism. Since they could easily fix that, they should be granted more federal funds to try a third launch. Alexander Graham Bell became a public spokesman for Langley, and announced that the Great Aerodrome "was a perfectly good flying machine, and . . . the first flying machine ever constructed capable of carrying a man. . . . There was nothing the matter with it. It stuck in the launching ways."[53]

In March 1904, Langley made a pitch to the BOF for more federal funding. The launching mechanism caused the failure the first two times, he explained, and "a cessation of these experiments at this point will be unfortunate." He requested $25,000 for "a new launching apparatus" and for "some slight change" in the aerodrome to bring "the experiments . . . to a successful conclusion." Bell and Octave Chanute supported Langley's request. "To do otherwise," Chanute explained, "would be to confess that the Board of Ordnance did not know what it was about in providing funds." Langley, in fact, refused new offers of money from private donors. His Great Aerodrome was his gift to his country, and he thought the federal government should pay for it.[54]

As Langley struggled with his problems, the Wright brothers had their own set of challenges. They were startled by skeptics, but Will and Orville had proof they had flown from pictures taken of their plane in the air. And they would be prepared to fly again, and longer, during 1904. In their public statement, the Wrights said,

"From the beginning, we have employed entirely new principals [*sic*] of control; and as all the experiments have been conducted at our own expense without assistance from any individual or institution, we do not feel ready at present to give out any pictures or detailed description of the machine." If they talked too much and showed their pictures, they believed others would evade patents, copy their machine, and deny them the profits of their labor.[55]

Meanwhile, as the weather improved, the brothers moved their testing to Huffman Prairie, Ohio, near Dayton. They had to learn how to turn an airplane in a circle. Flying only in straight lines wasn't practical or safe; airplanes had to get back to where they started, and circling a landing strip made sense. On September 20, 1904, Will flew the first complete circle in history in a manned plane, staying aloft about a minute and a half and traveling almost one mile. In later years they converted Huffman Prairie into the nation's first airport.[56]

Even though the Wright brothers' accomplishments weren't fully recognized for several years, Langley didn't get his new subsidy from Congress. "You can tell Langley for me," one congressman said, "that the only thing he ever made fly was government money." Congress and the War Department were embarrassed by Langley's crashes, but they still wanted flying machines for the military if they could be proved to be functional and reliable. They hatched a solution that improved on their subsidy idea. The army would be willing to buy airplanes, but only after a successful flight demonstration, not before.[57]

The Wrights endorsed that new policy. "We have not thought of asking financial assistance from the government," Will said. "We propose to sell the results of experiments finished at our own expense." Without subsidies, the Wright brothers continued to improve their airplane. In 1905, they designed the Wright Flyer III with improved hand controls for the pilot. Will, at one point, set a new record when he dazzled spectators by circling Huffman Prairie thirty times in thirty-nine minutes.[58]

"We had hoped in 1906," Will later said, "to sell our invention to governments for enough money to satisfy our needs and then devote our time to science." Instead, they were involved in patent disputes—and they were also rebuffed by skeptical purchasers in the War Department. In 1905, the Wright brothers, through their congressman, Robert M. Nevin, had written to the BOF offering to sell their proven Wright Flyer to the government for military defense. In the letter, the Wright brothers announced that "one hundred and five flights were made at our experimenting station on the Huffman prairie east of this city." Two of their flights, they boasted, were each about five minutes long and covered three miles.[59]

The BOF, in a remarkable move, rejected the Wrights' offer. The BOF members had the chance to redeem themselves for their failed subsidy to Langley, but either they didn't believe the Wright brothers, or didn't read their letter carefully. They concluded that the Wright brothers' "machine has not been brought to the stage of practical operation." Consequently, during 1906 the Wrights began negotiating with leaders in France to sell them the airplane the U.S. government didn't want.[60]

The event that really cemented the Wright brothers' place in history finally came in 1908. For five years, ever since their first successful flight in 1903, Wilbur and Orville had been perfecting their airplane. They knew that stability in flight was crucial, or else their plane could crash, just as Langley's had. In five years of experiments, they learned not only how to stabilize flight but to circle and land smoothly. They had also developed better controls for the three axes of motion during flight: pitch, roll, and yaw.

When the U.S. government rejected their airplane, the Wright brothers had offered to show the French military what they could do. Will and his sister Kate traveled to Le Mans, France, in the summer of 1908, while Orville prepared for a flight for U.S. military leaders at Fort Myer, Virginia. They would show the world how maneuverable their flying machine really was and prove their critics wrong.[61]

In France, Wilbur and an assistant put together the latest model of the Wright Flyer from the packing crates used to ship the plane overseas. French papers had been calling the Wright brothers "bluffeurs" (bluffers) and ridiculing their claims to have flown hundreds of miles over the past five years. But on August 7, Wilbur was finally airborne over French soil. The onlookers were amazed as he executed a perfect figure eight with the grace of a bird on the wing. François Peyrey, a young journalist who knew something about the problems of aviation, was transfixed as Wilbur's flight continued: "To behold this flying machine turn sharp round at the edge of the wood . . . and continue on its course is an enchanting spectacle," Peyrey reported. "The wind does not seem to trouble him." The Wright brothers were no "bluffeurs." They were the real deal.[62]

Meanwhile, Orville traveled to Fort Myer with the latest model of their plane in several packing crates. On September 3, he was ready for a flight similar to Wilbur's French triumph. As Orville's plane lifted from the ground—and stayed airborne—a reporter from the *Washington Star* heard "a long, in-drawn breath from the crowd." Orville also turned the plane to circle over the field. Some in the crowd wept as they realized the accomplishment they had just witnessed. Man had conquered the air.[63]

The Wright brothers, making headlines on both sides of the Atlantic, were the undisputed inventors of the airplane. That year, the U.S. government agreed to pay twenty-five thousand dollars for the Wright Flyer, with more cash to come later.[64]

The idea of awarding contracts for airplanes on the basis of merit improved government purchases. The Wrights dominated the early sales, but other entrepreneurs soon emerged with ideas of their own and innovations to improve flights. Glenn Curtiss, for example, a car racer, developed seaplanes and sold them to the navy.[65]

Starting in 1908, some countries, and some organizations within those countries, began awarding prizes for flying achievements. France often took the lead. The Coupe Michelin prize of twenty thousand francs was made available for the pilot making the longest flight for 1908. Wilbur Wright won the prize that year with a flight time of two hours, eighteen minutes. In England, the *Daily Mail* dangled a prize of one thousand pounds for the first pilot to fly across the English Channel. The Wrights won some of these early prizes, but younger pilots emerged with better planes and the energy to surpass the Wrights' achievements. The awarding of prizes, not government subsidies, spurred innovation and competition, which spared taxpayers the costs of backing more losers.[66]

Will's health let him down once more in 1912, when he was traveling on business. He struggled to get back to Dayton, where doctors diagnosed typhoid fever. He died a few days later, at age forty-five. Orville and Will had been partners in their work ever since Orville could remember. Without Will, Orville became more interested in documenting past triumphs than in creating new ones.

Today the accomplishments of the Wright brothers continue to amaze experts. With less than two thousand dollars of their own funds in their small bicycle shop in Dayton, the two men created the first machine that really flew. Their propeller, which took so much study and effort to design, has been proved to be over 80 percent efficient. Today's wooden propellers are about 85 percent efficient, which is only a small improvement on Wilbur and Orville's original design. The Wrights showed more than possibly any other entrepreneur what men with ingenuity, persistence, and commitment can produce when they have the freedom to develop their ideas.

7

The D.C. Subsidy Machine

In the 1930s, the United States made a crucial transition in the history of government intervention. Before then, government subsidies were damaging, but infrequent. After the 1930s, government subsidies proliferated and became part of American life. Why did this happen? First, before 1930 subsidies were usually found to be inconsistent with the Constitution. Second, Congress was held accountable for them. When Congress funded Collins's steamship company, the Union Pacific Railroad, or Samuel Langley's aerodrome, congressmen—who had to run for reelection—were accountable to voters for the results. In all three of these examples, the failure of the subsidy created a political backlash; Congress, often after much public embarrassment, stopped these subsidies.

Both of those barriers were knocked down in the 1930s. The Great Depression hit the nation, and the presidencies of Herbert Hoover and Franklin Roosevelt changed the way government operated. First, the new appointees to the Supreme Court increasingly viewed the Constitution as a mere guide, not binding law. Second, Congress—with much help from Hoover and FDR—created new government agencies with the power to award many subsidies. Congress funded the agencies through annual appropriations, but the bureaucrats in the agencies, not Congress, doled out the federal cash. In other words, unelected government bureaucrats would be liberally funded by Congress to give away other people's money on whatever projects they chose.

In many ways, the most dramatic new government agency of the 1930s was the Reconstruction Finance Corporation (RFC). Designed to lend or give cash to industries, the RFC was a new type of government entity, one not even imagined by the Founders. Never in U.S. history (except during World War I) had the United States established an independent agency with power to lend millions, and later billions, to corporations. The board of the RFC, not Congress, gave this money away to the corporations it chose. And the RFC chose many corporations in many different industries.[1]

President Hoover first promoted the idea for the RFC in 1931, during the Great Depression. When he saw thousands of banks going broke, and Americans losing their savings, he reacted. Also, many key corporations—railroads, for example—were going bankrupt, which disrupted commerce and threw millions of Americans out of work. The RFC, Hoover insisted, should be instituted to make loans (or gifts) to these banks and railroads, which would halt the cycle of bankruptcy and unemployment. Thus, in October 1931, Hoover approached congressional leaders with his idea for a heavily funded RFC. In the meeting, Hoover said he "hoped those present would approve my program in order to restore confidence, which was rapidly degenerating into panic." Most congressmen, according to Hoover, "seemed shocked at the revelation that our government for the first time in peacetime history might have to intervene to support private enterprise."[2]

Hoover's statement overlooked the government interventions that had already helped to cause the Great Depression and then made it worse. First, in 1928 and 1929, the Federal Reserve raised interest rates four times, which made it harder for businessmen to borrow money to invest, and that hindered economic growth. Second, the Smoot-Hawley Tariff, which Hoover signed in 1930, was the highest tariff in American history. It sharply raised rates on 887 items and virtually stopped foreign trade: Because the United States refused to buy from other countries, other countries would not buy from the United States. Third, Hoover raised tax rates across the board—from 24 to 63 percent on rich people. Wealthy Americans, when faced with such high tax rates, slowed down their investing and often took their capital out of the U.S. economy, making it much more difficult for entrepreneurs to establish new companies.[3]

Ten years earlier, in the recession of 1921, President Warren G. Harding had done the opposite of Hoover. Harding cut federal spending by more than half, from a $6.4 billion budget in 1920 to $3.1 billion in 1923. Also, he and his successor in the White House, Calvin Coolidge, cut tax rates on all income taxpayers during the 1920s—from 73 to 24 percent on the wealthiest Americans. The results were astonishing: Unemployment plummeted from 11.7 percent to 2.4 percent from 1921 to 1923, and remained low for the rest of the decade. During the 1920s, living standards went up, gross national product increased almost 25 percent, and the federal government recorded budget surpluses every year—until the Federal Reserve raised interest rates and Congress passed the Smoot-Hawley Tariff. Increasing the role of government during the 1930s, then, was not Hoover's only option, but it was the one he chose.[4]

Hoover announced the RFC as a minor program in his December 1931 State of the Union message. "It may not be necessary to use such an instrumentality very extensively," he said, and it would be liquidated "at the end of two years." Hoover introduced

his RFC as an emergency measure, a temporary solution that would
be more for show than action. The RFC, Hoover believed, had no
place in a normal American economy.[5]

Some congressmen were instantly skeptical of the RFC idea.
John Nance Garner, the Speaker of the House, thought an RFC
might help in the emergency, but "when that need is past, it will
linger on as a pipe line to the United States Treasury for chiselers
and drone businesses." In January 1932, Congress funded the RFC
with $500 million, almost 10 percent of the entire federal budget
that year. Congress gave the RFC the right to spend $1.5 billion
if necessary, and more was soon added to that. The RFC had the
power to bail out banks, railroads, and other corporations of its
choosing. The RFC's directors were supposedly experts who would
make sound choices in spending the money. The first president,
Eugene Meyer, was also chairman of the Federal Reserve.[6]

Chester Morrill, the secretary of the Board of Governors of the
Federal Reserve, watched the RFC in action and issued this devastating indictment of the negative effects of such an uncontrolled
agency:

> It became apparent almost immediately, to many Congressmen and
> Senators, that here was a device which would enable them to provide
> for activities that they favored for which government funds would be
> required, but without any apparent increase in appropriations, and
> without passing any appropriations bill of any kind to accomplish its
> purposes. After they had done that, there need be no more appropri-
> ations and its activities could be enlarged indefinitely, as they were
> almost to fantastic proportions.[7]

As Morrill observed, congressmen could promote funding of
corporations of their choosing—perhaps key industries in their
districts—and bear no real responsibility for spending errors or
budget deficits. Unelected RFC officials, who were supposedly ex-

perts, would choose who received bailouts and who didn't. After two years, the RFC spent $2 billion, and the new president, Franklin Roosevelt, gladly persuaded Congress to get its charter extended.

But after two years of RFC's unprecedented spending, unemployment was still high. That should not be surprising. First, many of the RFC loans were bad investments. Second, the RFC quickly became subject to politics. On the first point, the banks, railroads, and other corporations receiving the RFC money were bad risks, and they could not get conventional loans from banks or other institutions that had to make a profit to survive. Economists Charles Calomiris and Joseph Mason, who studied the RFC loans, estimated that 50 percent of the banks receiving RFC loans were poor risks.[8] In other words, these companies resembled the projects of Collins, McKenney, and Langley more than those of Vanderbilt, Astor, and the Wright brothers. When Collins, McKenney, and Langley lost government money, it detracted from U.S. economic development in a small way; when the same result occurred with hundreds of corporations receiving RFC loans, U.S. economic development was hindered in a larger way.

In the case of railroads, RFC loans may have done actual damage to the railroads themselves (as well as to taxpayers). Almost two-thirds of the largest twenty railroads receiving RFC loans from 1932 to 1937 failed anyway. When railroad owners received the government aid, they avoided long-term care and maintenance on their railroads and spent the new cash instead on slashing debt and making interest and dividend payments. Economists Joseph Mason and Daniel Schiffman argue that "RFC loans often merely delayed the inevitable [bankruptcy]; had the government allowed these roads to enter bankruptcy earlier, the economy would have benefitted from bankruptcy-related increases in maintenance."[9]

On the second point, the RFC quickly became a political cash cow for the party in power. RFC board members gave taxpayer subsidies to their friends. Eugene Meyer, the first president of the RFC, approved a $5.75 million grant to the Missouri Pacific Railroad to repay its bank loan to J. P. Morgan & Company. Meyer's brother-in-law, George Blumenthal, just happened to be a member of J. P. Morgan & Company, and the Missouri Pacific went into bankruptcy after repaying its loan to Blumenthal's bank.[10]

Such "coincidences" were common. The RFC provided $14 million to the Union Trust Company of Cleveland—and Joseph R. Nutt was chairman of the Union Trust's board. Nutt was also treasurer of the Republican National Committee. The Baltimore Trust Company received $7.4 million from the RFC, and that bank's vice chairman was Republican senator Phillips Lee Goldsborough of Maryland. Roy Chapin, Hoover's secretary of commerce, wangled $13 million from the RFC for his Union Guardian Trust Company, where he served as director.[11]

One final example is that of Charles Dawes, former U.S. vice president under Calvin Coolidge. Dawes, a loyal Republican, followed Eugene Meyer as president of the RFC, but then Dawes resigned suddenly on June 7, 1932. Within three weeks of Dawes's resignation, he received an RFC loan of $90 million for the Central Republic Bank and Trust Company, which he also headed. Dawes's bank went broke even with the RFC loan, although he repaid the loan many years later. The Democrats were frustrated by these loans and passed a bill through Congress requiring all RFC loans to be made public. No longer would Republicans make loans to other Republicans in secret. To protect the RFC, Hoover appointed more Democrats to its board. When the Democrats came to power in 1933, they took over the RFC. What happened? The Democrats often made loans even more unsound than those the Republicans made. President Roosevelt, for example, was able to get RFC loans for his son Elliott and his brother-in-law Hall Roosevelt.[12]

FDR liked to use the RFC to strengthen the Democratic Party. Jesse H. Jones, Roosevelt's appointee to head the RFC, was a rich

Texas businessman, and he was always on the lookout for ways to use the RFC to help the Democratic Party. For example, Roosevelt wanted to improve coverage of his presidency from reporters. The *Chicago Tribune* regularly criticized FDR, so Jones tried to help by offering Walter Trohan, a leading reporter on the *Tribune*, RFC loans to run a variety of small businesses. Trohan, who had an independent streak, turned down Jones's offer of RFC help. "I didn't think I would be honest in accepting," Trohan said.[13]

Sometimes even Jesse Jones was embarrassed by RFC loans going for such obviously political purposes. Thus Jones sometimes used his position of power not to make direct loans, but to leverage loans through private banks to key Democratic leaders, like J. David Stern, publisher of the *Philadelphia Record*, a key Democrat paper. Critics would have trouble tracing loans made by private bankers, who, as a favor to Jesse Jones, lent cash to needy Democrats.

Roosevelt repealed the two-year limit set for the RFC and extended the agency through his entire presidency. During World War II, the RFC made many large gifts and loans to industries making weapons for the war effort. The RFC, in effect, became a large bank, and many of its loans helped the United States defeat Germany. Jones wrote a book defending the RFC as needed during the wartime emergency.[14]

After the war, however, unemployment dropped to 3.9 percent in 1946 and 1947. The Great Depression was clearly over, but the life of the RFC went on as a patronage agency for the party in power. Harry Truman, the new president, controlled the RFC, and his administration used it, as Hoover and FDR had earlier done, to make loans and gifts to corporate friends. Only this time there was no Great Depression as an excuse for the RFC's existence. Many complaints about corruption and political manipulation within the RFC led Congress to investigate. Senator J. William Fulbright (D-Ark.), chairman of the Senate Banking and Currency Committee, headed the bipartisan inquiry, and during 1950 they steadily interviewed a parade of witnesses about RFC activities.[15]

After an abundance of testimony, Fulbright released his shocking RFC report in February 1951. It revealed three kinds of ethical problems in the RFC. First, RFC men were taking jobs with the companies they had recommended for loans. Second, Truman protégés at the RFC were taking free services from the companies they helped get RFC loans. Third, wives and children of the president's (or a U.S. senator's) staff were helping companies get RFC loans, and then receiving payment from those companies.

One much-discussed example was the Lustron Corporation, a manufacturer of prefabricated houses, which secured a series of RFC loans for $37 million starting in 1946. Lustron won these loans with only $36,000 in assets, and an expensive and untested method of making prefabricated houses with "enameled steel." The Fulbright committee discovered that E. Merl Young, the RFC official administering the loan, had resigned from the RFC within days after Lustron received a $10 million installment from the RFC. Young then took a new job with Lustron for two-and-one-half times his RFC salary— even though Lustron was losing $1 million each month. The Fulbright committee also discovered that Young gave his wife a $9,450 mink coat and sent the bill to a lawyer in another firm that had just received an RFC loan. Lustron then went into bankruptcy, after spending all of its RFC cash building a mere 2,500 houses. Young, however, didn't become unemployed; he was discovered to be on the payroll of another company seeking an RFC loan.[16]

Senator Fulbright found it troubling that RFC officials would recommend loans to shaky corporations, and then, when the loans were granted, take highly paid positions with the shaky corporations. In another example, John J. Hagerty, head of the RFC office in Boston, endorsed a $6 million loan to the Waltham Watch Company. Then Hagerty resigned his RFC position and took a new job with the Waltham Watch Company at triple his RFC salary. When the watch company went broke the next year, Hagerty went back to work for the RFC.[17]

President Truman didn't personally manipulate the RFC, but several of his close staff members had done so. Donald Dawson, an old Missouri friend and part of Truman's White House staff, had helped secure an RFC loan for a Florida hotel, and then he accepted three nights of free lodging from that hotel. "Is there anything wrong with that?" Dawson retorted to the Fulbright Committee. The *Los Angeles Times* responded, "Men in responsible public office can no more accept favors than grant them. That used to be an elementary point of honor." The *Washington Post* concluded: "His [Dawson's] unfitness for a post in the White House seems abundantly demonstrated."[18]

Other examples struck close to Truman. American Lithofold, a St. Louis printing company, tried three times to win an RFC loan, and finally succeeded two weeks after putting William Boyle Jr., a Truman protégé from Missouri, on the company payroll. Shortly thereafter, Boyle, citing health concerns, resigned his position as head of the Democratic National Committee. E. Merl Young, who helped Lustron get its loan, was also a Missouri friend of Truman's, and Young's wife, who received the mink coat, was a stenographer in the Truman White House.[19]

President Truman, although personally not guilty, became defensive and called the Fulbright Report "asinine." He insisted in a press conference that his administration had a clean house. Under further pressure, he began pointing fingers at Congress and at Republicans. "A great many members of Congress [from both parties]," Truman announced, "had accepted fees for their influence in getting RFC loans for constituents." Under Truman, the five-member RFC board had both Republicans and Democrats. Thus the political manipulation was bipartisan. Senator Joseph McCarthy, for example, secured a personal loan from the president of Lustron, and then received a $10,000 payment from soon-to-be-bankrupt

Lustron to produce a magazine article. Guy Gabrielson, in another example, was chairman of the Republican National Committee, and the Democrats accused him of receiving a fee from the officers of the Carthage Hydrocol company for trying to get them an RFC loan.[20]

The Fulbright Report ignited a national debate on government subsidies and ethics in government. Many wanted to abolish the RFC. Those who sought RFC loans, the *Wall Street Journal* pointed out, "turn to the R.F.C. either because the soundness of their project doesn't impress the money markets or because they are looking for bargain rates." Jesse Jones, who headed the RFC under FDR, and Herbert Hoover, who founded the RFC, both agreed. "There is no lack of justifiable private credit for either small or large business," Jones pointed out, "and any business that cannot succeed without government loans in such good times as we have been having the last few years should be liquidated." Hoover agreed: Small business "can get all the credit it needs from private sources."[21]

The corruption within the RFC, however, worried Hoover and others more than the wasted money. "Corruption in government is far wider in effect than corruption in private business," Hoover noted. And corruption in government "affects the pockets of all taxpayers" and "affects the morals of a people and lowers their respect for government." According to the *Wall Street Journal*, "the only way to end political loans is to take the R.F.C. out of politics by abolishing it entirely." The *Los Angeles Times* agreed: "It is impossible to drive all the knaves from Washington, but they can be denied access to the taxpayers' money." "Today," the *Boston Herald* observed, "the RFC is nearer FFA—free for all."[22]

Senator Fulbright suggested the nation needed "a restatement of the moral standards of governmental conduct." He added, "What seems to be new about these scandals is the moral blindness or callousness which allows those in responsible positions to accept the practices which the facts reveal." Graft had always been present but the growth of government, Fulbright believed, made graft more acceptable. The politicians, RFC bureaucrats, and leaders of the subsidized companies seemed to have less compunction about benefiting from government loans. "It is bad enough," Fulbright said, "for us to have corruption in our midst, but it is worse if it is to be condoned and accepted as inevitable."[23]

The presence of huge amounts of government money and the resulting decline in national ethics alarmed many political observers. President Truman, despite the scandals, wanted to keep the RFC, and so the subsidies kept on coming. "In the realm of morals," columnist Walter Lippmann noted, "the example set by the prominent is decisive." He added, "A civilized society must demand of those who have ambition to lead it a higher standard of disinterestedness" than that demanded of others "with no political ambitions."[24]

If Lippmann was correct, and many believed he was, then the RFC was a threat to national survival. "Without confidence in their government," Fulbright said, "the people will not make the sacrifices necessary to oppose Russia successfully." In the 1952 presidential election, the Republicans, in their party platform, attacked "favoritism and influence in the RFC." Most Republicans wanted to abolish it. The *New York Daily Mirror* called the RFC a "corrupting agency" and argued that "lending billions is a peril to national decency. Let's kill it." The *Philadelphia Inquirer* agreed: "Abolish the RFC," the editor urged. "No other agency . . . has . . . been in the kind of business—making loans to a large variety of enterprises— which laid it open to so many temptations from outside influences."[25]

Led by war hero Dwight Eisenhower, the Republicans won big in 1952 and carried both houses of Congress. With some Democratic support, the RFC was officially abolished in 1953. George M. Humphrey, the new Treasury secretary, estimated that liquidating the RFC's assets would add "[up] to a billion dollars toward balancing the budget." Thus Congress actually abolished a major government agency, the RFC, after it had made billions of dollars of corporate loans over a twenty-one-year period.[26]

In politics it's hard to stop the flow of federal funds, once allocated, because those dollars always spur visions of political gain in elected officials. The Republicans, in a way, were sorry to see the RFC die because its corporate loans always had such potential to gain votes. Secretary Humphrey, therefore, argued that with the RFC gone, it was "politically essential" that Republicans make government loans to smaller businesses—which would cultivate the support of middle-class voters. Even though the RFC was abolished, the Republicans created the Small Business Administration (SBA) to make government loans to "small business." Robert Taft, the Republican majority leader, agreed that Republicans could gain politically from the SBA because "the Administration has appointed so many big businessmen to important jobs." Thus, on July 30, 1953, Eisenhower signed the bill creating the SBA with a two-year charter—just like the RFC—to make special government loans to small businessmen and women.[27]

Wendell B. Barnes, Eisenhower's appointment to head the RFC, made the SBA as partisan for Republicans as the RFC had been for Democrats. The SBA, Barnes boasted, "employed 197 persons who have been recommended by the Republican National Committee, Republican congressional members, and Republican state organizations." Barnes concluded, "There is no other Federal agency which can approach this [high] percentage of Republicans employed." Leonard Hall, chairman of the Republican National Committee, praised the SBA and said, "No federal agency has worked as closely and as cooperatively with the Republican National Committee as has the SBA." Historian Jonathan Bean, who wrote a book on small business, thus concluded that "the Republicans replaced the scandal-ridden RFC with an agency equally committed to political ends."[28]

The SBA, with its $275 million initial funding, was much

smaller than the billion-dollar RFC. But with SBA's value to Republicans, its charter, like that of the RFC earlier, was extended indefinitely. During the 1970s, the SBA was able to expand its loan guarantee commitments almost tenfold, from $450 million to $3.6 billion—which made it larger than the old RFC. According to those who have studied the SBA, much of that money appears to have been used for political ends; small businesses, as a group, were unaffected. Government again was unable to spot market opportunities and pick winners. According to historian Pearl Rushfield Willing, the SBA, in its first twenty-five years of existence, had "a record of scandals, inadequate management assistance and repetitive contract assistance to a limited number of small businesses, many of which did not 'graduate' from the nurturing provided by government contracts and did not become self-sustaining firms."[29]

The RFC lived on through the SBA, but the long-run impact of the RFC must also be measured by the new organizations created directly with RFC funds. Those organizations include the Commodity Credit Corporation, which tried to raise farm prices, and the Federal National Mortgage Association (Fannie Mae), which lent millions of dollars to homeowners.[30] The RFC also supplied funding for the Export-Import Bank (often called Ex-Im), which gave loans to corporations and foreign governments, and for the Emergency Relief and Construction Act of 1932 (ERCA), which gave loans to state governments and was the first direct federal relief program in American history. Because the Export-Import Bank and the ERCA made federal loans to corporations and state governments, those two agencies, as children of the RFC, need special attention.

FEDERAL WELFARE

Before 1932, charities and churches gave relief to individuals on a case-by-case basis. Sometimes the Red Cross or the Salvation Army would organize national relief efforts during major disasters, such as fires in Michigan or an earthquake in San Francisco. People would give to those in trouble in other parts of the country. Usually, however, aid was local—churches or relief boards in Chicago, for example, helped those in need in Chicago.

During the Great Depression, with its high unemployment, the RFC changed the idea that relief raised locally ought to go to local citizens. Instead, relief raised nationally by the federal government through taxes would go to those states with the best political connections. In the tangled web of Washington bureaucracy, the Emergency Relief and Construction Act of 1932 meant that the RFC had a grant of $300 million for well-connected political friends, including mayors and governors. State governors had the chance to argue that more federal dollars should come into their state. Many governors, with the help of big-city mayors, used their political clout to win big chunks of federal relief money. Illinois, for example, was a swing state politically and its officials used their influence to grab $55,443,721, or almost 20 percent of the entire $300 million. Illinois received more than New York, California, and Texas combined.[31]

Illinois's leaders were taking a chance because the relief money was technically a loan. That made some states hesitate pushing for federal cash as hard as Illinois did. But many observers believed, as Senator Robert Wagner of New York predicted, "that the repayment would never take place, so that in effect, that $300,000,000, if we look at it realistically, was a gift to the states." Illinois guessed correctly, and the "loans" became gifts over time. Edward A. Williams, who carefully studied this first money for federal relief, also noted, "The R.F.C. did not make a serious attempt to supervise relief administration in the states." Williams describes "the looseness of federal control" and notes that states were relatively unsupervised in the way they spent the relief money.[32]

The next year, President Roosevelt continued federal relief. He signed bills that sharply increased funding available to states.

Almost all governors and many mayors again began lobbying to receive large chunks from Roosevelt's new Federal Emergency Relief Administration (FERA), another layer of bureaucracy on top of ERCA.[33]

This historic shift to using federal dollars for local relief profoundly changed the American work ethic. Before the RFC and the Hoover-Roosevelt presidencies, state and city leaders had incentives to be frugal in order to aid more of their residents. They took care of their own, and in emergencies they sometimes received assistance from national charities such as the Red Cross or the Salvation Army. During the New Deal years, states had new incentives to look to Washington to solve their relief needs. In fact, they had incentives to do a poor job raising local funds and then exaggerate their needs. That way they could secure more cash for their states, and disperse to other states the costs of raising the taxes to cover these funds.

These new political realities weren't lost on politicians. For example, Governor Joseph Ely of Massachusetts had asked for no federal funds in 1932 because he believed aid should be raised privately, and his state raised millions to help the residents of Massachusetts. But in 1934, James Michael Curley, who eagerly pleaded tales of woe to Washington to bring federal money to Massachusetts, replaced Ely. By 1935, Massachusetts had solicited and received more than $114 million in federal funds for relief. In retirement, Governor Ely observed, "Whatever the justification for relief, the fact remains that the way in which it has been used makes it the greatest political asset on the practical side of party politics ever held by any administration."[34]

THE EXPORT-IMPORT BANK

Created in 1934, the Export-Import Bank was a product of Roosevelt's New Deal. FDR initially wanted the Ex-Im Bank as a foreign policy tool to make easy credit available to nations he liked.

The bank could also give incentives, like low-interest loans, so that other nations would buy American exports.

In traditional finance, large commercial banks often helped Americans trade with other countries by lending money to other countries so they could buy American products. Obviously, the bankers lost money if they made bad loans, so they evaluated the foreign debtors (and sometimes the American exporters) very carefully. If the risk was high, so were the interest rates the banks charged.

The Ex-Im, by contrast, often expected to lose money because it was making risky loans, or giving subsidies, to favored countries or favored American corporations. Unlike large commercial banks, which had to make profits to survive, the Ex-Im could lose money regularly and get replenished in annual appropriations by Uncle Sam. The Ex-Im Bank started with a $10 million grant from the RFC, and, once on its own, it secured millions and even tens of billions of dollars in annual appropriations from Congress. It became both a giver of special loans to favored nations as well as one of the biggest subsidizers of large corporations in America.[35]

In 1934, the first loan the Ex-Im Bank ever made was to Cuba, again showing the ruinous effects of government-subsidized loans and political interference. Cuba was often in political turmoil, but more so after 1930, when the United States passed the highest tariff in U.S. history, the Smoot-Hawley Tariff. The high duties on imported Cuban sugar were put in place to protect American sugar growers from cheaper imports. Senator Reed Smoot, coauthor of that tariff, was from Utah, and he wanted Americans to buy his state's expensive beet sugar rather than cheaper Cuban sugar.[36]

With the United States slashing its use of imported sugar, the total U.S. exports to Cuba shrank from $160 million in 1926 to $27 million in 1932. Two years later, Cuba asked for, and received, an Ex-Im loan to initiate a public works program, similar to what FDR was doing in the United States with the Works Progress Administration. In other words, the Ex-Im Bank gave Cuba special government help perhaps to compensate for earlier government harm from the tariff. By 1938, U.S. trade with Cuba had increased but was barely more than half of what it was before Smoot-Hawley. Much to the distress of Ex-Im officials, Cuba refused to make any payments on its current loan and, in fact, asked for another loan.[37]

When other Latin American countries saw Cuba tap the United States, they requested Ex-Im loans as well. Many of those loans were never paid back, and some were unsound from the start. Haiti, for example, had already defaulted on earlier U.S. loans, but the Ex-Im Bank made yet another loan to Haiti in 1938 to build public works.[38] If we did it for Cuba, why not do the same for Haiti?

W. D. Whittemore, vice president of the Ex-Im Bank, admitted that the loan to Haiti was financially unsound, but he defended the high risks as "dwarfed into insignificance" by the political advantages to the United States. "It has been represented to us," Whittemore explained, "that if the Good Neighbor [the United States] does not come to her rescue in her hour of need, distress will force Haiti to appeal to Europe (probably Continental)." He argued that U.S. interests would be hurt by having "another European power acquire a political and economic (if not military) base right in our front yard."[39]

The implications of Whittemore's comments are astonishing. First, it shows how far the United States had come in the 1930s in giving federal aid. The United States, Americans were told, should make an economically unsound loan to Haiti, or else some European country might make the money-losing loan and thereby secure a presence in Latin America. But Europeans had always had a strong presence in Latin America. In the early 1800s, when the United States was much weaker, Spain and Portugal owned almost all of Central and South America. Britain in the 1930s still had control over whole countries in Latin America. Even Germany, the probable source of Whittemore's alarm, already had historic trading relations in Central and South America. Also, if aid to Haiti is important to U.S. foreign policy, shouldn't that be decided through the State Department, not the Ex-Im Bank?

A second point is that Ex-Im loans were being used to promote public works—roads and infrastructure. These were the very government projects that historically had been so disastrous for the United States. The National Road, America's first federal road, was a shambles. The canal mania, after two decades of debt, left the states eager to stop building, or turn the projects over to private enterprise. The Union Pacific Railroad was an expensive failure; James J. Hill, with his privately built Great Northern Railway, had finally showed the nation how to build a profitable transcontinental railroad. Why should politicians in Cuba and Haiti be expected to outperform those who had failed in the United States?

One reason President Roosevelt encouraged public works in other countries was that he was financing public works in the United States, through the Works Progress Administration (WPA), which he thought would increase employment and attack the Great Depression. Unemployment, however, can't be cut in the long run by taxing citizens to pay for it. The money sucked in by higher taxes eliminates investment capital in mainstream America, which means fewer jobs are created.

Henry Morgenthau, FDR's secretary of the Treasury, confessed that point in May 1939, when unemployment, after massive spending—especially in public works—reached 20.7 percent. "We have tried spending money," Morgenthau lamented. "We are spending more than we have ever spent before and it does not work."[40] Of course, in Cuba and Haiti, the United States was subsidizing their roads and building, so that might make it profitable to those countries, especially if they could later default on the loans.

Much of public works building, however, is not about economics, but politics. Just as with the National Road, canal building, and the Union Pacific, the construction on these projects in foreign countries was a way for politicians to entrench themselves with voters and hand out jobs as political favors. The leaders in Cuba and Haiti clearly saw that possibility, as did FDR with his WPA. David Lawrence, editor of *U.S. News & World Report*, has shown that areas receiving large amounts of WPA aid voted heavily Democratic in the 1936 presidential election.[41]

Many politicians freely admitted this connection. V. G. Coplen, a Democratic county chairman in Indiana, said, "What I think will help is to change the WPA management from top to bottom. Put men in there who are . . . in favor of using these Democratic projects to make votes for the Democratic Party." James Doherty, a New Hampshire Democrat, agreed. "It is my personal belief that to the victor belongs the spoils and that Democrats who should be holding most of those [WPA] positions so that we might strengthen our fences for the 1940 elections." One WPA director in New Jersey answered his office phone, "Democratic headquarters."[42] Public works, then, were not an economic solution but a political opportunity.

Another major group that favored the Ex-Im Bank was American exporters. They liked subsidized loans because they increased their trade. Some exporters even wangled Ex-Im loans for their own businesses. An early example was International Telephone and Telegraph (ITT), which owned telegraph service throughout South America. In 1938, ITT considered selling its South American assets to pay off debts that were due. But before doing that, ITT turned to Ex-Im for $10 million cash on the grounds that if ITT sold off its telegraph businesses in South America, Europeans might acquire them and gain a foothold in those countries. The Ex-Im Bank agreed and made the loan. Frederick Adams, the author of a book on Ex-Im, concluded that the "IT&T transaction . . . indicated that the bank would become more aggressive in expanding United States interests in the hemisphere." The ITT aid marked the beginning of Ex-Im–directed subsidies for large U.S. exporters.[43]

As the ITT example illustrates, Ex-Im loans amounted to a federal subsidy for exporters. Ex-Im, not the exporter, took the risk on foreign loans. Also, the exporter, because of government help, either received a direct infusion of cash, as ITT did, or could sell his products abroad with the advantage of special low-interest loans to the foreign buyer. Over the decades, exporters began to seek Ex-Im loans instead of commercial loans because Ex-Im's subsidies gave exporters a special advantage against competitors. In a 1972 audit, the General Accounting Office called Ex-Im a lender of "first resort," not "last resort." Commercial banks, the GAO concluded, could have made many of the Ex-Im loans, but large commercial banks couldn't replenish their funds annually with tax dollars given by Congress. Commercial banks would have made the loans at market rates, and the exporters wouldn't have had any special advantage.[44]

Boeing, one of America's largest exporters, has become the largest receiver of Ex-Im loans over the last forty years. Here, for example, is how the politics of Ex-Im loans often works: In 1977, when Jimmy Carter became president, he appointed fellow Georgian John L. Moore Jr. to be president of the Ex-Im Bank. In February 1980, when Carter was running for reelection, Moore met with Rupert Murdoch, the head of Ansett Airways in Australia, to encourage Murdoch to buy Boeing airplanes. Murdoch was willing to buy Boeing 767s for his fleet, but he wanted a special low-interest loan from Ex-Im. Moore obliged and endorsed the special loan. After the successful meeting with Moore, Murdoch had lunch with President Carter. Three days after Murdoch's meetings with Moore and Carter, the New York Post, which was owned by Murdoch, publicly endorsed Jimmy Carter for reelection. A week later, Ex-Im officially announced the special deal for Boeing planes for Murdoch. Six months later, in August 1980, Carter signed a bill sharply hiking Ex-Im's lending limit from $3.75 to $5.1 billion. The winners in this transaction were Boeing, Ansett Airways, and the

Ex-Im Bank. President Carter won his endorsement from the *New York Post* but lost his reelection bid. The American taxpayers were the biggest losers.[45]

In many of the last twenty years, Boeing has received more financial help from Ex-Im than all other companies combined. In fact, from 1998 to 2005, Boeing received $33 billion in Ex-Im loans or gifts—more than half of Ex-Im's total funds. Under President Obama, Boeing's share of the Ex-Im pot has increased even more. In 2012, for example, Boeing grabbed 82.7 percent of all loan guarantees from Ex-Im—$12.2 billion out of Ex-Im's $14.7 billion total went to subsidize Boeing's sales.[46]

Boeing's political connections to the Obama administration are strong. David Plouffe, Obama's campaign manager in 2008, was a "management consultant" to Boeing and other companies after Obama became president. Bill Daley went from the Boeing board of directors to White House chief of staff in 2011. And when Gary Locke, Obama's former secretary of commerce, was governor of Washington, he signed more than $3 billion to Boeing in state subsidies in one legislative session alone. For special help, Boeing hired as lobbyists Linda Daschle, the wife of former Democratic senator Tom Daschle, and the Podesta Group, cofounded by John Podesta, Obama's transition director.[47]

Boeing argues that it needs political connections and Ex-Im help to compete with its main competitor, Airbus, a French company. Boeing has a point. Airbus is a virtual government company, heavily subsidized in its operations. Former French prime minister Lionel Jospin said bluntly, "We will give Airbus the means to win the battle against Boeing."[48]

Thus we have dueling subsidies. The Ex-Im supports Boeing, and the French prop up Airbus. But dueling subsidies have been a historical disaster. When Britain subsidized Cunard, the United States responded by subsidizing Collins. Then both Cunard and Collins increased their subsidies, but both were inefficient and exposed by Vanderbilt as being so. Why not let the French subsidize Airbus, and the United States would save money and buy whichever plane—Boeing or Airbus—was the cheapest and best built? We do that with products from shirts to shampoo. Why not passenger airplanes?

Boeing argues that unlike shirts and shampoo, airplanes are essential in case of war. Therefore, Boeing must be protected. In our study of federal subsidies, we can see that the argument of emergency, and war in particular, is a strong one often used to justify unwarranted subsidies. The government fur company, through its forts, was supposed to protect us from British encroachment on our Northwest Territory. McKenney failed to do that, but British encroachment didn't become a military threat (except during the War of 1812). The Collins subsidy was supposed to give us a competitive steamship company, which would have ships usable in case of war. Collins wasn't competitive and his ships were unusable as war ships. Langley was supposed to give us an airplane useful for military defense, but he also failed.

One might argue that in a nuclear age, any miscalculation is fatal. If we did need Boeing for war, and if Boeing had gone bankrupt, we might not have time to recover. That argument has two problems. First, if true, shouldn't that decision to protect Boeing be made by the Pentagon, and not by the Ex-Im Bank? Second, the argument probably isn't true. It assumes Boeing will not be competitive if Airbus is subsidized. Many examples in U.S. history show the subsidized company losing to the privately funded entrepreneur, but examples of subsidized companies defeating entrepreneurs are hard to find. Also, Boeing, even if it lost all European customers, would still be competitive outside of Europe if it produced the better product.[49]

Throughout the history of Boeing, it has often produced the better product. William Boeing, the company's founder, was a remarkable entrepreneur along the lines of Vanderbilt and the Wright brothers. Boeing founded the company in 1916 because he had ridden a Curtiss seaplane and thought he could build a better one. He did, and sold several seaplanes to the U.S. Navy during World War I. After the war, with no government contracts, most airplane companies went out of business. Boeing even had his company selling furniture to survive, but he always believed he could build sound planes at competitive prices for customers in peacetime. William Boeing tried to succeed by developing commercial planes to carry passengers and mail.[50]

Boeing delivered more than 30 percent of the nation's airmail until February 1934, when FDR decided the mail contracts were too lucrative for Boeing and the other carriers. The president abruptly canceled them, and had the army deliver the mail again. In the first week, five army pilots were killed; by the end of March seven more army pilots died, and FDR decided to give mail delivery back to private carriers.[51]

William Boeing was so infuriated with FDR that he left the business, but he had established Boeing as a company that succeeded not so much by selling to the military, but by building innovative and safe airplanes for commercial use at competitive prices. After he left the company, his successors were also innovative. They built the B-17 bomber in 1937 largely at their own expense, and during World War II American B-17s accounted for about half of the bombing of Germany. Most of the bombs dropped on Japan came from Boeing's B-29s, including the atomic bombs.[52]

After the war, Boeing's B-47, with its swept-wing design, was a favorite with the U.S. Air Force. On the commercial side, Boeing's 707 and subsequent models were so successful that most other companies had to merge or shift to other parts of airplane production in order to survive. On the current 787 Dreamliner, according to Boeing president Jim McNerney, "We're out to about 1,000 in our backlog; you can't get one until 2019." With all of those sales and back orders, the Boeing Company obviously is very competitive.

The idea that Boeing would need Ex-Im loans to stay in business is refuted by almost one hundred years of company history. Those Ex-Im loans mainly padded Boeing's profits and gave politicians a way to leverage tax dollars for votes.[53]

The Ex-Im Bank, the first federal welfare program, and Fannie Mae all began with funds from the RFC. In other words, the RFC launched the D.C. subsidy machine, which still supplies funds to a bevy of political entrepreneurs—with minimal oversight from Congress. No longer must Congress be responsible for misplaced subsidies run amok. When the RFC was finally killed, other government entities, like a hydra-headed monster, were born and matured with power independent of Congress to dole out grants and pry into businesses. The Environmental Protection Agency, for example, has the power to support some businesses, investigate others, and set aside a law of Congress if necessary. After Hoover and FDR, the era of the political entrepreneur was truly at hand.

8

Uncle Sam Invents
the Energy Crisis

Energy is the great force in economic growth. No energy, no Industrial Revolution. Energy is the grand prize of prosperous nations. In the 1700s, that energy came from wind, water, and wood; in the 1800s from coal; and in the 1900s mostly from oil and natural gas.

England may have begun the Industrial Revolution in the 1700s, but Americans captured it in the 1800s, and then used cheap energy to transform the world. The United States has often been at the forefront in the quest for energy, in part because of its abundant supply and in part because producing energy has attracted many of the greatest entrepreneurs and inventors in the nation's history.

Relatively free markets were the means to American abundance in energy. Coal, for example, replaced wood as a chief energy source in the early 1800s. Key entrepreneurs like Joseph Scranton mined Pennsylvania coal to heat homes; then he used it to fuel other industries. When he and his Scranton cousins used coal on nearby iron deposits, they made the rails for the majestic Erie Railroad—the first large-scale railroad that was American-made. Even today, American coal reserves are plentiful enough to supply our nation for hundreds of years.[1]

In the next generation, oil entered the market, first as kerosene to light homes and then as gasoline to power the newly invented automobile. John D. Rockefeller, perhaps the greatest entrepreneur in U.S. history, was the mastermind who discovered how to refine oil so cheaply he could supply light to most American homes for one cent an hour. His Standard Oil Company sold oil to most of America and most of the world in the late 1800s. "Good news for whales," crowed one newspaper at the triumph of kerosene over whale oil. Rockefeller, meanwhile, became the first billionaire in American history, and oil was his way to touch the world. "We must ever remember," Rockefeller wrote one of his partners in 1885, "we are refining oil for the poor man and he must have it cheap and good."

Rockefeller not only was making profits; he was a prophet. Naysayers gloomily noted that oil, as a fossil fuel, was limited. Pennsylvania's oil reserves were running out. Oil, the critics predicted, would be here today and gone tomorrow. But Rockefeller always had faith in the future of oil. He was the first industrial giant to invest heavily in research and development. He believed that in a free market, man's ability to find oil would outstrip his use of it for centuries to come. Oil was not just the here-and-now solution for energy needs but the future solution as well.

As Pennsylvania ran out of oil, for example, it was discovered in Ohio. But the Ohio oil was high in sulfur and therefore unusable in household lamps. Rockefeller, when faced with America's first "energy crisis," bought the Ohio oil anyway—over loud shrieks from his board of directors at Standard Oil. In the midst of great stress, Rockefeller's triumph was soon at hand. His research and development team discovered a process that made high-sulfur oil usable in households across America. Standard Oil would continue to refine almost 60 percent of all oil used in the world in the 1890s.[2]

In his old age, Rockefeller watched so-called energy shortages come and go. In 1901, Texas emerged as the next major source of oil. Oklahoma and California chipped in, too. Then came off-shore drilling—all just in time to fuel the gigantic auto industry of the twentieth century. In fact, until 1973, the story of energy in America in the twentieth century is the story of abundance. Before World War II, coal accounted for more than 50 percent of the fuel Americans used. Even so, oil was so plentiful that Texas had to cap wells to keep the price from plummeting. American oil fueled the tanks and jeeps of the Allies in World War II, and after that U.S. reserves in oil continued to outpace use. Middle Eastern oil was a mere backdrop on a world stage dominated by American oil, coal, and natural gas.[3]

One of the key issues energy producers had to address after World War II was the environment. Extracting coal, oil, and natural gas from the earth often damaged the land; burning these fuels polluted the air. Many of the best entrepreneurs in energy knew this and worked hard to make the industry more friendly to the earth.

John D. Rockefeller was probably the first, and the most effective, environmentalist in early U.S. history. When Rockefeller entered the oil business after the Civil War, oil drilling was destroying the environment of northwest Pennsylvania. Those who struck oil often wasted more than they used. Thousands of barrels of oil poured into Oil Creek, not into tanks. Local creek bottoms were often flooded with runaway oil; the Allegheny River smelled and glistened with it for many miles toward Pittsburgh. Gushers of wasted oil were bad enough; sometimes a careless smoker would turn a spouting well into a killing inferno. Other wasters torpedoed holes with nitroglycerine, sometimes losing the oil and their lives.[4]

Right from the start, Rockefeller believed that the path to success was to cut waste and produce the best product at the lowest price. Sam Andrews, his early partner at Standard Oil, worked on getting more kerosene per barrel of crude. Both men searched for uses for the by-products from oil, which were often dumped into rivers or left on the ground. They used the gasoline for fuel, some of the tars for paving, and shipped the naphtha to gas plants. They also sold lubricating oil, Vaseline, and paraffin for making candles. Rockefeller and his chemists in research and development discovered three hundred oil by-products, ranging from paint and varnish to dozens of lubricating oils and even anesthetics. "We saw the vast possibilities of the oil industry," Rockefeller said, "stood at the center of it, and brought our knowledge and imagination and business experience to bear in a dozen, in twenty, in thirty directions."[5]

With Rockefeller using all that was in a barrel of oil, the landscape from Titusville to Cleveland was cleaner at last. To talented entrepreneurs, waste is an abhorrent loss of raw materials. Rockefeller, for example, spent an entire day trying to seal cans of his Standard oil with thirty-nine drops of solder instead of the usual forty (he succeeded). In a similar manner, Herbert Dow took Michigan brine that others threw away and used it to make valuable bromine and challenge the Germans. The Wright brothers wanted the lightest, most economical materials to build the fastest planes they could fly. James J. Hill built his Great Northern Railway straighter and with a flatter grade than any other transcontinental.

Even though the world demand for energy skyrocketed after World War II, the U.S. supply of coal, natural gas, and oil was still abundant. From 1948 to 1972, the U.S. use of oil tripled, from 5.8 million barrels a day to 16.4 million barrels. The nations of Western Europe, and Japan, too, saw even greater proportional increases. As plentiful oil became steadily cheaper to produce, it began to replace dirtier coal as the fuel of choice in homes around the world. Where coal was mined, it marred the landscape; where coal was burned, it polluted the air. In fact, during the 1950s and 1960s, oil or natural gas replaced coal as the fuel of choice in many countries. More than ever, consumers could not only afford energy, they could afford the cleaner options. Britain and France largely converted from coal to oil by 1960; American utilities companies, led by Consolidated Edison in New York, began the switch in the late 1960s. Abundance had provided competition, discounts, and choices for fuel.[6]

Given the abundance of energy, the so-called energy crisis of the 1970s shocked many Americans. If we had a four-hundred-year supply of coal, if we had oil so abundant that drillers had to slow down their production, if we had a booming natural gas industry in the Southwest, and if we had nuclear energy in reserve, why was there an energy crisis? Why were oil prices spiking from less than $4 per barrel in 1973 to $32 per barrel eight years later? Why were we importing half of our oil from the Organization of the Petroleum Exporting Countries (OPEC)?

The answer is that government intervention in energy stifled production. The oil, the natural gas, and the coal were still plentiful, but an onslaught of federal laws killed the incentives to extract and sell them. These laws, most of them new, fell into two categories: laws on the environment, and laws that fixed the prices of energy. In the first category, coal, as we have seen, declined because of environmental restrictions. Nuclear energy was also restricted.

The oil industry was, to some extent, also held hostage by environmentalists. Oil can be depleted and must be replaced by drillers who explore for new reserves. Discovering and then drilling for new oil almost came to a standstill after Richard Nixon became president in 1969. In that year, interventionists used government to halt drilling in California's Santa Barbara Channel, after an oil spill stirred up understandable complaints. In Alaska, the largest oil fields in North American history were discovered at Prudhoe Bay, but environmentalists blocked drilling there even though no safety standards had been violated. Interventionists also used government to block the building of nine refineries along the east coast, and then imposed emissions standards on cars that added "an estimated

300,000 barrels a day to U.S. oil demand."[7] As historian Allen Matusow noted, "the Alaskan caribou got a reprieve, but energy supplies tightened and dependence on foreign oil grew."[8]

The second problem was price-fixing. Price controls on oil became part of Nixon's presidency, destroying incentives for entrepreneurs to explore and drill for oil. The energy crisis became a national problem in 1973, but Nixon laid its foundation in 1971 through "the stupidities of price controls."[9] He believed that inflation was an obstacle to his reelection campaign in 1972, so he instituted price controls the year before, hoping that stable prices would please voters. Price-fixing, however, changes incentives. When the president, for example, fixed the price of home heating oil, refiners had no incentive to search for and supply the increased demand for oil. Why take the risk when the reward was so small? By the winter of 1972–73, with the supplies of heating oil almost exhausted, many Americans wore heavy sweaters in their cold houses. Some states imposed their own controls to limit the use of heating oil, and the city of Denver shut its schools for a few days because it didn't have the fuel to keep students warm. Finally, in January 1973, with Nixon safely reelected, new regulations took effect that allowed heating oil prices to rise by 8 percent.

When the oil companies raised their prices by the permitted 8 percent, they came under fire from the Cost of Living Council, which had been created by the price-control laws. On March 6, 1973, the Cost of Living Council reinstated price controls on the twenty-four largest oil firms, but left the others virtually free to charge what they wanted. The "Big 24" had no incentive to refine oil, or to import it to sell to shivering Americans eager to raise their thermostats.[10] The voters may have been cold, but the politicians warmed to the idea of choking the profits of big oil companies. When voters complained about short supplies, the politicians could say they were fighting against the power and profits of large oil companies.

Given the emphasis on the environment, the big winner would appear to be natural gas, which is the cleanest of fuels. But price-fixing in natural gas created shortages in that industry, too. The Federal Power Commission (FPC) was created under FDR to set "fair" prices for natural gas. Roosevelt always searched for the policy that would gain the most votes, and price controls on natural gas did this. If controlled rates kept prices low and supplies plentiful, he could take credit for the good results; if the FPC set prices too low and natural gas producers refused to take the risks to ensure a strong supply, then FDR, or other politicians, could blame the gas companies for selfishness. And there seemed to be no real harm to consumers because, before 1973, plentiful oil and coal were available for alternate use. The FPC set prices of natural gas so low that producers steadily lost money during the 1960s. In the early 1970s, they had to cancel contracts because they had no gas to deliver.[11] In the midst of plenty, the United States was in a government-created energy crisis.

The first step to solving the energy shortage of 1973 would have been to repeal the price controls on oil and natural gas. That would have spurred drillers to search for new sources of fuel. Once politicians get the power to control prices, however, it is hard to oust them. President Nixon, for example, worried that if he decontrolled either oil or gas he would be blamed if prices shot up. In the case of shortages, however, he and other politicians had scapegoats. They could castigate the oil companies for shirking on their drilling, or he could blame OPEC for being so greedy. Another point: Using market solutions to fix oil prices appears passive and weak to skeptics in the public arena; slapping price controls on large corporations looks bold and forceful. In a crisis, the political bias is for action, even when it makes the problem worse.

The use of price controls, then, was unsound economically, but the concerns for clean air and water were legitimate. The question on the environment is this: Is a healthful environment and plentiful

fuel better achieved by government, which is subject to much political manipulation, or by markets, which have incentives to correct
some mistakes? In 1870, as we have seen, the rivers in northwest
Pennsylvania were full of oil, and the land was soaked in sludge. No
EPA existed in 1870, but the oil region had something better: John
D. Rockefeller. As an entrepreneur, he abhorred the waste, and his
improvements in refining and his use of by-products forced competitors to use their oil more wisely, or else go out of business. The
land, the air, and the water of Pennsylvania proved to be resilient.
It did recover. So have areas with oil spills, less frequent now, but
sometimes tragic for a year or two. Even coal has become somewhat
cleaner by installing scrubbers, which use limestone to diminish
the sulfur in the smoke. Entrepreneurs have incentives to improve
their products and capture the waste. Politicians have incentives to
pass restrictive laws that gain votes but raise the costs of business for
corporations, which are then easy targets for blame.

The Nixon presidency, with all of its price controls, was a stunning disaster. Even without the Watergate scandal, Nixon's energy
policy doomed his legacy in the White House. His 1973 energy
crisis infuriated Americans who had to wait in long gas lines, turn
down their thermostats at home, pay more for food at their stores,
and drive more slowly on the highways because speed limits were
capped at 55 miles per hour. President Nixon goes down in history
as the man who staked his energy policy on his ability to manipulate prices, not on the ability of entrepreneurs to find oil if given the
incentives to explore for it.

What is most remarkable? That Nixon's successors, Gerald Ford
and Jimmy Carter, did roughly the same thing—with roughly the
same results. All three presidents of the 1970s made similar mistakes
because they had the same wrong assumptions. They assumed that
the 1970s energy shortage, unlike all those in the past, was permanent, that fossil fuels were nearly exhausted. They assumed that
energy had to be imported at high prices, and that American power

in the world therefore would likely diminish. They assumed that more government, not greater freedom, was the best way out of the energy crisis. The government, so they assumed, needed to impose measures for conservation of fuel, and government also needed to give subsidies to create fuel from alternate sources.[12]

When Jimmy Carter defeated Gerald Ford for the White House in 1976, Carter decided to stake much of his presidency on his energy policy. In his third month in office he gave a televised address announcing his major ideas. Above all, Carter stressed, the energy shortage was permanent. It was, he told the country, "the greatest challenge our country will face during our lifetimes," and "it is likely to get progressively worse." The president spoke with certainty. "We could," he told the country, "use up all the proven reserves of oil in the entire world by the end of the next decade." Sure, oil production might go up for a brief period, "but some time in the 1980s it can't go up much more. Demand will overtake production. We have no choice about that." Why? Because "we can't substantially increase our domestic production." It was fixed, and it was "running out."[13]

Doing something about the pending energy collapse was, to Carter, "the moral equivalent of war." That meant massive government involvement to conserve what remaining energy we had. Carter, through his newly created Department of Energy, proposed tax credits to promote conservation, plans for rationing gas, and new taxes for gas-guzzling cars. In fact, Carter further taxed oil drillers because he didn't want them to reap gains from jumps in international oil prices. That meant a $13 billion windfall profits tax, and new price controls on oil.[14]

The gloom of Jimmy Carter's presidency became self-fulfilling. He said oil was disappearing, and his policies made it do so. U.S. oil production dropped from 11 to 9 million barrels a day during the 1970s while oil imports rose sharply. With prices fixed on oil and natural gas, entrepreneurs had no incentives to take risks exploring and drilling to find new sources. Inflation during the Carter presidency skyrocketed to 14 percent, and middle-class and poor Americans fared poorly. From 1978 to 1981 real income for middle-class families dropped from $32,319 to $30,916. For the bottom one-fifth of American households, income dropped from $9,650 to $8,906 during Carter's last three years in office.[15]

In the 1980 presidential election, Ronald Reagan swept to victory over Jimmy Carter with the promise to try something new. "There's more oil in Alaska than in Saudi Arabia," he liked to say—let's go get it! On the day he was inaugurated, President Reagan, through executive order, removed all price controls on oil and natural gas. "With the stroke of a pen," economist Arthur Laffer observed, "the oil crisis ended."[16] Prices for oil and natural gas plummeted, and Americans were paying for gas at the pump less than half of what they paid under President Carter. Economist Robert Crandall studied prices in the natural gas industry and in four other industries that deregulated in the late 1970s and early 1980s. He found that prices fell by at least 25 percent, and sometimes up to 60 percent, in all five industries. Oil prices fell even more, from almost $32 barrel in 1981 to under $13 per barrel five years later.[17] When producers had incentives to take risks, they did so; in oil and natural gas the United States discovered new wells and put this abundance at the disposal of consumers across the country.

The free-market solutions in the oil and natural gas industries worked well under President Reagan, but the "energy crisis" of the 1970s had also spawned more federal subsidies for renewable energy. The number of experts praising the benefits of renewable energy grew during the 1980s, and the term "green energy" took root in American society. Presidents Nixon, Ford, and Carter had supported funding for wind power, solar energy, and ethanol for fuel. Carter in particular talked about the need to create "renewable energy sources" to offset the decline in domestic oil production. In a nationally televised speech in 1979, he said, "I am asking for the most massive peacetime commitment of funds and resources in our nation's history to develop America's own alternative sources of fuel—from coal, from oil shale, from plant products for gasohol, from unconventional gas, from the sun."[18]

The idea of using subsidies to create energy was new. In the past, energy crises always had market solutions. In the 1800s, as we have seen, coal replaced wood as fuel. In the late 1800s and into the 1900s, oil and natural gas began edging out coal. In the same way, kerosene, a by-product of oil, replaced whale oil in the 1870s for lighting homes. Three decades later, cheaper and cleaner electricity replaced kerosene as an illuminant.

The larger point is that sources of energy and lighting had always been market driven. They were major capital investments—among the largest in the country—and entrepreneurs, willing to take risks for the possibility of profits, drilled for oil, and then tried to refine it competitively to capture the huge demand for energy and lighting. Also entering the competition was electricity. Thomas Edison performed hundreds of experiments and invested millions of dollars to develop electricity as a major source of energy. Markets led the way in supplying the energy that powered America and the world.[19]

Long before Jimmy Carter, entrepreneurs had tried to process farm crops into fuel for cars. Ethanol, for example, is corn that has been ground up and soaked until it ferments into alcohol. Then it can be distilled to make it even stronger. Henry Ford, when building the Model T, made its gas engines usable for either gasoline or ethanol because he didn't know which one would ultimately be more competitive. Ford loved agriculture and tried to promote ethanol, but he and others discovered that corn was too expensive to grow, harvest, and then convert to fuel.[20] Gasoline was thus the market choice—until the energy crisis.

In the 1970s, President Carter embraced the argument that green energy, with strong federal support, would be the effective long-run alternative to oil, natural gas, and coal. New "renewable" sources—using the sun, wind, and corn—would, with government subsidies, be competitive with oil and would be safer for the environment as well. In the 1970s, the RFC was defunct, and so Congress relied on other federal agencies, such as the Environmental Protection Agency, and on acts of Congress to help promote green energy companies. Some of these green energy ideas may yet work out, but most have already failed.[21]

The biggest winner of federal subsidies has been ethanol. Under market conditions, as Henry Ford proved, ethanol is inferior to gasoline. Ethanol is relatively expensive to produce, and it takes 1.4 gallons of ethanol to take a car as far as one gallon of gas. On the environmental side, ethanol is better than gas on carbon dioxide emissions, but not as efficient with hydrocarbon emissions. In fact, ethanol needed a special exemption to escape the terms of the Clean Air Act. Before 1973, hardly any corn was converted to ethanol.[22]

With federal subsidies come political entrepreneurs, and green energy has produced the most ambitious political entrepreneur in American history: Dwayne Andreas, president of Archer Daniels Midland (ADM) in the 1970s. Andreas has spent much of his life lobbying senators and presidents to create the federal subsidies for his businesses in ethanol and other products.

Born in Minnesota in 1918, Andreas dropped out of college to work at the family business, Honeymead Products Company, processing soybeans into a variety of products.[23] During World War II, he secured a draft deferment and helped produce fifty thousand bushels of soybeans daily for the war effort. The profits he made from government subsidies and the price controls helped fix his mind on the money to be made from special government favors. He sold his share in Honeymead after the war and became an officer for Cargill, also a major soybean producer; later he became president of Archer Daniels Midland (ADM).[24]

During the 1950s, the opportunities for political entrepreneurship in America were limited, but Andreas exploited them when he could. For a start he collected politicians. His first was Thomas Dewey, the Republican governor of New York, and both men did favors for each other. Dewey, as governor, had soybeans used in the baked bread in prisons throughout New York; and Andreas got Dewey lucrative jobs, such as general counsel for the National Soybean Processors Association.[25] In politics, Andreas found politicians in both parties could help him, and he attached himself early to Senator Hubert Humphrey of Minnesota. Humphrey, not a wealthy man, was impressed with large campaign contributions from Andreas and, in turn, Andreas appreciated Humphrey's efforts to get more soybeans and processed food included in the new Food for Peace program, a federal effort to promote peace through farm exports.

During the 1960s, Andreas gave large gifts to both Humphrey and Richard Nixon, even when they ran against each other for president. Once elected, Nixon tried to help Andreas with wheat exports to China and by including soy products in school lunches. Andreas, in turn, gave generously to Nixon, but often secretly because he had had to pay fines in the past for illegal contributions. During the 1972 presidential campaign, for example, Andreas came to the West Wing of the White House, and gave a large folder of hundred-dollar bills—one thousand in all—to Nixon's reelection campaign.[26]

The big returns to Andreas came during the energy crisis when he helped persuade President Carter to give large subsidies to the ethanol industry. Archer Daniels Midland became the largest ethanol producer in the nation, and President Carter steered much of the federal aid for ethanol in Andreas's direction. He made federal aid for ethanol an explicit part of his administration.

Under Carter, for example, Congress passed an act that would "invest" $60 million in guaranteed loans for distillers of ethanol. Then Congress passed the Energy Tax Act, which gave a credit of 5.2 cents per gallon of gas that contained at least 10 percent ethanol.

According to reporter Frank Greven, "During the 1978 Persian Gulf oil crisis, he [Andreas] convinced Carter that using ADM's ethanol as a lead-free octane booster in gasoline would promote energy independence and cleaner air."[27]

Andreas also needed Carter's help with a tariff. Corn ethanol, Andreas discovered, was not only more expensive than gasoline to produce but also more expensive than ethanol made from sugar. Thus, with Carter's help, the United States slapped a tariff on imported ethanol, especially from Brazil, which protected Andreas but made ethanol more expensive for consumers. And if American corn-based ethanol needs both subsidies and a tariff to survive, will it ever become a fuel of choice instead of a fuel of force? As financial analyst John McMillan emphasized, "There's no question that ethanol would not exist without federal subsidies."[28]

In 1980, Carter tried to use ethanol subsidies to reward supporters and to win votes for his reelection campaign. One month before the election, his secretary of agriculture announced $341 million in federal cash for new loans to build fifteen ethanol plants. According to Bruce Yellen of the Better Government Association, "Two loan guarantees were approved for individuals who had contributed to the Democratic National Committee or the Carter campaign. And 10 of the 15 guarantees went to states that were, at the time, considered critical to the president's re-election bid." Yellen added, "These elements suggested that this last-minute rush was politically inspired, and our interviews with agency officials substantiated this point."[29] When President Reagan discovered all the procedures violated in awarding these quick subsidies, he had them rescinded. Despite this setback, Andreas continued to influence policy under Presidents Reagan, Bush, and Clinton. And, perhaps to return so many favors, Andreas bought ex-president Carter's peanut farm for $1.5 million.[30]

As with the RFC, questions of corruption quickly followed the subsidies. For example, in 1977 President Carter named David

Gartner, who was Senator Humphrey's chief of staff, to head the Commodity Futures Trading Commission. In the two years before that appointment, however, Andreas had given $72,000 in ADM stock to Gartner's children. When that revelation came out, Vice President Walter Mondale urged Gartner to resign "on the grounds that the ethical appearances surrounding the matter were such that he could not operate without public questioning of his integrity and the independence of his judgment." The power of political entrepreneurs had increased since the RFC scandals of 1951—Gartner refused to resign.[31]

The diversion today of 40 percent of the nation's corn crop into ethanol also costs consumers with higher prices for corn, which means higher prices for beef, pork, and chicken. As ethanol expert James Bovard has noted, "That fits the historical pattern of farm policy intentionally sacrificing relatively unsubsidized farmers to subsidized farmers and making all farm profits and losses increasingly a question of political pull."[32]

Green energy advocates, with bipartisan support, passed major federal laws in 2005 and 2007 that mandated greater use of corn ethanol, and other biofuels, each year until 2022. Under these bills—the Energy Policy Act of 2005 and the Energy Independence and Security Act of 2007—even more of the U.S. corn crop is blended into gasoline. The tariff and the tax credit for ethanol were still in place as well, aiding farmers and corporations in the ethanol business. With so much federal loot at stake, more and bigger companies have emerged to capture the large subsidies. A corporation named Poet, for example, has even surpassed ADM as an ethanol producer. After the 2007 law, Poet also snagged an $80 million federal grant to build an ethanol plant in Iowa.[33]

The ethanol mandates of 2005 and 2007 had strong bipartisan support in Congress. The 2007 bill passed by votes of 86–8 in the Senate and 314–100 in the House. President George W. Bush was perhaps the most enthusiastic cheerleader for ethanol, and strongly encouraged the 2007 bill. In his 2007 State of the Union message, Bush said, "We must continue changing the way America generates electric power, by even greater use of clean coal technology, solar and wind energy, and clean, safe nuclear power." Then he added, "We need to press on with battery research for plug-in vehicles, and expand the use of clean diesel vehicles and biodiesel fuel." He insisted on "investing in new methods of producing ethanol," and urged Congress to set "a mandatory fuels standard to require 35 billion gallons of renewable and alternative fuels in 2017." Bush patted himself, and his predecessors, on the back for their bipartisan support for green energy: "We have made a lot of progress, thanks to good policies here in Washington and the strong response of the market."[34]

Just as Carter supported "investment" in green energy, so did Bush thirty years later. Federal support for green energy was strong and still undiminished by the consistent failure of ethanol to be economical or friendly to the environment. With more funds from government, Congress and the presidents believed the political entrepreneurs would make green energy work so well that the energy crisis—which they had created—would eventually go away.

9

Uncle Sam Heals
the Planet

"We will harness the sun and the winds and the soil to fuel our cars and run our factories." Thus spoke President Obama in his first inaugural. He had promised to be the greatest green energy president ever, and he moved to fulfill that goal. During the 2008 campaign, he best captured the spirit of the green energy movement when he said, "I am absolutely certain that generations from now, we will be able to look back and tell our children that . . . this was the moment when the rise of the oceans began to slow and our planet began to heal."[1]

Green energy appeals to President Obama because it is "renewable," meaning naturally replenished. Sunlight, wind, tides, geothermal heat—all are renewable in nature, and therefore provide green energy. Strongly tied to the green energy movement is the belief that the most dangerous threat to mankind is global warming, defined as a gradual increase in the overall temperature of the earth's atmosphere, generally attributed to the greenhouse effect caused by increased levels of carbon dioxide, chlorofluorocarbons, and other pollutants.

Many so-called experts, with support from politicians such as former vice president Al Gore, have proclaimed that global warming is a proven fact, and therefore levels of carbon dioxide in the atmosphere must be reduced worldwide. What does Gore blame for the increase in carbon dioxide levels? The use of fossil fuels. Environmentalists who believe in global warming have predicted that warmer temperatures will melt the polar ice caps, raising the levels of the oceans until lower Manhattan is under water. They blame droughts in sub-Saharan Africa on global warming. Stronger hurricanes occur, they say, because of global warming. "Global warming is no longer a political issue but rather, the biggest moral challenge facing our civilization today."[2]

Barack Obama embraced the "fact" of global warming as fully as Jimmy Carter embraced the "fact" that the United States would run out of oil in about ten years. Both presidents, therefore, took immediate action to encourage political entrepreneurs. To President Obama, for example, the ethanol mandates, in place from the Bush administration, were just the start. Right away, he promoted a cap-and-trade law. Under cap-and-trade, people would pay to emit carbon by purchasing from the government special permits. Those permits are "permission rights" to emit certain amounts of carbon into the air. In the cap-and-trade bill that passed the House, the Waxman-Markey bill, 15 percent of the permits would be auctioned off to the highest bidders, and fully 85 percent of the permits would be given away to corporations free of charge. Such a corporate giveaway was, at first, too much even for Obama, whose budget director observed, "All of the evidence suggests that what would occur is that corporate profits would increase by approximately the value of the permits." But President Obama later endorsed the Waxman-Markey bill as passed.[3]

Many corporate leaders supported cap-and-trade even though it would sharply raise the costs of energy for every family in America. General Electric was in the forefront. "On climate change," John Rice of GE wrote, "we were able to work closely with key authors of the Waxman-Markey climate and energy bill, recently passed by the House of Representatives. If this bill is enacted into law it would benefit many GE businesses."[4]

With ethanol heavily mandated, and corporations lining up for their government subsidies, the United States was in danger of being drowned in corn, swallowed by debt, and sucked dry by political entrepreneurs. During President Obama's first term, green energy finally began to be challenged. Many Republicans changed from being quietly skeptical to publicly critical. The much higher cost of food and the expensive subsidies finally began to erode the bipartisan support for green energy. Also, the newly formed Tea Party urged politicians to balance the budget and slash subsidies for ethanol and other special interests. The massive Tea Party rallies in early 2010 fortified the Republican minority in Congress. They became more serious about the rising national debt, corporate subsidies, and new revelations about pollution from ethanol and its perverse effects on car engines. Some complained that corn, from its growth to the gas tank, was creating more pollution and even more carbon emissions than gasoline.

Some scientists still supported President Obama's view of global warming, but others did not. As scientist Bjorn Lomborg has noted, "We are told that very expensive carbon regulations are the only way to respond to global warming, despite ample evidence that this approach does not pass a basic cost-benefit test. We must ask whether a 'climate-industrial complex' is emerging, pressing taxpayers to fork over money to please those who stand to gain."[5]

The first break in the bipartisan consensus for green energy emerged in 2009. The Republicans stalled the cap-and-trade bill, and it didn't become law. Second, Republicans challenged the massive growth of government—in part on energy issues, but more so on the huge stimulus bill and Obamacare. Not one Republican voted for Obamacare, the president's interventionist health-care program, and Republicans ran in the 2010 midterm elections on the issue of cutting federal spending. When they captured the House by winning sixty-three new seats, more than had been gained by any party in more than sixty years, they became more fortified in resisting federal expansion in energy and other areas. "We shouldn't be giving corporate farms, these large agribusiness companies, subsidies," said Paul Ryan, chairman of the House Budget Committee. "I strongly believe that."[6]

In 2011, Senator Tom Coburn (R-Okla.) tested the resolve of the new Republican resistance when he forced a Senate vote to repeal both the ethanol tax credit and the ethanol tariff. It was a legislative assault on ethanol unheard-of ever since Dwayne Andreas began playing golf with Hubert Humphrey. The taxpayers could save $3 billion, Coburn said, if Congress would end those two government favors for ethanol. Coburn lost, but he did corral forty votes to repeal. "I'm proud," Coburn said, "so many of my Republican colleagues put common sense, good judgment, and free-market conservative economic principles ahead of political expediency." Later that month, a repeal bill endorsed by Coburn and Senator Dianne Feinstein (D-Calif.) won seventy-three votes, a majority from both parties. President Obama opposed the bill, and the House never considered it. Coburn's work paid off at the end of 2011, however, when the ethanol tax credit and tariff came up for renewal. Ethanol supporters couldn't muster enough support, and those subsidies ended.[7]

The 2012 Republican primary became the next test of enthusiasm for ethanol. The Iowa caucuses have long been the first test for Republican candidates, and they had always come to Iowa full of praise and promises of cash for ethanol. Bob Dole, for example, who won the 1996 Republican nomination, was known as "Senator Eth-

anol." In 2012, however, that glowing Republican support for ethanol was often muted, and sometimes even negative. As Bloomberg
reporter Laura Litvan noted, "The declining political allegiance to
ethanol, once required for political gains in rural states, also was on
display in the 2012 Republican presidential campaign, where for
the first time support for corn-based biofuels didn't play much of a
role." Only Newt Gingrich showed much enthusiasm for ethanol,
and he finished the Iowa caucuses a distant fourth—even trailing
Ron Paul, who explicitly opposed subsidies for ethanol. "This isn't
2000 or even 2008," said columnist Kathie Obradovich of the *Des
Moines Register.* "Concern over the national deficit and debt, and
the tea party's scorn for government handouts, has moved ethanol
subsidies off the third rail of Iowa politics."[8]

The Republican indifference, and even hostility, to ethanol
contrasted sharply with President Bush's support of the ethanol
mandate. In 2013, some Republicans, in fact, tried to repeal that
mandate. Their effort "lost a little wind in its sails" when the EPA
changed the gasoline and ethanol quotas for 2014, which made
them more attainable and less disruptive. Even so, the mandate as it
still exists will force about 40 percent or more of future corn crops
into the gas blenders. The National Academy of Sciences, however,
did a 2009 study that concludes, "Plowing up more land to grow
crops has also increased water pollution and emissions of air pollutants, including particulate matter." The National Research Council, created by Congress in 2008, also points to ethanol's harmful
effects on the environment. Before the ethanol tax credit expired at
the end of 2011, "it was increasing carbon emissions by five million
tons every year, at a cost of $5.26 billion." In other words, we may
actually have more carbon dioxide from ethanol, and it has raised
food prices, raised gas prices, and made the gasoline in our cars less
efficient.[9]

What's so outrageous is that green energy subsidies, even if they
had worked, were never needed. The United States was already

heading toward energy independence when President Reagan lifted price controls on oil and natural gas in the early 1980s. During the 1980s, American drillers not only discovered new sources of energy; they invented new methods of extracting it from the ground. The key invention was hydraulic fracturing (fracking), and the entrepreneur was Texas oilman George P. Mitchell.

Fracking, which Mitchell popularized, is a process for capturing more oil and natural gas from wells. Some wells are rich in oil, but it is trapped behind a massive rock formation. Mitchell discovered that shooting lots of water and sand down a well causes the sand to seep into cracks in the rock, and the blasts of water over time shatter the rock. That opens a path for the oil (or natural gas) to escape and be captured by the driller. Many sources of oil and natural gas, which had been trapped behind impermeable rock, could suddenly be extracted after 1998, when Mitchell scored his first big success with fracking.[10]

Mitchell, the son of a Greek immigrant, became an independent oilman in Texas after serving in the Army Corps of Engineers in World War II. Like John D. Rockefeller, Mitchell always envisioned a great future for oil, and invested all he had in his own company, Mitchell Energy. Conventional wisdom of the 1980s said that Mitchell, like Rockefeller a century earlier, was too heavily invested in a declining industry. Rockefeller trusted in the high-sulfur oil of the Lima, Ohio, oil fields, and Mitchell had faith in the Barnett shale near Fort Worth, Texas. In 1982, shortly after President Reagan lifted price controls on energy, Mitchell began a sixteen-year, multimillion-dollar investment in fracking to break up the hard shale rock in the Barnett oil formation.[11]

"My engineers kept telling me, 'You are wasting your money,'" Mitchell said. But he continued the risk because the Barnett formation was 250 feet thick, and Mitchell believed millions of untapped barrels lay within reach if he could only figure out how to pump it out. In fairness, we should note that the Department of Energy and the tax-funded Gas Research Institute assisted Mitchell along the way. But mostly it was tens of millions of Mitchell's dollars funding the experiments. Dan Steward, a geologist with Mitchell Energy, said, "George told us, 'If you don't think you can do it, fine, I will put people in the positions that can.'" In 1998, he finally broke open the shale and began harvesting gushers full of oil.[12]

Once fracking proved to be successful, American oil drillers experimented with it in the Bakken formation in North Dakota, the Eagle Ford formation in South Texas, and the Marcellus formation in Pennsylvania. The newer drillers combined fracking with horizontal drilling and the result has been to discover about 1,000 trillion cubic feet of natural gas and countless billions of barrels of oil. American energy independence could be just around the corner.[13]

The drilling in these gas-rich areas has sometimes been slow because of environmental restrictions on fracking. Mitchell believed that fracking was both profitable and environmentally sound. "There are good techniques to make it safe that should be followed properly," he argued. If fracking can prove to be both safe and effective, it could unleash oil and gas abundance that might rival the days when John D. Rockefeller captured almost 70 percent of the world's oil market for his company alone. Dwayne Andreas didn't give us a competitive fuel with his ethanol, but George Mitchell may have done so with much less federal aid through fracking innovations that have unlocked a wealth of natural resources. Only 1 percent of natural gas came from fracking in 2000, but that figure climbed to 40 percent by 2012. Energy imports to the United States were 60 percent in 2008, but dropped to 42 percent by 2012.[14]

Concerns about fracking and the environment, however, continue to delay progress. In the meantime, the Republicans in Congress have supported building a 2,100-mile oil pipeline from Alberta to Houston, called the Keystone XL Pipeline. President Obama has opposed it, but several votes in Congress in 2011, 2012, and 2013 revealed strong support for the Keystone Pipeline from Republicans, and even votes from some Democrats.[15]

Construction of the Keystone Pipeline would create tens of thousands of jobs, yet President Obama refuses to support that project while vigorously supporting federal funding for solar energy. One example has been Solyndra, a California company founded in 2005 to build solar panels. Solyndra claimed that its solar panels, consisting of unique cylindrical tubes, could capture more sunlight than conventional flat solar panels.

Solyndra's leaders eagerly sought federal subsidies for their solar panels. They promised the creation of about four thousand new jobs as well as solar panels that would make Americans glad they had switched to solar energy. Tulsa, Oklahoma, businessman George Kaiser, a major investor in Solyndra, became a strong contributor to Barack Obama's presidential campaign in 2008. Kaiser personally gave $53,500 to the Obama election, and other Solyndra executives and board members also kicked in enough to make $87,050 in contributions to Obama.[16]

After Obama was elected, Solyndra spent $550,000 lobbying Congress, and almost that much in support of the American Clean Energy Leadership Act of 2009 and the Solar Manufacturing Jobs Creation Act. George Kaiser also visited the White House on several occasions, and the president cited Solyndra as a model green energy corporation. Obama backed Solyndra for a successful $535 million federal loan, and then he came to California and toured a company factory in 2010. He publicly called Solyndra "a testament to American ingenuity and dynamism." The president added: "Less than a year ago, we were standing on what was an empty lot. But through the Recovery Act this company received a loan to expand its operations." Obama concluded, "This new factory is the result of these loans."[17]

Within about one year of the president's visit, Solyndra went bankrupt, closed its doors, and laid off all of its employees. The federal money was gone. But the Obama administration was still confident of its strategy of giving subsidies to green energy companies. "The project [Solyndra] that we supported succeeded," insisted an official at the Department of Energy. At the White House, spokesman Eric Schultz said in an email, "While we are disappointed by this particular outcome, we continue to believe the clean-energy jobs race is one that America can, must and will win."[18] As usual, politics was paramount. Solyndra, at the request of the White House, delayed its announcement of bankruptcy until one day after the 2010 midterm elections.[19]

Shortly after Solyndra went broke, another key green energy company, Ener1, was also in the news. Ener1 made electric car batteries and Vice President Joe Biden had visited its Indiana plant to tout the company and the $118 million federal subsidy it received to "expand its operations." The White House had earlier praised Ener1 for its promise of adding 1,400 jobs to the economic recovery. In fact, the Obama administration called Ener1 one of the "100 Recovery Act Projects that are changing America." Then, in January 2012, Ener1 declared bankruptcy.[20]

Another source of federal subsidies for green energy is the Production Tax Credit (PTC), passed in 1992 under President George H. W. Bush. PTC, according to reporter Tim Carney, has given $1.4 billion each year in federal subsidies to corporations for producing wind or solar power. PTC, according to the Congressional Budget Office, was the biggest subsidizer of renewable energy except for ethanol.

A key supporter for the bill that extended the PTC subsidy in 2012 was Jeffrey Immelt, chairman and chief executive officer of General Electric. GE is the leading American producer of wind turbines, and Immelt has actively supported President Obama, serving in his administration as the jobs czar.[21] GE has the biggest lobbying budget of any corporation in America, and the company gave more to Obama in 2008 than any presidential candidate in its history. Since Obama's election, Immelt has had regular contact

with the White House. As he once said, "Things that are good for
the environment are also good for business." All forms of green
energy subsidies interest GE. As Lorenzo Simonelli, then head of
GE Transportation, said, for example, "We are ready to partner
with the federal government and Amtrak to make high-speed rail
a reality."[22]

Another CEO of green energy companies who is also a major
donor for President Obama, is Elon Musk. According to reporter
Tim Carney, "Musk is the paradigmatic political entrepreneur,
launching businesses that seek to capitalize on government favors
and lobbying clout rather than provide goods or services that consumers demand." Musk was born in 1971 in South Africa, but came
to the United States in 1992 to attend the University of Pennsylvania. Of the United States, Musk said, "It is where great things are
possible." He is the founder of Tesla Motors, which makes electric
cars; of SpaceX, which seeks federal subsidies to explore space; and
of SolarCity, which claims to be the largest provider of solar power
systems in the United States.[23]

Musk seeks federal subsidies for all three of his companies, and
he was a major supporter of President Obama. In 2012, for example,
Musk gave more than $100,000 to Obama's reelection campaign.
Musk also benefited from strategically placed donors. Steve Westly,
who has invested in Tesla and served on its board, also raised more
than $1.5 million for President Obama. The president put Westly
on an energy policy advisory board, which gives advice on federal
subsidies for electric carmakers. Musk also hired as lobbyists McBee
Strategic, which deals heavily in green energy subsidies, and the
Podesta Group, led by John Podesta, who was Obama's transition
director when he became president.

Musk has received a high return for his businesses from his expensive lobbying of Congress, including some Republicans, and
the White House. Tesla, for example, won a $465 million loan
from the Department of Energy to make all-electric plug-in cars.

Tesla's Model S, even with subsidies, sells for fifty thousand dollars. In the case of SpaceX, the federal government is both the subsidizer and the customer. SpaceX has received $824 million in federal cash through specific Space Act Agreements.[24]

In the green energy debate in Washington, some senators don't bother to hide their connections with lobbyists and political entrepreneurs. Senator Max Baucus (D-Mont.), for example, "tops the list of recipients from business PACs," says reporter Tim Carney. Baucus's staff members work for him for several years and then resign to work for Washington lobbyists, who then buttonhole the senator to support subsidies for their corporate clients.[25]

Here is how Senator Baucus's system works. After the 2006 elections, Baucus became chairman of the Senate Finance Committee. After that, he actively courted lobbyists and invited them to various private gatherings he held. Much seems to have come from this intermingling. Peter Prowitt, for example, a former Baucus chief of staff, became a lobbyist and vice president at General Electric, which leads the United States in making wind turbines. Prowitt, GE filings reveal, was "on the lobbying team that won wind-tax credits, electric-vehicle tax credits," and a provision that allowed foreign subsidiaries to avoid taxation. GE, in fact, exploited that provision, which helped the company pay zero in corporate taxes in 2011 when it earned $5.1 billion in profits.[26]

David Castagnetti, another former Baucus chief of staff, lobbied for at least a dozen health-care companies. Senator Baucus was the point man for President Obama on the passing of Obamacare in 2010. Another Baucus staffer, Shannon Finley, left him to work for a lobbying firm that supported the American Wind Energy Association, which won a tax credit for wind power. Michael Evans, a legislative director for Senator Baucus, left to help the algae industry "extend the biofuels tax credit and expand the subsidy to include ethanol made from algae."[27]

The connections here between politics and the granting of federal cash are not illegal. Many no longer see these connections as even unethical. But they are only made possible because over time federal subsidies have been liberally granted to many corporations. These subsidies have rarely added value to the American economy; instead, they have deepened the national debt, and they have undermined trust and faith in the American system of government.

U.S. oil independence was declared to be impossible by President Carter, and unlikely to happen ever again by Presidents Nixon, Bush, Clinton, and Bush. A host of experts agreed. Market entrepreneurs are proving them wrong.

President Obama has poured money into the hands of political entrepreneurs who have promised great results. These subsidies, thus far, have failed abysmally and have created more corruption. But the president clings tenaciously to his faith that green energy will "heal the planet" from the evils of global warming. This, despite growing protests from scientists around the world, who now declare that earlier computer models "involving water vapor and clouds greatly amplify the small effect of CO_2." Even the Nobel Prize–winning physicist Ivar Giaever recently resigned from the American Physical Society (APS). Giaever supported Obama in 2012, but in a letter to the APS a year later, he stated, "I did not renew [my membership] because I cannot live with the [APS policy] statement: 'The evidence is incontrovertible: Global warming is occurring. If no mitigating actions are taken, significant disruption in the Earth's physical and ecological systems, social systems, security and human health are likely to occur. We must reduce emission of greenhouse gases beginning now.'" In other words, Giaever resigned because global warming is not a fact; global warming is a theory that is not substantiated by current scientific data. Yet in 2013, the APS had not changed its statement.[28]

What we have here is a conflict between two faiths. Most Republicans now have faith that markets can solve the energy problem. They believe that entrepreneurs can find energy faster than the world can use it. They believe that current and future innovations will bring energy safely and cheaply into American homes with few environmental hazards. President Obama and most Democrats, by contrast, argue that fossil fuels are running out and that substitutes must be found. They have little faith that drillers can safely extract the remaining energy from the ground and deliver it cheaply to American homes without damaging the environment. They have faith that green energy is safer to use and friendlier to the earth, and that someday political entrepreneurs will make green energy competitive with fossil fuels. To them, green energy is America's future.

This is a contrast of visions. And, many would ask, are President Obama, Al Gore, and the environmentalists using the "emergency" of global warming as an opportunity to tighten control of American society? In the 1790s, President George Washington, alarmed by a perceived threat of British intrusion, set up a federal fur company. In the 1840s, Congress worried that American shipping would fall further behind international competitors and therefore subsidized Edward Collins's steamships. Samuel Langley received a small fortune to build a flying machine for the U.S. military during the Spanish-American hostilities. Franklin Roosevelt used World War II to pass new taxes and regulations for every aspect of society. Politicians know that threats to national security provide a quick and easy means to rally public support. The energy crisis and global warming have served as such an emergency, but scientists and market entrepreneurs are coming forward to debunk this manufactured crisis.

Conclusion

The United States did not become great by chance. The life-changing inventions that have transformed the American economy in the last two hundred years have all been created and mostly developed by entrepreneurs through the profit motive, not by government through subsidies. John Jacob Astor innovated in the fur trade, Cornelius Vanderbilt developed steamships, James J. Hill perfected the transcontinental railroad, and the Wright brothers invented and marketed the first airplane. Those entrepreneurs had no federal funds, and they had to beat rivals who did. Those men who received federal subsidies usually went broke, sometimes retarded innovation, and always produced products inferior in quality and price to those produced by Astor, Vanderbilt, Hill, and the Wright brothers.

The Founders intended for the federal government to be active in national defense, in holding honest elections, and in enforcing the laws of the land—not in economic development (except for occasional tariffs). But even the Founders, committed though they were to limited government, made serious blunders. George Washington believed that federal funds to support the fur trade in the Northwest would halt British encroachment into American territory. Washington was wrong. Thomas Jefferson believed that federal funds to build a National Road would create a strong flow of settlers into the new Louisiana Territory. Jefferson was wrong. Robert Livingston believed that a steamboat monopoly in New York would advance the public interest. Livingston was wrong. All of these moves lost money and may have retarded growth.

The Founders trusted markets and freedom, but they believed that when the nation faced big projects, especially when an emergency seemed to be at hand, federal subsidies were both constitutional and prudent. The Founders believed, and those who came after them also believed, that Congress and the president could effectively pick the right industries and the right political entrepreneurs to bless with federal aid.

But what is astonishing here is that even though Congress often did carefully pick its experts, those experts still failed. Samuel Langley, for example, with his experience and credentials, was seemingly the most qualified man in the world to bet on to invent the airplane. No one in 1900 would have thought that Langley would fail abysmally, and instead, two bicycle mechanics from Dayton, Ohio, would reveal the talent and persistence to unlock the principles of flight for mankind. One reason the government followed one blunder (funding Langley) with another (refusing to buy a Wright Flyer) was that it was hard for the mind to grasp that the modest Wright brothers had succeeded where the highly acclaimed Langley had failed.

Others who received federal funds looked like winners at first glance. Thomas McKenney would seem to be the man to earn profits in the fur trade. His three-volume *History of the Indian Tribes of North America* revealed his expertise on Indians. Edward Collins had been successful in shipping and so had his father. Grenville Dodge seemed to be the best man for chief engineer of the Union Pacific. Abraham Lincoln was told that Dodge knew more about railroads than any "two men in the country," which was close to the truth.[1] Governor Leland Stanford, who headed the Central Pacific, had been a fiscally responsible governor of California and reduced the state's debt. In chemicals, the powerful German Bromkonvention included great scientists and seemed unbeatable. Yet all of these subsidy recipients, with powerful help from the government, were beaten by less educated and seemingly less qualified men.

Finally, Governor Stevens T. Mason may have been the smartest man in Michigan. He seemed to be the perfect choice to plan and direct the state-funded railroads and canals. He failed miserably, but to his credit he owned up to his mistake and called the system of subsidies "the false spirit of the age."

Experts Langley and Mason failed. Others, with lesser credentials and their own money, succeeded. That's the beauty of letting markets serve as testing grounds for budding entrepreneurs. We never know who will surprise us with remarkable inventions and products. Astor was a German immigrant who at first sold musical instruments. Hill was a one-eyed immigrant with no start-up capital. Vanderbilt came from a meager background and so did Herbert Dow.

Most of the world thought these men were eccentrics: Hill's railroad was dubbed "Hill's Folly," and Dow was called "Crazy Dow." Just as Steve Jobs said, "Here's to the crazy ones—the misfits, the rebels, the troublemakers, the round pegs in the square holes. The ones who see things differently—they're not fond of rules. You can quote them, disagree with them, glorify or vilify them, but the only thing you can't do is ignore them because they change things."[2] When they first began, the plans of the market entrepreneurs in this book seemed laughable: the Wright brothers flying gliders at Kitty Hawk; Vanderbilt planning a steamship route through Nicaragua; Herbert Dow challenging the German monopoly in the chemical industry. But they did it—they changed the world.

Lesson number one seems to be that incentives and freedom spark creativity from the nation's entrepreneurs. But it is still puzzling that the subsidized experts failed so dramatically and failed so often. Lesson number two seems to be that Congress, and the president as well, *always* respond to political influence. Federal subsidies thus corrupt politics and often retard innovation. When Samuel Morse first went to Congress in 1838 to seek funding for his telegraph, he was immediately faced with a key congressman who agreed to help only if he got a one-fourth share in the new invention. Also, Edward Collins, to expand his steamship subsidies, hired the finest lobbying firm in Washington, D.C., to influence Congress. President Lincoln told Oakes Ames, the president of the Union Pacific Railroad, that he could have double the subsidies if he needed them. But Ames was so corrupt with what he already had that he was formally censured by Congress for bribing congressmen with UP stock.

The modern subsidies have been an even larger disaster. That is because modern subsidies have empowered bureaucrats (and politicians) to dole out large amounts of federal cash to assorted political entrepreneurs. Presidents Hoover and Roosevelt launched the modern subsidy system during the Great Depression, when Congress gave authority to the Reconstruction Finance Corporation and other agencies to dispense subsidies to corporations. In other words, just as the historical record was clearly showing federal subsidies to be counterproductive, Congress and Presidents Hoover and Roosevelt declared an economic emergency as an occasion for expanding subsidies.

The results with the RFC were corrupt right from the start. Republicans in power helped Republicans; when the Democrats gained power they funded Democrats. RFC officials who helped administer the loans often left the RFC to work at sharply increased pay for the corporations that won the subsidies. At the Export-Import Bank, Boeing year after year has been wangling most of the federal cash available, and then using some of it to support key politicians, who then support increased funding for the Export-Import Bank. Congress has little oversight over these government agencies, and they dole out federal cash to whomever they want to receive it. Corporations like Boeing and General Electric, with the best lobbyists and best political connections, walk away with the most loot.

Green energy has been a haven for political entrepreneurs since the 1970s. The promise of making ethanol competitive with oil attracted Dwayne Andreas, former president of Archer Daniels Midland, who may be the all-time king of federal subsidies. He started by showering campaign contributions, and ADM stock, on Senator Hubert Humphrey. But after Nixon defeated Humphrey for the presidency, Andreas came calling on President Nixon with one thousand hundred-dollar bills, which his secretary quickly locked away in a safe. Andreas supported President Bush, but when he lost to Clinton, Andreas helped pay for Clinton's presidential inaugural, and the door to the White House was again open to him. Even with the federal help for ethanol, Andreas could never make it competitive with oil—even when oil prices skyrocketed under President Carter.

In 1951, the *Los Angeles Times* said, "Men in responsible public office can no more accept favors than grant them. That used to be an elementary point of honor."[3] But in those days, there were fewer federal subsidies to tempt politicians. During the RFC era, 1932 to 1953, Americans often allowed politics to determine which corporations received federal subsidies and which didn't. After a debate on this subject, leaders from both parties allowed the practice to continue, and even encouraged it. Today it is practiced more blatantly, and increasing amounts of debt and distrust are the result. The major legacy of corporate welfare in the United States has been high debt, minimal economic development, and perverse ethical standards for running the federal government. Corporate subsidies, especially the ethanol subsidies, erode the confidence in government that is necessary to hold a free society together.

The inability of ethanol, even with all of its subsidies, to be competitive in price with oil helps illustrate a truth. Successful industries are created by markets, not by government. From the fur trade to steamships to railroads, oil, and autos, the market has determined what works and what doesn't. No subsidy has ever sustained a popular product.

Once the choices of consumers in the marketplace have picked the successful industries, then comes the creation of infrastructure to support the industry. In other words, if we look at U.S. economic history, the market has created the products that only later demanded infrastructure. The product always came first, then the infrastructure followed. And the product created the surge in productivity and jobs much more than the infrastructure.[4]

For example, steamboats, as we have seen, were first perfected by Robert Fulton in 1807, which predated the canal era by at least a decade. Steamboats chugged down all major rivers before states began using funds to build canals and harbors. Congress tried to get the federal government involved by passing a massive canal and road building bill in 1817, but President Madison vetoed it. Thus the state of New York built the Erie Canal. Most of the state-supported canals lost money, and Pennsylvania in 1857 and Ohio in 1861 finally sold their canal systems to private owners.

The Erie Canal is the exception as a successful state project. But New York had excellent topography—relatively flat terrain and a good river system—and the Erie Canal ultimately connected the Great Lakes with the Atlantic Ocean, a huge potential market. Thus New York's natural advantages created an excellent economic opportunity, whether developed quickly by the state or more slowly by private entrepreneurs. Eventually New York politics ended the profitability of the state's canal system. Politicians in New York demanded that the state add many feeder canals to the Erie system, and all of those branch canals cost so much to build and operate that the state went into debt. So in the end, even the Erie Canal was not a great example of government-built infrastructure.

Neither were railroads. Before the 1860s, almost all railroads were privately financed and built. Michigan, as we have seen, was an exception. The state of Michigan built two railroads, but the job was poorly done and in 1846 the railroads were sold to private owners, who finished them and finally ran them profitably. When the federal government decided to fund infrastructure in the 1860s, and build the transcontinental railroads, they were politically corrupt and often—especially in the case of the Union Pacific and the Northern Pacific—went broke. Part of the failure was because the track was laid ahead of the settlements. The Great Northern Railway, privately built by immigrant James J. Hill, grew slowly, and each segment became profitable before Hill moved farther west. His was the only transcontinental to be consistently profitable, and the Great Northern was the only transcontinental to receive no federal aid.

In airplanes, as we have seen, the Wright Brothers invented them in part to carry passengers from one place to another. Juan Trippe, the head of Pan American World Airways, began flying passengers overseas by the mid-1930s. The building of airports, as infrastructure, followed the successful flights. The Wright brothers created the first airport at Huffman Prairie in Dayton in 1910; St. Louis and Tucson followed with private airports by 1919. Public airports didn't appear in large numbers until the World War II airfields were converted after 1945.

The infrastructure-follows-entrepreneurs point is important because many politicians have been arguing for federal subsidies for infrastructure without considering the industry. Barack Obama, for example, ever since he became president, has been arguing for massive federal spending for highways, airports, and high-speed rail—"putting people back to work rebuilding America's infrastructure"—without considering which industries of the future will need what infrastructure.[5] The story of steamships, railroads, and oil suggests that entrepreneurs will create the industries, and then the infrastructure, usually privately built, will logically follow—not the other way around.

Are there any occasions where subsidies might work? What about national defense and national security emergencies? That argument has been a popular appeal for many a failed subsidy. George Washington, as we have seen, wanted to establish forts in the American Northwest for the fur trade to prevent the British from encroaching there. Fifty years later, Edward Collins appealed to national pride and national defense when he requested his steamship subsidies. Fifty years after that Samuel Langley received a subsidy to build an airplane that had potential for national defense. And one hundred years after that, Boeing officials requested subsidies for their airplanes for national defense even though their planes were already better than their competitors'. In any case, Boeing already has a backlog in production until 2019. "Emergency" and "national defense" is the battle cry of many a subsidy seeker.

What about modern wars? The larger point here is that the United States has done well in wars because Americans are free. Freedom builds patriotism, loyalty, and appreciation among citizens for the many opportunities present in a free country. From ancient times to the present, historians have described the effectiveness of free people fighting to preserve their liberty against assaults from stronger dictatorships. Athens defeated Persia, although the Athenians and their Greek allies had a smaller army and navy. Two millennia later, the Americans defeated a much stronger British empire to secure independence. Pericles in his Funeral Oration and Lincoln in his Gettysburg Address remind us how attached free people are to their country during war. But no subsidy can win a war if the receivers of the subsidy don't earnestly want to exert themselves to win. And freedom is preserved and enjoyed by avoiding federal interventions (such as subsidies) except in real emergencies—not the phony ones conjured up over the years by political entrepreneurs from Collins to Boeing.

Corporate subsidies can have a positive effect under two conditions: first, if you have a major war—a genuine national emergency—against a sinister and clearly identified foe; and second, if the government allows those creative people with talent to co-operate with minimal interference from outside bureaucrats. The United States had that during World War II, especially in the Manhattan Project.

General Leslie Groves directed the project and seems to have been an honest and patriotic officer who keenly wanted to defeat Germany and Japan. In many ways, Groves was the Vanderbilt or James J. Hill of the Manhattan Project. He didn't personally unlock the secrets of physics that made the bomb possible or design the actual products, but he kept a close eye on his project and all the top people answered to him.[6]

General Groves and his staff, the scientists, and all the production workers in the atomic facilities—they produced the weapons that ended the war with Japan and saved hundreds of thousands of lives, both American and Japanese. Sure, there was some waste and mismanagement, but the Manhattan Project stands as one of the very few huge government projects that worked well. Perhaps the project's extreme degree of secrecy helped ward off political entrepreneurs. In any case, wars are exceptional and should be avoided unless the freedom of the nation is threatened.

The rare government efforts that work—a moon walk or a military victory—usually occur during a national emergency through a highly motivated core of people imbued with patriotism to overcome a specific short-term obstacle. But most government activity, from the RFC to promoting green energy to steamship subsidies, has almost none of that. As Jonah Goldberg observes, "The NASA that sent men to the moon was imbued with a culture not just of excellence and patriotism but the kind of awe and wonder that cannot be replicated by the Department of Health and Human Services."[7] Nor by Obamacare, the Post Office, or most other government programs. Many government employees work hard and are dedicated, but few achieve what those working in free markets have achieved and will continue to achieve if given the incentives to do so.

Throughout American history, we can see the clash between market entrepreneurs and political entrepreneurs. Both groups talk about the tradition of freedom in the United States, and how much they want to make the country better. But which group actually improves society? Time after time, it is the market entrepreneurs. Why? To use the words of Steve Jobs, "They push the human race forward, and while some may see them as the crazy ones, we see them as genius because the ones who are crazy enough to think that they can change the world, are the ones who do." The United States became a world economic power when its statesmen showed character, and its market entrepreneurs were encouraged to dream. Let us always remember that.

Acknowledgments

We can't count the number of years *Uncle Sam Can't Count* has been in the making. The idea that government subsidies not only fail but also cause harm to the economy—and to the people receiving the subsidies—is so counterintuitive that we have only grasped the truth of it over many years of study.

We have many people to thank for helping us write this exciting book. Robert Higgs, Aileen Kraditor, and Forrest McDonald have been mentors and sources of wisdom to both of us for many decades. Lawrence Reed, president of the Foundation for Economic Education, and Ron Robinson, president of Young America's Foundation, have steadily encouraged us over many years in developing these ideas, and both men have offered us opportunities to teach and to refine our ideas through give-and-take with many different audiences. Michelle Easton, president of the Clare Boothe Luce Policy Institute, has done the same. Larry Arnn, the president of Hillsdale College, took the chance in hiring both of us at Hillsdale College. We thank him for helping preserve Hillsdale College as a bastion of freedom, and we thank Mark Kalthoff for his fine leadership of the history department, and Doug Jeffrey for his help in External Affairs. John Cervini and Ellen Donohoe have been so encouraging to us that we simply had to finish this book to show them that their faith was not misplaced.

We developed earlier versions of some of the chapters in this book for Young America's Foundation (Vanderbilt and Hill) and the Mackinac Center for Public Policy (Astor, Mason, and Dow). We thank both of these groups for the confidence they had that we could show the advantages entrepreneurs have in a relatively free economy.

Specific scholars also helped us with several of our chapters. On Astor, John Denis Haeger, the foremost expert on Astor, read our first draft and offered wise counsel. On Vanderbilt, Glenn Porter and Bill Mulligan read our first draft many years ago and helped point us in the right direction. The Hagley Foundation in Wilmington, Delaware, has a wealth of information on steamships, Collins, and Vanderbilt, and that got our research started. On Hill, we learned from Albro Martin and Maury Klein about railroads and mobility in the 1800s. On Dow, we were blessed to work in a good research facility at the Post Street Archives in Midland, Michigan. Ned Brandt, the curator, has written a definitive book on Dow and he was a sure guide through the maze of information. Herbert Dow's grandson, Ted Doan, gave us an interview that helped us focus on Dow and his challenges. On U.S. energy, Burt had several lunches with Allen Matusow, history professor at Rice University and author of an outstanding book on Richard Nixon. Matusow's insights on price controls and the energy crisis were indispensable to writing our chapter. Richard H. K. Vietor, author of a fine book on energy policy, was Burt's colleague in graduate school and his insights on energy and government have been useful. On the modern energy subsidies, Tim Carney has constantly been full of insights. We have been blessed in our conversations with him and by reading his many fine articles in the *Washington Examiner.*

HarperCollins has been a fine publisher to work with on this project. Our editor, Adam Bellow, has been an enthusiastic supporter of this book's publication, and Eric Meyers has assisted us many times. Tom Pitoniak did excellent copyediting on this book, and we are grateful to him for his improvements. Alex Hoyt is the best agent there is; when he speaks, we listen.

The students at Hillsdale College have been a wonderful sounding board for these ideas. Special thanks go to Ian Swanson for his fine work as our research assistant, and also to Thomas Waters, Robert Ramsey, and Doug Williams for their suggestions. We also want to thank Joseph Rishel, Blaine McCormick, Kendra Shrode, Mitchell Rutledge, Sally Pavalis, Thomas Folsom, Winston Elliott, Margaret Britt, and Gary Dean Best for support and kind words at the right time. Our son, Adam, to whom we dedicate this book, is central to our lives, and we want him to enjoy the liberty in his life that we have had so abundantly in ours.

Notes

INTRODUCTION

1. Walter Isaacson, *Steve Jobs* (New York: Simon & Schuster, 2011), 329.
2. President Barack Obama speaking in Roanoke, Virginia, on July 13, 2012. For the text and discussion of this passage, see Kathleen Hennessey in the *Los Angeles Times*, July 18, 2012.
3. Isaacson, *Steve Jobs*, 213–17, 284–92.
4. Burton W. Folsom Jr., *The Myth of the Robber Barons* (Herndon, Va.: Young America's Foundation, 2014).
5. The latest book on the National Road is Theodore Sky, *The National Road and the Difficult Path to Sustainable National Investment* (Newark: University of Delaware Press, 2011). However, we still prefer Philip D. Jordan, *The National Road* (Gloucester, Mass.: Peter Smith, 1966). See also Karl Raitz, ed., *The National Road* (Baltimore: Johns Hopkins University Press, 1996), 93–223.
6. Jordan, *National Road*, 79.
7. George Rogers Taylor, *The Transportation Revolution, 1815–1860* (New York: Harper & Row, 1951), 30.
8. Jordan, *National Road*, 95–102.
9. Ibid., 92, 98–99.
10. Ibid., 98, 283–85; Billy Joe Peyton, "Surveying and Building the Road," in Raitz, ed., *The National Road*, 147–49.
11. Jordan, *National Road*, 282–85.
12. Ibid., 172.

13. Peyton, "Surveying and Building the Road," 144; Gregory S. Rose, "Extending the Road West," in Raitz, ed., *The National Road*, 187; Jordan, *National Road*, 175; and Sky, *The National Road and the Difficult Path to Sustainable National Investment*.

14. Daniel Walker Howe, *What Hath God Wrought* (New York: Oxford University Press, 2007), 691–98, 826–27.

15. Kenneth Silverman, *Lightning Man: The Accursed Life of Samuel F. B. Morse* (New York: Knopf, 2003), 220–23.

16. Robert L. Thompson, *Wiring a Continent: The History of the Telegraph Industry in the United States, 1832–1866* (Princeton, N.J.: Princeton University Press, 1947), 27, 33; Howe, *What Hath God Wrought*, 693.

17. Thompson, *Wiring a Continent*, 32–34.

18. Silverman, *Lightning Man*, 225–34, 249–96; Howe, *What Hath God Wrought*, 691–98.

19. Larry Schweikart and Lynne Doti, *American Entrepreneur* (New York: Amacom, 2010), 107–108; Taylor, *Transportation Revolution*, 151–52.

20. Thompson, *Wiring a Continent*.

21. Franklin D. Roosevelt, "The Third 'Fireside Chat'—'The Simple Purposes and the Solid Foundations of Our Recovery Program,'" July 24, 1933, in Samuel I. Rosenman, ed., *The Public Papers and Addresses of Franklin D. Roosevelt* (New York: Random House, 1938), II, 295–303.

22. Roosevelt, "Inaugural Address, March 4, 1933," in Rosenman, *Public Papers*, II, 11–16.

23. Roosevelt, "Campaign Address at Madison Square Garden, New York City, 'We Have Only Just Begun to Fight,'" October 31, 1936, in Rosenman, *Public Papers*, V, 566–73.

24. Burton Folsom Jr. and Anita Folsom, *FDR Goes to War* (New York: Simon & Schuster, 2011).

25. For example, Professors John D. Black and Milburn Wilson wrote the foundation of the Agricultural Adjustment Act.

CHAPTER 1: BEAVER PELTS, BIG GOVERNMENT, AND JOHN JACOB ASTOR

1. Two classic works on the fur trade are Hiram M. Chittenden, *The American Fur Trade of the Far West*, 2 vols. (Lincoln: University of Nebraska Press, [1901], 1986); and Paul Phillips, *The Fur Trade*, 2 vols. (Norman: University of Oklahoma Press, 1961). A useful recent account is Eric Jay Dolan, *Fur, Fortune, and Empire* (New York: Norton, 2010).

2. Good accounts of the early fur trade are found in Chittenden, *American Fur Trade*, and Phillips, *Fur Trade*.

3. Francis Paul Prucha, *The Great Father: The United States Government and the American Indians* (Lincoln: University of Nebraska Press, 1986), 31–36. See also Prucha's *American Indian Treaties* (Berkeley: University of California Press, 1997).

4. Prucha, *The Great Father*, 35–40; Phillips, *Fur Trade*, II, 76.

5. Prucha, *Great Father*, 35–40; Chittenden, *American Fur Trade*, I, 12–15.

6. Herman J. Viola, *Thomas L. McKenney: Architect of America's Early Indian Policy, 1816–1830* (Chicago: Swallow Press, 1974), 5.

7. Viola, *McKenney*, 2, 25–26; Phillips, *Fur Trade*, II, 76.
8. Viola, *McKenney*, 13, 25–26, 48–49, 68–69.
9. An early and usually reliable biography of Astor is Kenneth Wiggins Porter, *John Jacob Astor: Businessman*, 2 vols. (Cambridge, Mass.: Harvard University Press, 1931). A useful short essay is William James Ghent, "John Jacob Astor," in Allen Johnson, ed., *Dictionary of American Biography* (New York: Charles Scribner's Sons, 1957), I, 397–99. The most reliable and most informative book on Astor is John Denis Haeger, *John Jacob Astor: Business and Finance in the Early Republic* (Detroit: Wayne State University Press, 1991).
10. Haeger, *Astor*, 42–43, 46–56, 63.
11. Ibid., 57–60, 78–92, 203–204, 230–32.
12. Ibid., 57, 59, 67, 78.
13. Carolyn Gilman, *Where Two Worlds Meet: The Great Lakes Fur Trade* (St. Paul: Minnesota Historical Society, 1982).
14. Haeger, *Astor*, 99–102, 105, 185–88, 205–43.
15. Porter, *Astor*, 711–12. An excellent and reliable historical novel that shows the fur trade in action is Kenneth Roberts, *Northwest Passage* (New York: Doubleday, 1937).
16. Gilman, *Where Two Worlds Meet*, 86; Haeger, *Astor*, 9, 13–14, 186.
17. Haeger, *Astor*, 14, 25–26, 68.
18. Viola, *McKenney*, 34.
19. Haeger, *Astor*, 238–39.
20. Ibid., 213, 221, 223.
21. Ibid., 228–29, 232–33; Porter, *Astor*, 589–638.
22. Viola, *McKenney*, 16–17, 19–20, 35, 48.
23. Porter, *Astor*, 686–790; Haeger, *Astor*, 226–27, 237.
24. Phillips, *Fur Trade*, II, 87; Viola, *McKenney*, 48, 54–55.
25. Viola, *McKenney*, 55.
26. Ibid., 57.
27. Ibid., 59; Prucha, *The Great Father*, 39; Phillips, *Fur Trade*, II, 89.
28. Viola, *McKenney*, 34–35, 56–57.
29. Viola, *McKenney*, 55–56; Porter, *Astor*, 706–707, 712–13; Haeger, *Astor*, 193; Phillips, *Fur Trade*, II, 69.
30. Haeger, *Astor*, 233–34.
31. Ibid., 208, 210–11; Prucha, *The Great Father*, 38.
32. Viola, *McKenney*, 57–58.
33. Ibid., 61.
34. Ibid.
35. Ibid., 48, 64; Haeger, *Astor*, 196–98, 209; Ida A. Thompson, *The Michigan Fur Trade* (Lansing: Michigan Historical Commission, 1919), 147–48.
36. Viola, *McKenney*, 48, 61–62.
37. Jedidiah Morse, *A Report to the Secretary of War* (Washington, D.C.: Davis & Force, 1822), 12.
38. Morse, *Report*, 13–15.
39. Ibid., 56.
40. Ibid., 61.

41. Viola, *McKenney*, 68–69; Thomas Hart Benton, *Thirty Years View* (New York: Appleton, 1854), I, 13, 20–21.
42. Phillips, *Fur Trade*, II, 94–95; Viola, *McKenney*, 68–69; Benton, *Thirty Years View*, I, 20–21.
43. Viola, *McKenney*, 71–80 (quotations on 74, 76); Francis Paul Prucha, *Lewis Cass and American Indian Policy* (Detroit: Wayne State University Press, 1967), 10–11.
44. Viola, *McKenney*, 80.
45. Haeger, *Astor*, 220–23, 232–38.
46. Ibid., 234; Prucha, *Lewis Cass*, 10–11.
47. Haeger, *Astor*, 236.
48. Ibid., 107–109, 186, 236.
49. Ibid., 238–40.
50. Ibid., 236–37; Viola, *McKenney*, 201.
51. Viola, *McKenney*, 92–95.
52. Ibid., 98, 176.
53. Ibid., 173–75.
54. Ibid., 200–203.
55. Haeger, *Astor*, 242–43, 244–79, 282.
56. Viola, *McKenney*, 223, 268–77, 281, 292, 295–300.

CHAPTER 2: VANDERBILT GOES UPSTREAM AGAINST THE SUBSIDIES

1. Kirkpatrick Sale, *The Fire of His Genius: Robert Fulton and the American Dream* (New York: Free Press, 2001), 21.
2. John S. Morgan, *Robert Fulton* (New York: Mason/Charter, 1977), 21.
3. Ibid., 27.
4. Ibid., 66–67, 81–82, 132.
5. Fulton's monopoly rights are clearly spelled out in a pamphlet titled *The Right of a State to Grant Exclusive Privileges in Roads, Bridges, Canals, Navigable Waters, etc. Vindicated by a Candid Examination of the Grant from the State of New York to and Contract with Robert R. Livingston and Robert Fulton for Exclusive Navigation* (New York: E. Conrad, 1811). For a good description of the steamboat monopoly, see Maurice G. Baxter, *The Steamboat Monopoly: Gibbons v. Ogden, 1824* (New York: Knopf, 1972), 3–25. See also Morgan, *Fulton*, 178–88.
6. Baxter, *Gibbons v. Ogden*, 25–26; and Robert G. Albion, "Thomas Gibbons" and "Aaron Ogden," *Dictionary of American Biography*, 20 vols. (New York: Charles Scribner's Sons, 1928–37), VII, 242–43; VIII, 636–37 (hereafter cited as *DAB*). Two useful studies of Vanderbilt are Wheaton J. Lane, *Commodore Vanderbilt: An Epic of the Steam Age* (New York: Knopf, 1942); and William A. Croffut, *The Vanderbilts and the Story of Their Fortune* (Chicago: Belford Clarke, 1886). More recent and also helpful is T. J. Stiles, *The First Tycoon: The Epic Life of Cornelius Vanderbilt* (New York: Random House, 2009).
7. Chief Justice Marshall's written decision has been reprinted in John Roche, ed., *John Marshall: Major Opinions and Other Writings* (Indianapolis: Bobbs-Merrill, 1967), 206–25. A lively account of the *Gibbons v. Ogden* case is in Albert J.

Beveridge, *The Life of John Marshall*, 4 vols. (Boston and New York: Houghton Mifflin, 1916–19), IV, 397–460. See also Baxter, *Gibbons v. Ogden*, 37–86; David W. Thomason, "The Great Steamboat Monopoly," *American Neptune* 16 (January and October 1956), 23–40, 279–80; George Dangerfield, "Steamboats' Charter of Freedom: Gibbons vs. Ogden," *American Heritage*, October 1963, 38–43, 78–80; and Robert G. Albion, *The Rise of New York Port* (New York: Charles Scribner's Sons, 1939), 152–55. For a newer study, see Erik F. Haites, James Mak, and Gary M. Walton, *Western River Transportation: The Era of Internal Development, 1810–1860* (Baltimore: Johns Hopkins University Press, 1975).

8. David L. Buckman, *Old Steamboat Days on the Hudson River* (New York: Grafton Press, 1907), 53–55.

9. Lane, *Vanderbilt*, 43–49; Morgan, *Fulton*, 179, 187; Albion, *New York*, 152–55.

10. Lane, *Vanderbilt*, 47, 50–51.

11. Albion, *New York*, 154–55; Lane, *Vanderbilt*, 56–62.

12. *Harper's Weekly*, March 5, 1859, 145–46; Lane, *Vanderbilt*, 50–84, 231; Albion, *New York*, 156–57.

13. Sailing ships (called "packets") and clipper ships were still competitive carriers of freight (not passengers) before 1860. Their reliance on wind, not coal, made them cheaper, if not faster. During the 1850s, clipper ships captured a lot of trade to the Orient. The most thorough account of steamships is William S. Lindsay, *History of Merchant Shipping and Ancient Commerce*, 4 vols. (London: Sampson, Marston, Low, & Searle, 1874). See also John G. B. Hutchins, *The American Maritime Industries and Public Policy, 1789–1914* (Cambridge, Mass.: Harvard University Press, 1941), 348–62.

14. For a good history of the Cunard line, see Francis E. Hyde, *Cunard and the North Atlantic, 1840–1973* (Atlantic Highlands, N.J.: Humanities Press, 1975). See also David B. Tyler, *Steam Conquers the Atlantic* (New York: Arno Press, 1972), 142–45; Royal Meeker, *History of the Shipping Subsidies* (New York: Macmillan, 1905), 5–7; Hutchins, *American Maritime Industries*, 349; and Lindsay, *Merchant Shipping*, IV, 184. For an excellent critique of shipping subsidies, see Walter T. Dunmore, *Ship Subsidies: An Economic Study of the Policy of Subsidizing Merchant Marines* (Boston: Houghton Mifflin, 1907), esp. 92–103.

15. *Congressional Globe*, 33rd Congress, 2nd session, 755–56. Cunard later began weekly mail and passenger service. See also Tyler, *Steam Conquers the Atlantic*, 136–48; and William E. Bennet, *The Collins Story* (London: R. Hale, 1957).

16. For a defense of mail subsidies, see "Speech of James A. Bayard of Delaware on the Collins Line of Steamers Delivered in the Senate of the United States, May 10, 1852" (Washington: John T. Towers, 1852). See also Thomas Rainey, *Ocean Steam Navigation and the Ocean Port* (New York: Appleton, 1858). For other views of the subsidies, see Lindsay, *Merchant Shipping*, IV, 200–203; Hutchins, *American Maritime Industries*, 358–62; and Dunmore, *Ship Subsidies*, 96–103.

17. French E. Chadwick, *Ocean Steamships* (New York: Charles Scribner's Sons, 1891), 120–22; John H. Morrison, *History of American Steam Navigation* (New York: W. F. Sametz, 1903), 420–23; and N.A., "A Few Suggestions Respecting the United States Steam Mail Service" (n.p., 1850), 9–17.

18. Tyler, *Steam Conquers the Atlantic*, 206.
19. Ibid., 202–14; George E. Hargest, *History of Letter Post Communications Between the United States and Europe, 1845–1875* (Washington, D.C.: Smithsonian Institution Press, 1971). See also Henry Cohen, *Business and Politics in America from the Age of Jackson to the Civil War: The Career Biography of W. W. Corcoran* (Westport, Conn.: Greenwood, 1971), 109–13.
20. *Congressional Globe*, 33rd Congress, Appendix, 192. See also Lane, *Vanderbilt*, 143–44.
21. Tyler, *Steam Conquers the Atlantic*, 225–29; Lane, *Vanderbilt*, 143–48; Hutchins, *American Maritime Industries*, 367; Dunmore, *Ship Subsidies*, 92–103; Roy Nichols, *Franklin Pierce* (Philadelphia: University of Pennsylvania Press, 1958), 377. For Seward's comment, see *Congressional Globe*, 33rd Congress, Appendix, 301.
22. *Congressional Globe*, 33rd Congress, 2nd session, 1156–57; *New York Evening Post*, March 3 and 5, 1855; *Baltimore Sun*, March 5, 1855; Mark W. Summers, *The Plundering Generation* (New York: Oxford University Press, 1987), 105–106, 206.
23. Summers, *The Plundering Generation*, 106.
24. *New York Tribune*, March 8, 1855; Lane, *Vanderbilt*, 147–48, 150.
25. Stiles, *First Tycoon*, 257–65; Lane, *Vanderbilt*, 147–48. In a letter to the *New York Tribune*, March 8, 1855, Vanderbilt complained that the Collins subsidy was "paralyzing private enterprise, and in fact forbidding it access to the ocean."
26. Lane, *Vanderbilt*, 148–51, 167; Tyler, *Steam Conquers the Atlantic*, 238–41.
27. *Congressional Globe*, 35th Congress, 1st session, 2826, 2827, 2843. See also Tyler, *Steam Conquers the Atlantic*, 231–46; James D. McCabe Jr., *Great Fortunes* (Philadelphia: G. MacLean, 1871); and Meeker, *Shipping Subsidies*, 156.
28. Lane, *Vanderbilt*, 151–56; Meeker, *Shipping Subsidies*, 5–20.
29. Meeker, *Shipping Subsidies*, 10–11.
30. Ibid.; Henry Fry, *The History of North Atlantic Steam Navigation* (New York: Charles Scribner's Sons, 1896), 42–53, 77–78, 81; Hyde, *Cunard*, 27–34.
31. Robert Macfarlane, *History of Propellers and Steam Navigation* (New York: George P. Putnam, 1851); Tyler, *Steam Conquers the Atlantic*, 117–18, 138–42; Lane, *Vanderbilt*, 93–94.
32. *Congressional Globe*, 33rd Congress, Appendix, 354–55; Tyler, *Steam Conquers the Atlantic*, 128–32, 138–42; Lane, *Vanderbilt*, 175–78.
33. Earnest A. Wiltsee, *Gold Rush Steamers* (San Francisco: Grabhorn Press, 1938), 50–89; Lane, *Vanderbilt*, 85–107; Hutchins, *American Maritime Industries*, 359–60.
34. Hutchins, *American Maritime Industries*, 359–63.
35. Lane, *Vanderbilt*, 108–38; Wiltsee, *Gold Rush Steamers*, 112–51.
36. Lane, *Vanderbilt*, 123–24, 135; Stiles, *First Tycoon*, 272–91; William D. Scroggs, "William Walker," *DAB*, XIX, 363–65.
37. *Congressional Globe*, 35th Congress, 1st session, 2843–44.
38. Lane, *Vanderbilt*, 124, 136.
39. In 1855, with Vanderbilt paid off, the California lines raised the New York to San Francisco fare from $150 to $300. They also doubled the steerage fare from $75 to $150. Many passengers—real and potential—were angry, but one point needs to be made. This fare was only one-half of what it was before Vanderbilt arrived. The effect of Vanderbilt's competition was to shrink the fare from $600

to $150; when he left, it was still only $300. For the California lines to have raised the fare any higher would have probably meant two things: first, a decline in the number of passengers wanting to go to California; second, the appearance of a new rival ready to cut fares and capture what traffic was left. Since the California lines had only one-fourth of their subsidy left, they could ill afford the arrival of another Vanderbilt, so they kept the fares moderately low. See Wiltsee, *Gold Rush Steamers*, 21–26, 55–56, 139–42, 149.

40. Meeker, *Shipping Subsidies*, 156.
41. Harry H. Pierce, *Railroads of New York: A Study of Government Aid, 1826–1875* (Cambridge, Mass.: Harvard University Press, 1953), 14–16; George Rogers Taylor, *The Transportation Revolution* (New York: Harper & Row, 1951), 128–31; Julius Rubin, *Canal or Railroad? Imitation and Innovation in Response to the Erie Canal in Philadelphia, Baltimore, and Boston* (Philadelphia: American Philosophical Society, 1961); Douglass C. North, *Growth and Welfare in the American Past* (Englewood Cliffs, N.J.: Prentice-Hall, 1974). After the Civil War, Vanderbilt sold his steamships and began building the New York Central Railroad from New York to Chicago. Vanderbilt again had to battle political entrepreneurs (this time city councilmen and state legislators) in New York who demanded bribes from Vanderbilt before they would approve a right-of-way for his railroad. But Vanderbilt never took his eyes off the main task: building the best railroad and delivering goods at the lowest possible prices. He spearheaded America's switch from iron to steel rails, standardized his railroad's gauge, and experimented with the four-track system. He improved roadbeds and rolling stock and cut his cost in half in seven years—all the time maintaining an 8 percent dividend to stockholders.

CHAPTER 3: THE BOY GOVERNOR ENDORSES STATE SUBSIDIES

1. Willis F. Dunbar and George S. May, *Michigan: A History of the Wolverine State* (Grand Rapids, Mich.: Eerdmans, 1980), 222; Lawton T. Hemans, *Life and Times of Stevens Thomson Mason* (Lansing: Michigan Historical Commission, 1920), 17, 55.
2. Two books have been written on Mason. They are Hemans, *Mason*; and Kent Sagendorph, *Stevens Thomson Mason: Misunderstood Patriot* (New York: Dutton, 1947).
3. For the material in this and the following paragraphs on Mason's early life, see Hemans, *Mason*, 11–37; and Sagendorph, *Mason*, 15–73.
4. Hemans, *Mason*, 23–34; Sagendorph, *Mason*, 59–67, 76.
5. Sagendorph, *Mason*, 86–89; Willard C. Klunder, *Lewis Cass and the Politics of Moderation* (Kent, Ohio: Kent State University Press, 1996); Frank B. Woodford, *Lewis Cass: The Last Jeffersonian* (New York: Octagon Books, 1973).
6. Sagendorph, *Mason*, 121–22, 126–31; Woodford, *Lewis Cass*, 187–89.
7. Sagendorph, *Mason*, 135–40.
8. Ibid., 143–44.
9. Ibid., 147–48.
10. Ibid., 22, 45–46; Helen Hill, "George Mason," *Dictionary of American Biography* (New York: Charles Scribner's Sons), VI, 361–64.

11. Emily V. Mason, Governor Mason's sister, has written a valuable account of the Mason administration. See Emily V. Mason, "Chapters from the Autobiography of an Octogenarian, 1830–50," *Michigan Pioneer and Historical Society* 35 (1905): 248–58; Sagendorph, *Mason*, 155–62.

12. Mason, "Autobiography," 250; Sagendorph, *Mason*, 162–68.

13. George N. Fuller, *Messages of the Governors of Michigan* (Lansing: Michigan Historical Commission, 1925), I, 121–290; Sagendorph, *Mason*, 191–95.

14. Sagendorph, *Mason*, 232–58; Fuller, *Messages of the Governors*, 158–69.

15. For a description of the Erie Canal, and its impact, see John Lauritz Larson, *Internal Improvement: National Public Works and the Promise of Popular Government in the Early United States* (Chapel Hill: University of North Carolina Press, 2001); Nathan Miller, *The Enterprise of a Free People: Aspects of Economic Development in New York State During the Canal Period, 1792–1838* (Ithaca, N.Y.: Cornell University Press, 1962); Evan Cornog, *The Birth of Empire: DeWitt Clinton and the American Experience* (New York: Oxford University Press, 1998); and Ronald E. Shaw, *Canals for a Nation: The Canal Era in the United States, 1790–1860* (Lexington: University Press of Kentucky, 1990). An old but useful study is Alvin F. Harlow, *Old Towpaths: The Story of the American Canal Era* (New York: Appleton, 1926).

16. George Rogers Taylor, *The Transportation Revolution, 1815–1860* (New York: Harper & Row, 1951), 32–37; Madeline S. Waggoner, *The Long Haul West: The Great Canal Era, 1817–1850* (New York: G. P. Putnam's Sons, 1958), 32, 100, 180–81, 271–72.

17. Ronald E. Shaw, *Erie Water West: A History of the Erie Canal, 1792–1854* (Lexington: University of Kentucky Press, 1966).

18. Shaw, *Erie Water West*, 39–40, 47.

19. James Madison, "Veto of Federal Public Works Bill," March 3, 1817. Online at constitution.org/JM/18170303_veto.htm. For recent criticism of Madison, see Larson, *Internal Improvement*, 67–69.

20. Shaw, *Erie Water West*, 39, 45–48, 61, 77–79, 86–111. For a recent treatment, see Peter Bernstein, *Wedding of the Waters: The Erie Canal and the Making of a Great Nation* (New York: Norton, 2005), 211–19.

21. Shaw, *Erie Water West*, 73, 136, 406.

22. Dunbar and May, *Michigan*, 189–90; Thomas M. Cooley, *Michigan: A History of Governments* (Boston: Houghton Mifflin, 1885), 203; Sagendorph, *Mason*, 92; Frank Woodford, *Yankees in Wonderland* (Detroit: Wayne State University Press, 1951), 13–20; Ronald Shaw, "Michigan Influences upon the Formative Years of the Erie Canal," *Michigan History* 37 (March 1953): 1–19. The impact of the Erie Canal is developed in the Pulitzer Prize–winning book by Daniel Walker Howe, *What Hath God Wrought: The Transformation of America, 1815–1848* (New York: Oxford University Press, 2007), 116–24.

23. Julius Rubin, *Canal or Railroad? Imitation and Innovation in the Response to the Erie Canal in Philadelphia, Baltimore, and Boston* (Philadelphia: American Philosophical Society, 1961); Reginald C. McGrane, *Foreign Bondholders and American State Debts* (New York: Macmillan, 1935).

24. Hill, "George Mason," 361–64.

25. Harold M. Dorr, *The Michigan Constitutional Convention of 1835–36* (Ann Arbor: University of Michigan Press, 1940), 394, 479.
26. Fuller, *Messages of the Governors*, 169, 192.
27. Ibid., 194–95.
28. Ibid., 170; Robert J. Parks, *Democracy's Railroads: Public Enterprise in Jacksonian Michigan* (Port Washington, N.Y.: Kennikat Press, 1972), 71–72.
29. Cooley, *Michigan*, 280; Parks, *Democracy's Railroads*, 39–41, 84–87, 91.
30. Rubin, *Canal or Railroad?*, 6, 10–11. Professor Rubin was Burt's mentor in graduate school, and Burt benefited from many conversations with Professor Rubin on the Erie Canal. See also an important book by Rubin's mentor: Carter Goodrich, *Government Promotion of American Canals and Railroads, 1800–1890* (New York: Columbia University Press, 1960), 52–61. See also Larson, *Internal Improvement*, 80–82.
31. Rubin, *Canal or Railroad?*, 5–8, 38–41; Julius Rubin, "An Innovative Public Improvement: The Erie Canal," in Carter Goodrich, ed., *Canals and American Economic Development* (New York: Columbia University Press, 1961); Robert G. Albion, *The Rise of New York Port, 1815–1860* (New York: Charles Scribner's Sons, 1970); Howe, *What Hath God Wrought*, 120, 216–17, 220, 393–94.
32. Fuller, *Messages of the Governors*, 196–97; Parks, *Democracy's Railroads*, 84–86; Dunbar and May, *Michigan*, 271–77.
33. Mason, "Autobiography," 255–56; Sagendorph, *Mason*, 293–94, 327, 339–40.
34. Parks, *Democracy's Railroads*, 186–208; McGrane, *Foreign Bondholders*, 143–67.
35. Dunbar and May, *Michigan*, 274; Ronald P. Formisano, *The Birth of Mass Political Parties: Michigan, 1827–1861* (Princeton, N.J.: Princeton University Press, 1971), 117; Gene Schabath, "Cross-State Canal Stayed Just a Dream," *Detroit News*, April 24, 1995, B3.
36. Parks, *Democracy's Railroads*, 134–38; Schabath, "Cross-State Canal," B3.
37. Parks, *Democracy's Railroads*, 85, 91–117; Larson, *Internal Improvement*, 219–20.
38. Parks, *Democracy's Railroads*, 225.
39. Ibid., 118–31, 224.
40. Ibid., 134, 138–39.
41. Fuller, *Messages of the Governors*, 284.
42. Parks, *Democracy's Railroads*, 219–33.
43. Ibid., 63–90, 120–22, 154–85; Fuller, *Messages of the Governors*, 194–95.
44. Parks, *Democracy's Railroads*, 120–23, 128, 162–67.
45. Ibid., 92–94.
46. Ibid., 125, 224.
47. Taylor, *Transportation Revolution*, 21, 36, 51; Clifford Thies, "Infrastructure's Forgotten Failures," *Free Market* 10 (July 1994): 6; Sagendorph, *Mason*, 397, 404–13.
48. Shaw, *Erie Water West*, 313–34; Walter Stahr, *Seward: Lincoln's Indispensable Man* (New York: Simon & Schuster, 2012), 14–15, 61–62, 85.
49. Taylor, *Transportation Revolution*, 36; Thies, "Infrastructure's Forgotten Failures," 6; Shaw, *Canals for a Nation*, 45–46. See also www.nycanals.com/Black_River_Canal.
50. Shaw, *Erie Water West*, 330–60, 417.

51. Larson, *Internal Improvement*, 80–87, 220–21; Shaw, *Canals for a Nation*, 81; Taylor, *Transportation Revolution*, 43–45; Goodrich, *Government Promotion*, 61–75.
52. Rubin, *Canal or Railroad?*, 10, 15–47; Albion, *Rise of New York Port*.
53. Harry N. Scheiber, *Ohio Canal Era: A Case Study of Government and the Economy, 1820–1861* (Athens: Ohio University Press, 1969), 306. See also Taylor, *Transportation Revolution*, 45–46; Shaw, *Canals for a Nation*, 208–10, 226–27.
54. Shaw, *Canals for a* Nation, 215–16; Thies, "Infrastructure's Forgotten Failures," 6; Taylor, *Transportation Revolution*, 47.
55. Shaw, *Canals for a Nation*, 211–12, 218.
56. Taylor, *Transportation Revolution*, 48; Shaw, *Canals for a Nation*, 216–18; Thies, "Infrastructure's Forgotten Failures," 6.
57. Fuller, *Messages of the Governors*, 284, 382–86, 512–13.
58. Ibid., 516.
59. Cooley, *Michigan*, 290.
60. Fuller, *Messages of the Governors*, II, 45.
61. Willis F. Dunbar, *All Aboard! A History of Railroads in Michigan* (Grand Rapids, Mich.: Eerdmans, 1969), 29–56.
62. Cooley, *Michigan*, 291–93.
63. *Grand Rapids Enquirer*, October 9, 1850. See also Dunbar and May, *Michigan*, 366; Milo M. Quaife and Sidney Glazer, *Michigan: From Primitive Wilderness to Industrial Commonwealth* (New York: Prentice Hall, 1948), 188.
64. Jeremy Atack and Peter Passell, *A New View of Economic History* (New York: Norton, 1994), 150–56; Roger Ransom, "Social Returns from Public Transport Investment: A Case Study of the Ohio Canal," *Journal of Political Economy* 78 (September–October 1970): 1041–64. For a good discussion of these issues, see Larry Schweikart and Lynne Pierson Doti, *American Entrepreneur* (New York: Amacom, 2010), 88–90.

CHAPTER 4: JAMES J. HILL VS. SUBSIDIZED RAILROADS

1. Stephen E. Ambrose, *Nothing Like It in the World* (New York: Simon & Schuster, 2000), 23–62, 90; John A. Garraty, *The American Nation: A History of the United States*, 7th ed. (New York: HarperCollins, 1991), 497.
2. Richard White, *Railroaded: The Transcontinentals and the Making of Modern America* (New York: Norton, 2011), 1–8; James F. Stover, *American Railroads* (Chicago: University of Chicago Press, 1961), 67; Henry Kirke White, *History of the Union Pacific Railway* (Chicago: University of Chicago Press, 1895).
3. Ambrose, *Nothing Like It*, 132; Maury Klein, *Union Pacific: Birth of a Railroad, 1862–1893* (Garden City, N.Y.: Doubleday, 1987).
4. Robert G. Athearn, *Union Pacific Country* (Chicago: Rand McNally, 1971), 37–38, 43–44.
5. J. R. Perkins, *Trails, Rails, and War: The Life of General G. M. Dodge* (Indianapolis: Bobbs-Merrill, 1929), 207. See also Stanley P. Hirshson, *Grenville M. Dodge: Soldier, Politician, Railroad Pioneer* (Bloomington: Indiana University Press, 1967).
6. Athearn, *Union Pacific Country*, 200–203.

7. Perkins, *Dodge*, 231–33, 238. See also William F. Rae, *Westward by Rail: The New Route to the East* (London: Longmans, Green, 1871).
8. Athearn, *Union Pacific Country*, 139–42.
9. Perkins, *Dodge*, 205–206; Athearn, *Union Pacific Country*, 153.
10. Athearn, *Union Pacific Country*, 224, 337–40, 346.
11. Julius Grodinsky, *Transcontinental Railway Strategy, 1869–1893: A Study of Businessmen* (Philadelphia: University of Pennsylvania Press, 1962), 70–71.
12. For a full description of the Central Pacific, see Oscar Lewis, *The Big Four: The Story of Huntington, Stanford, Hopkins, and Crocker, and of the Building of the Central Pacific* (New York: Knopf, 1938).
13. Grodinsky, *Transcontinental Railway Strategy*, 137. For a fuller account of Villard's career, see James B. Hedges, *Henry Villard and the Railways of the Northwest* (New Haven, Conn.: Yale University Press, 1930).
14. White, *Railroaded*, 1.
15. Hedges, *Villard*, 112–211; Grodinsky, *Transcontinental Railway Strategy*, 140, 185.
16. Mildred H. Comfort, *James Jerome Hill, Railroad Pioneer* (Minneapolis: T. S. Denison, 1973), 64–65.
17. Grodinsky, *Transcontinental Railway Strategy*, 137.
18. Albro Martin, *James J. Hill and the Opening of the Northwest* (New York: Oxford University Press, 1976), 16–45; Stewart Holbrook, *James J. Hill: A Great Life in Brief* (New York: Knopf, 1955), 9–23.
19. Stover, *American Railroads*, 76; Holbrook, *Hill*, 13–42.
20. Martin, *Hill*, 122–40, 161–71, passim; Holbrook, *Hill*, 44, 54–68.
21. Martin, *Hill*, 183; Robert Sobel, *The Entrepreneurs: Explorations Within the American Business Tradition* (New York: Weybright & Talley, 1974), 140; Howard L. Dickman, "James Jerome Hill and the Agricultural Development of the Northwest" (Ph.D. diss., University of Michigan, 1977), 67–144.
22. Holbrook, *Hill*, 93; Martin, *Hill*, 366.
23. Martin, *Hill*, 381–83; Comfort, *Hill*, 67–70.
24. The source for this paragraph and the following five paragraphs can be found in Martin, *Hill*, 225, 233, 236, 239–43, 264–70, 298, 300, 307, 338, 346, 410–15, 442, 494.
25. Robert W. Fogel, *The Union Pacific Railroad* (Baltimore: Johns Hopkins University Press, 1960), 99–100.
26. Ibid., 25. Carl Degler has a variant of this viewpoint. He says, "In the West, where settlement was sparse, railroad building required government assistance." Later, he adds, "By the time the last of the four pioneer transcontinentals, James J. Hill's Great Northern, was constructed in the 1890s, private capital was able and ready to do the job unassisted by government." This argument suggests that the key variable is the timing of the building, not the subsidy itself. The main problem here is that Hill's transcontinental across the sparse Northwest, especially with the Canadian Pacific above him and the Northern Pacific below him, was just as risky as the Union Pacific was. That's why it was called "Hill's Folly." Also, Hill was building at roughly the same time as the Northern Pacific; but Hill succeeded, while the Northern Pacific failed. Finally, we need to remember that, in 1893, Hill flourished, while the Union Pacific, the Northern Pacific,

and the Santa Fe all went into receivership. This brings us back to the subsidy as the problem, not the timing of the gift. See Carl Degler, *The Age of the Economic Revolution, 1876–1900* (Glenview, Ill.: Scott, Foresman, 1977), 19–20.

27. For a development of much of this argument, see Albro Martin, *Enterprise Denied: Origins of the Decline of American Railroads, 1897–1917* (New York: Columbia University Press, 1971). See also Martin, *Hill*, 535–44.

28. Fogel, *Union Pacific Railroad*, 41.

29. Holbrook, *Hill*, 161–63; Sobel, *Entrepreneurs*, 138; James J. Hill, *Highways of Progress* (New York: Doubleday, Page, 1910), 156–69.

30. Holbrook, *Hill*, 162–63.

31. Ibid., 161; Sobel, *Entrepreneurs*, 135; Martin, *Hill*, 464–65. By the early 1900s, the UP began to compete seriously with the Great Northern. Toward the end of the Gilded Age, daring entrepreneurs bought the Union Pacific and paid off its federal debts. The UP, fully privatized, became one of the nation's major railroads.

32. Martin, *Hill*, 298–99, 307, 347, 442, 462.

33. Hill, *Highways of Progress*, 156–184; Holbrook, *Hill*, 163; Martin, *Hill*, 540; Ari Arthur Hoogenboom and Olive Hoogenboom, *A History of the ICC: From Panacea to Palliative* (New York: Norton, 1976), 49–59.

CHAPTER 5: HERBERT DOW CHANGED THE WORLD

1. Bureau of the Census, *Historical Statistics of the United States: Colonial Times to 1970* (Washington, D.C.: U.S. Bureau of the Census, 1975), II, 1104. See also Allan Nevins, *Grover Cleveland: A Study in Courage* (New York: Dodd, Mead, 1932); and John Pafford, *The Forgotten Conservative: Rediscovering Grover Cleveland* (Washington, D.C.: Regnery, 2013).

2. Ralph W. Hidy and Muriel E. Hidy, *Pioneering in Big Business, 1882–1911* (New York: Harper, 1995), 130–54; Harold Livesay, *Andrew Carnegie* (Boston: Little, Brown, 1975).

3. Burton W. Folsom Jr., *The Myth of the Robber Barons* (Herndon, Va.: Young America's Foundation, 2010), 83–100.

4. Herbert Dow briefly describes his father's influence in a letter he wrote in 1928, in the Post Street Archives (hereafter PSA), Midland, Michigan, doc. #87001. Burt has benefited from many conversations at the Post Street Archives with Ned Brandt, the company historian of Dow Chemical Company. A good secondary account is Don Whitehead, *The Dow Story: The History of the Dow Chemical Company* (New York: McGraw-Hill, 1968), 19.

5. Whitehead, *The Dow Story*, 20. For an overview of the chemical industry, see Alfred D. Chandler Jr., *Shaping the Industrial Century: The Remarkable Story of the Evolution of the Modern Chemical and Pharmaceutical Industries* (Cambridge, Mass.: Harvard University Press, 2005).

6. Murray Campbell and Harrison Hatton, *Herbert H. Dow: Pioneer in Creative Chemistry* (New York: Appleton-Century-Crofts, 1951), 3.

7. Whitehead, *The Dow Story*, 21.

8. Ibid., 24; Campbell and Hatton, *Herbert Dow*, 15–19.

9. Campbell and Hatton, *Herbert Dow*, 28.

10. Whitehead, *The Dow Story*, 29.
11. Ibid., 31–32.
12. Campbell and Hatton, *Herbert Dow*, 41–42.
13. Ibid., 31–36.
14. For good summaries of the bleach war, see ibid., 55–60; and Whitehead, *The Dow Story*, 40, 53–54, 67. An excellent text is E. N. Brandt, *Growth Company: Dow Chemical's First Century* (East Lansing: Michigan State University Press, 1997), 20–21, 42–45.
15. Campbell and Hatton, *Herbert Dow*, 58.
16. Ibid., 60.
17. For helpful accounts of the bromine war, see Brandt, *Growth Company*, 42–48; Campbell and Hatton, *Herbert Dow*, 72–78; and Whitehead, *The Dow Story*, 55–56, 59–61, 66, 69, 71.
18. Herbert Dow, "The Dow Chemical Company's Experience with German Competitors," PSA, doc. #200047. See also Dow's description in an untitled paper, PSA, doc. #270065.
19. Dow's account of the Jacobsohn episode is in Dow, "The Dow Chemical Company's Experience with German Competitors," 1–3.
20. "German Yellow Dog Fund," from *American Economist*, February 4, 1921, PSA, doc. #210156.
21. Dow, "The Dow Chemical Company's Experience with German Competitors." See also "German Bromides," PSA, doc. #080017; and Whitehead, *The Dow Story*, 59–61.
22. Campbell and Hatton, *Herbert Dow*, 76.
23. Ibid., 75.
24. Ibid., 76.
25. Dow gives a full account of the price-cutting war in "Statement of Mr. Herbert H. Dow, of the Dow Chemical Company, Midland, Michigan," to the Federal Trade Commission, Detroit, July 22, 1915, 2–8. See also Whitehead, *The Dow Story*, 62.
26. Campbell and Hatton, *Herbert Dow*, 76–77; Brandt, *Growth Company*, 47.
27. Campbell and Hatton, *Herbert Dow*, 63–71; Whitehead, *The Dow Story*, 68.
28. Whitehead, *The Dow Story*, 58.
29. Ibid., 96.
30. Ibid., 76; Campbell and Hatton, *Herbert Dow*, 69.
31. Whitehead, *The Dow Story*, 20.
32. Two useful accounts of the dye business are Campbell and Hatton, *Herbert Dow*, 102–108; and Whitehead, *The Dow Story*, 81–82, 89.
33. Campbell and Hatton, *Herbert Dow*, 104.
34. Ibid. The textile producers also approached DuPont and other chemical companies with pleas for more experiments to make dyes.
35. Ibid., 106–107.
36. "Statement of Herbert Dow" to the Federal Trade Commission, 1.
37. Campbell and Hatton, *Herbert Dow*, 107–108.
38. Dow, "The Dow Chemical Company's Experience with German Competitors," 1.

39. The story of the iodine cartel is in Brandt, *Growth Company*, 152–53; and White-field, *The Dow Story*, 104–105, 131–33. Iodine had the potential to eliminate the knock in gasoline, but, with the success of ethylene dibromide, iodine was used primarily as a medicine.

CHAPTER 6: THE WRIGHT BROTHERS CONQUER THE AIR

1. Samuel P. Langley, "The 'Flying Machine,'" *McClure's Magazine* (June 1897), 658–60; Samuel P. Langley and Charles M. Manly, *Langley Memoir on Mechanical Flight* (Washington, D.C.: United States Government Printing Office, 1911), Part 1, 106–109; J. Gordon Vaeth, *Langley: Man of Science and Flight* (New York: Ronald Press, 1966), 45; and Robert V. Bruce, *Bell: Alexander Graham Bell and the Conquest of Solitude* (Boston: Little, Brown, 1973), 358–64.
2. Richard P. Hallion, *The Wright Brothers: Heirs of Prometheus* (Washington, D.C.: Smithsonian Institution Press, 1978), 8.
3. Cyrus Adler, *I Have Considered These Days* (Philadelphia: Jewish Publication Society of America, 1945), 188. Cyrus Adler was a museum expert, and Langley hired him from Johns Hopkins University to be chief librarian at the Smithsonian. Adler and Alexander Graham Bell were probably Langley's two best personal friends, and thus the almost sixty pages in Adler's book that he devotes to discussing Langley are very useful. For a comment on Adler and Bell and their close relationship to Langley, see Vaeth, *Langley*, 63.
4. Vaeth, *Langley*, 19–20, 23, 45, 60; Donald L. Obendorf, "Samuel P. Langley: Solar Scientist, 1867–1891" (Ph.D. diss., University of California, Berkeley, 1969), 223–31.
5. Adler, *I Have Considered These Days*, 184, 199; Obendorf, "Samuel P. Langley," 226–41.
6. Adler, *I Have Considered These Days*, 227; Obendorf, "Samuel P. Langley," 232, 236.
7. Russell J. Parkinson, "Politics, Patents and Planes: Military Aeronautics in the United States, 1863–1897" (Ph.D. diss., Duke University, 1963), 178–79.
8. James Tobin, *The Wright Brothers and the Great Race for Flight* (New York: Free Press, 2003), 28, 29. The Tobin book is a remarkable effort; we read it thoroughly and use it often.
9. Parkinson, "Politics, Patents and Planes," 105.
10. Ibid.; Tobin, *Wright Brothers*, 30.
11. Tobin, *Wright Brothers*, 30; Parkinson, "Politics, Patents and Planes," 180.
12. Adler, *I Have Considered These Days*, 183.
13. Parkinson, "Politics, Patents and Planes," 161, 166. The BOF was created in 1888 "to make all needful and proper purchases [of] . . . guns . . . and other implements and engines of war." The BOF became the go-to place for inventors and suppliers of military equipment for national defense. "The aim of the Board," it stated in an 1898 report, is "to keep in touch with the best inventive talent of the country in all that pertains to war material, to encourage the development of every suggestion and device of value presented, and to use the funds at its disposal to secure for our service the best products of American genius."
14. Tobin, *Wright Brothers*, 34.

15. Parkinson, "Politics, Patents and Planes," 159–64, 171; Tobin, *Wright Brothers*, 34. From 1896 to 1906, the BOF examined about one hundred proposals to build flying machines—men were trying to do it in many countries around the globe. The BOF rejected all the proposals except for Langley's, because only his, in their view, showed some kind of demonstrated promise of future success. Langley received his $50,000 subsidy in two installments—$25,000 immediately and the other $25,000 later.

16. Adler, *I Have Considered These Days*, 249–54; Langley and Manly, *Langley Memoir*, 133–74.

17. Fred C. Kelly, ed., *Miracle at Kitty Hawk: The Letters of Wilbur and Orville Wright* (Cambridge, Mass.: Da Capo Press, [1951], 2002), 15–16; Russell Freedman, *The Wright Brothers: How They Invented the Airplane* (New York: Holiday House, 1991), 17–20.

18. Tobin, *Wright Brothers*, 41; Tom Crouch, *The Bishop's Boys* (New York: Norton, 1989), 74–76.

19. Kelly, *Miracle at Kitty* Hawk, 212; Freedman, *Wright Brothers*, 2, 5; Tobin, *Wright Brothers*, 49.

20. Crouch, *Bishop's Boys*, 142–62; Freedman, *Wright Brothers*, 17–20.

21. Crouch, *Bishop's Boys*, 142–70; Tobin, *Wright Brothers*, 52.

22. Vaeth, *Langley*, 66–92; Langley and Manly, *Langley Memoir*, 126–32; Adler, *I Have Considered These Days*, 249–54; Tobin, *Wright Brothers*, 53.

23. Tobin, *Wright Brothers*, 58; Langley and Manly, *Langley Memoir*, 126–27.

24. Tobin, *Wright Brothers*, 67–77; Crouch, *Bishop's Boys*, 146–56, 229–32.

25. Adler, *I Have Considered These Days*, 249–63; Tobin, *Wright Brothers*, 165.

26. Tobin, *Wright Brothers*, 71, 73–74.

27. Freedman, *Wright Brothers*, 3; Tobin, *Wright Brothers*, 90.

28. Crouch, *Bishop's Boys*.

29. Ibid., 181–99; Kelly, *Miracle at Kitty Hawk*, 27.

30. Tobin, *Wright Brothers*, 145–46.

31. Ibid., 221–22.

32. Freedman, *Wright Brothers*, 40.

33. Tobin, *Wright Brothers*, 129–30; Crouch, *Bishop's Boys*, 229.

34. Tobin, *Wright Brothers*, 155; Crouch, *Bishop's Boys*, 229; Fred Howard, *Wilbur and Orville* (New York: Knopf, 1987), 76.

35. Tobin, *Wright Brothers*, 154.

36. Langley and Manly, *Langley Memoir*, 126; Vaeth, *Langley*, 69–74.

37. Tobin, *Wright Brothers*, 38, 77–79; Vaeth, *Langley*, 72–76.

38. Tobin, *Wright Brothers*, 142.

39. Langley and Manly, *Langley Memoir*, 261.

40. Tobin, *Wright Brothers*, 173.

41. Langley and Manly, *Langley Memoir*, 265–66.

42. *Washington Post*, October 8, 1903, 8, and October 9, 1903, 2. See also *Washington Star*, October 8, 1903, 4.

43. Langley and Manly, *Langley Memoir*, 271.

44. Ibid., 272–73; Adler, *I Have Considered These Days*, 257. For critical newspaper accounts, see *Washington Post*, December 9, 1903, 2, and December 10, 1903, 6;

Philadelphia Inquirer, December 9, 1903, 1; *Washington Star,* December 9, 1903, 4; *Chicago Tribune,* December 10, 1903, 6.

45. *Boston Herald,* December 10, 1903, 6; *New York Times,* October 9, 1903, 6.
46. "Failure of Langley's Aeroplane," *San Francisco Chronicle,* December 10, 1903, 6.
47. Howard, *Wilbur and Orville,* 106–107; Tobin, *Wright Brothers,* 158–59.
48. Tobin, *Wright Brothers,* 160.
49. Kelly, *Miracle at Kitty Hawk,* 104.
50. Tobin, *Wright Brothers,* 190.
51. Freedman, *Wright Brothers,* 74, 76; Crouch, *Bishop's Boys,* 267–70.
52. Tobin, *Wright Brothers,* 201.
53. Langley and Manly, *Langley Memoir,* 282; Bruce, *Bell,* 436; Tobin, *Wright Brothers,* 198.
54. Tobin, *Wright Brothers,* 200, 231.
55. Ibid., 202.
56. Ibid., 215–218, 234–5; Crouch, *Bishop's Boys,* 285, 297, 443.
57. Crouch, *Bishop's Boys,* 293; Langley and Manly, *Langley Memoir,* 279; Vaeth, *Langley,* 95–96.
58. Tobin, *Wright Brothers,* 261.
59. Parkinson, "Politics, Patents and Planes," 210–11.
60. After the Langley fiasco, some in the War Department renounced flying machines completely and considered balloons as the weapon of the future. Balloons had been tested for aerial reconnaissance in 1898 during the Spanish-American War, and had failed. Spanish soldiers shot thirteen holes in one of the balloons, grounded it, and in doing so exposed the American battlefield position. In May 1906, however, after the Wright brothers' rejection, the War Department's Signal Corps bought a ninth balloon for its military arsenal from France for $1,425—an amount almost as large as the entire expense the Wright brothers incurred from start to finish during the four years they spent inventing the airplane. Parkinson, "Politics, Patents and Planes," 142, 148, 210–22, 254–56.
61. Tobin, *Wright Brothers,* 301–306.
62. Ibid., 307–308.
63. Ibid., 314–16.
64. Ibid., 273, 361.
65. Seth Shulman, *Unlocking the Sky: Glenn Hammond Curtiss and the Race to Invent the Airplane* (New York: HarperCollins, 2002), 71–72.
66. Tobin, *Wright Brothers,* 330. Charles Lindbergh, with his New York to Paris flight in 1927, won the Orteig Prize and became the greatest prize winner of them all. See A. Scott Berg, *Lindbergh* (New York: G. P. Putnam's Sons, 1998), 102–31; Joe Jackson, *Atlantic Fever: Lindbergh, His Competitors, and the Race to Cross the Atlantic* (New York: Farrar, Straus & Giroux, 2012), 216, 227–316; and Charles A. Lindbergh, *The Spirit of St. Louis* (New York: Charles Scribner's Sons, 1953), 134–492.

CHAPTER 7: THE D.C. SUBSIDY MACHINE

1. A useful introduction to the RFC is James S. Olson, *Herbert Hoover and the Reconstruction Finance Corporation* (Ames: Iowa State University Press, 1977).

2. Vern McKinley, *Financing Failure: A Century of Bailouts* (Oakland, Calif.: Independent Institute, 2011), 52–53.

3. Burton Folsom Jr., *New Deal or Raw Deal?* (New York: Simon & Schuster, 2008); Douglas Irwin, *Peddling Protectionism: Smoot-Hawley and the Great Depression* (Princeton, N.J.: Princeton University Press, 2011).

4. Bureau of the Census, *Historical Statistics of the United States: Colonial Times to 1970* (Washington, D.C.: United States Government Printing Office, 1975), I, 135; II, 1095, 1104–1106, 1117. See also Allis Radosh and Ronald Radosh, "Time for Another Harding?," *Weekly Standard*, October 24, 2011.

5. *New York Times*, December 9, 1931, 1, 21; McKinley, *Financing Failure*, 51.

6. Bascom N. Timmons, *Portrait of an American: Charles G. Dawes* (New York: Henry Holt, 1953), 313.

7. James S. Olson, *Saving Capitalism: The Reconstruction Finance Corporation and the New Deal, 1933–1940* (Princeton, N.J.: Princeton University Press, 1988), 43.

8. Charles W. Calomiris and Joseph R. Mason, "How to Restructure Failed Banking Systems: Lessons from the U.S. in the 1930s and Japan in the 1990s," National Bureau of Economic Research, Working Paper No. 9624 (April 2003).

9. Joseph R. Mason and Daniel A. Schiffman, "Too Big to Fail, Government Bailouts, and Managerial Incentives: The Case of the Reconstruction Finance Corporation Assistance to the Railroad Industry during the Great Depression," in Benton E. Gup, *Too Big to Fail* (Westport, Conn.: Praeger, 2004), 61.

10. Murray Rothbard, *America's Great Depression* (New York: Richardson & Snyder, 1972), 262–63.

11. Ibid., 262–64.

12. Olson, *Herbert* Hoover, 52–54, 58–60; Rothbard, *Great Depression*, 158, 262–63; Timmons, *Charles G. Dawes*, 319–24; Jesse Jones, *Fifty Billion Dollars: My Thirteen Years with the RFC, 1932–1945* (New York: Macmillan, 1945), 265–66, 295–97.

13. Walter Trohan, *Political Animals* (Garden City, N.Y.: Doubleday, 1975), 75.

14. Jones, *Fifty Billion Dollars*, 315–484.

15. Randall B. Woods, *Fulbright: A Biography* (Cambridge: Cambridge University Press, 1995), 154–63; Robert J. Donovan, *Tumultuous Years: The Presidency of Harry S Truman, 1949–1953* (New York: Norton, 1983), 332–39; Jules Abels, *Truman Scandals* (Chicago: Regnery, 1956), 70–122.

16. *New York Daily Mirror*, March 3, 1951, 4; *Baltimore Sun*, February 3, 1951, 11; Andrew J. Dunar, *The Truman Scandals and the Politics of Morality* (Columbia: University of Missouri Press, 1985), 88; Thomas T. Fetters, *The Lustron Home: A History of a Postwar Prefabricated Housing Experiment* (Jefferson, N.C.: McFarland, 2002), 110–13.

17. *Boston Herald*, July 21, 1950, 1; *Boston Daily Globe*, July 21, 1950, 1, 9.

18. *Los Angeles Times*, March 15, 1951. The *Washington Post* quotation is in the *Los Angeles Times* article.

19. Abels, *Truman Scandals*, 64–68, 110–18.

20. *St. Louis Post-Dispatch*, March 10, 1951, 4A; Dunar, *Truman Scandals*, 89, 181.

21. *Wall Street Journal*, February 6, 1951, 8; *New York Times*, May 1, 1951, 22.

22. *New York Times*, May 1, 1951, 22; *Los Angeles Times*, March 15, 1951, 4; *Boston Herald*, July 20, 1950, 24; *Wall Street Journal*, February 6, 1951, 8.

23. *New York Times*, March 28, 1951, 22.
24. *Chicago Sun-Times*, March 30, 1951, 22.
25. *New York Daily Mirror*, March 7, 1951, 22; *Philadelphia Inquirer*, March 23, 1951, 14.
26. Jonathan J. Bean, *Beyond the Broker State: Federal Policies Toward Small Business, 1936–1961* (Chapel Hill: University of North Carolina Press, 1996), 136–37; McKinley, *Financing Failure*, 62–63.
27. Bean, *Beyond the Broker State*, 158.
28. Ibid., 147.
29. Ibid., 139, 162–63.
30. Vern McKinley, *Financing Failure*, 62. Also helpful is Olson, *Herbert Hoover*, 62–75.
31. Edward A. Williams, *Federal Aid for Relief* (New York: AMS Press, 1968), 48–52.
32. Ibid., 48, 56. For a more detailed description of the effects of federal relief, see Folsom, *New Deal or Raw Deal?*, 80–83.
33. Williams, *Federal Aid for Relief*, 58–86; Josephine C. Brown, *Public Relief, 1929–1939* (New York: Octagon, [1940], 1971), 145–298. A helpful study of the origins of welfare is Theda Skocpol, *Protecting Soldiers and Mothers: The Political Origins of Social Policy in the United States* (Cambridge, Mass.: Harvard University Press, 1992).
34. Joseph B. Ely, *The American Dream* (Boston: Bruce Humphries, 1944), 148; Williams, *Federal Aid for Relief*, 177, 217.
35. William H. Becker and William M. McClenahan Jr., *The Market, the State, and the Export-Import Bank of the United States, 1934–2000* (Cambridge: Cambridge University Press, 2003).
36. Frederick C. Adams, *Economic Diplomacy: The Export-Import Bank and American Foreign Policy, 1934–1939* (Columbia: University of Missouri Press, 1976), 136–39; Irwin, *Peddling Protectionism*.
37. Adams, *Export-Import Bank*, 136–39, 209–11.
38. Ibid., 198–204; Dana G. Munro, *The United States and the Caribbean Republics, 1921–1933* (Princeton, N.J.: Princeton University Press, 1974).
39. Adams, *Export-Import Bank*, 201.
40. Henry Morgenthau Diary, May 9, 1939, Franklin Roosevelt Presidential Library. For a copy of Morgenthau's entry on May 9, 1939, see "Morgenthau Quote" at BurtFolsom.com.
41. David Lawrence, *Who Were the Eleven Million?* (New York: Appleton-Century, 1937).
42. James Patterson, *The New Deal and the States* (Princeton, N.J.: Princeton University Press, 1969), 82–83; Lyle W. Dorsett, *Franklin D. Roosevelt and the City Bosses* (Port Washington, N.Y.: Kennikat Press, 1977), 102, 104.
43. Adams, *Export-Import Bank*, 208–209.
44. Becker and McClenahan, *Export-Import Bank*, 169.
45. Timothy P. Carney, *The Big Ripoff* (Hoboken, N.J.: John Wiley, 2006), 75–77.
46. Carney, *Big Ripoff*, 78–79; Timothy P. Carney, "Boeing and Obama Sitting in a Tree, K-I-S-S-I-N-G," *Washington Examiner*, November 30, 2012.

47. Timothy P. Carney, "Boeing Lives by Big Government, Dies by Big Government," *Washington Examiner*, March 19, 2012.
48. Carney, *Big Ripoff*, 79.
49. Ibid., 89–90.
50. Robert J. Serling, *Legend and Legacy: The Story of Boeing and Its People* (New York: St. Martin's Press, 1991), 2–7.
51. Ibid., 10–12, 16, 24–25, 31; Harold Mansfield, *Vision: A Saga of the Sky* (New York: Madison, 1986), 22–78; John B. Rae, *Climb to Greatness: The American Aircraft Industry, 1920–1960* (Cambridge, Mass.: MIT Press, 1968), 52–57.
52. Eugene Rodgers, *Flying High: The Story of Boeing and the Rise of the Jetliner Industry* (New York: Atlantic Monthly Press, 1996), 51–71, 146–206; Serling, *Legacy*, 25–26, 29–37, 50–69, 85–92.
53. Rodgers, *Flying High*, 146–206; Serling, *Legacy*, 85–92; Jim Cramer interview with Jim McNerney, June 26, 2013.

CHAPTER 8: UNCLE SAM INVENTS THE ENERGY CRISIS

1. Two excellent introductions to energy in general and the oil industry in particular are Daniel Yergin, *The Prize* (New York: Simon & Schuster, 1991); and Robert L. Bradley Jr., *Oil, Gas, and Government* (Lanham, Md.: Rowman & Littlefield, 1995). The Scranton story is in Burton W. Folsom Jr., *Urban Capitalists* (Baltimore: Johns Hopkins University Press, 1981).
2. Ralph W. Hidy and Muriel E. Hidy, *Pioneering in Big Business, 1882–1911* (New York: Harper, 1955); Ron Chernow, *Titan: The Life of John D. Rockefeller, Sr.* (New York: Random House, 1998). The best biography of Rockefeller is still Allan Nevins, *Study in Power: John D. Rockefeller*, 2 vols. (New York: Charles Scribner's Sons, 1953).
3. Richard H. K. Vietor, *Energy Policy in America Since 1945* (Cambridge: Cambridge University Press, 1984), 4–12, 22–23; E. Anthony Copp, *Regulating Competition in Oil: Government Intervention in the U.S. Refining Industry, 1948–1975* (College Station: Texas A&M University Press, 1976).
4. Harold F. Williamson and Arnold R. Daum, *The American Petroleum Industry: The Age of Illumination, 1859–1899* (Evanston, Ill.: Northwestern University Press, 1959), 82–194.
5. Nevins, *Rockefeller*, I, 666.
6. Yergin, *The Prize*, 541, 544, 568.
7. Allen J. Matusow, *Nixon's Economy* (Lawrence: University Press of Kansas, 1998), 244. For the spike in crude oil prices from $3.89 per barrel in 1973 to $31.77 in 1981, see www.eia.gov/dnav/pet/hist/LeafHandler.ashx?n=PET&s=F000000 3&f=A.
8. Matusow, *Nixon's Economy*, 245.
9. Ibid., 247.
10. Ibid., 249–50.
11. Vietor, *Energy Policy*, 64–90, 146–62; Copp, *Regulating Competition*, 159–62; Matusow, *Nixon's Economy*, 242–43.

12. John Robert Greene, *Gerald R. Ford* (Lawrence: University Press of Kansas, 1995), 71–81; Burton I. Kaufman, *James Earl Carter, Jr.* (Lawrence: University Press of Kansas, 1993), 32–33, 67, 137–38, 169–70, 177.

13. *New York Times*, April 19, 1977, and July 16, 1979. The Carter speech, given on April 18, 1977, was a major televised address, and is readily available online.

14. *New York Times*, April 19, 1977; Kaufman, *Carter*, 138; Arthur B. Laffer, Stephen Moore, and Peter Tanous, *The End of Prosperity* (New York: Simon & Schuster, 2008), 73–79.

15. Laffer, Moore, and Tanous, *End of Prosperity*, 82, 112.

16. Ibid., 78.

17. Ibid., 79. On Reagan's success, Brian Domitrovic stresses Reagan's actions with tax rate cuts and with the Fed as well as his lifting of price controls on energy. See Domitrovic, "Want Gasoline Prices to Decline? Do as Reagan Did," *Forbes .com*, April 10, 2012.

18. The televised Carter speech of July 15, 1979, is in *New York Times*, July 16, 1979.

19. Burton W. Folsom Jr., *The Myth of the Robber Barons* (Herndon, Va.: Young America's Foundation, 2010), 83–100; Williamson and Daum, *American Petroleum Industry*.

20. Bill Kovarik, "Henry Ford, Charles Kettering and the Fuel of the Future," *Automotive History Review* (Spring 1998): 7–27; James Day, "Ethanol: Indictment for Violation of the Laws of Physics and Economics," *Business Law Brief* (Spring 2009): 22–25.

21. James Bovard, "Archer Daniels Midland: A Case Study in Corporate Welfare," Cato Institute Policy Analysis, September 16, 1995.

22. Timothy P. Carney, *The Big Ripoff* (Hoboken, N.J.: John Wiley, 2006), 224–41.

23. E. J. Kahn Jr., *Supermarketer to the World: The Story of Dwayne Andreas* (New York: Time Warner, 1991), 71–78.

24. Ibid.; Carney, *Big Ripoff*, 223–24.

25. Kahn, *Supermarketer to the World*, 38–39, 106.

26. Carney, *Big Ripoff*, 223–24.

27. Bovard, "Archer Daniels Midland," 7.

28. Carney, *Big Ripoff*, 228–29.

29. Bovard, "Archer Daniels Midland," 8.

30. Carney, *Big Ripoff*, 228, 240.

31. Bovard, "Archer Daniels Midland," 4.

32. Ibid., 9.

33. Information on Poet is available online. See "What is POET?," www.poet.com /inspiration/index.asp. We have benefited from discussions on the renewable mandates and on Poet with reporter Timothy Carney of the *Washington Examiner*.

34. President Bush's 2007 State of the Union address was delivered on January 23, 2007, and is available at WashingtonPost.com.

CHAPTER 9: UNCLE SAM HEALS THE PLANET

1. *New York Times*, June 5, 2008, and January 21, 2009.

2. Al Gore's documentary on global warming is *An Inconvenient Truth*: http://www .takepart.com/an-inconvenient-truth/film.

3. Timothy P. Carney, *Obamanomics* (Washington, D.C.: Regnery, 2009), 108.
4. Ibid., 113.
5. Bjorn Lomborg, "The Climate-Industrial Complex," *Wall Street Journal*, May 22, 2009.
6. E. G. Austin, "Political Realities: The End of Ethanol Subsidies," *Economist*, January 2, 2012.
7. Nicolas Loris, "Coburn Moves to Eliminate Ethanol Subsidies," *Foundry*, April 5, 2011; Darren Goode and Robin Bravender, "Senators: Ethanol Deal Possible," *Politico*, July 6, 2011; "Dr. Coburn's Statement on Ethanol Vote," press release, www.coburn.senate.gov/public/index.cfm/2011/6/dr-coburn-s-statement-on -ethanol-vote.
8. Laura Litvan, "Bid to Repeal Ethanol Mandate Seen Diluted by EPA Change," Bloomberg, August 8, 2013; Kathie Obradovich, "Pawlenty's Straight Talk Not a Huge Risk," *Des Moines Register*, May 23, 2011; Austin, "Political Realities."
9. Scott Faber and Alex Rindler, "Reform the Ethanol Mandate," *Politico*, July 29, 2013; "Perverse Effects," *Wall Street Journal*, August 20, 2013. The quotation in the text is the wording of the *Wall Street Journal*.
10. For an introduction to fracking, see www.what-is-fracking.com.
11. Russell Gold, "The Man Who Pioneered the Shale-Gas Revolution," *Wall Street Journal*, October 23, 2012, www.online.wsj.com/article/SB10001422405297020 363060457807506368097342.html.
12. Ibid.; Christopher Helman, "Father of the Fracking Boom Dies—George Mitchell Urged Greater Regulation of Drilling," Forbes.com, July 27, 2013. See also Michael Shellenberger and Ted Nordhaus, "A Boom in Shale Gas? Credit the Feds," *Washington Post*, December 16, 2011. The Gas Research Institute was later absorbed into the Gas Technology Institute.
13. An excellent documentary is Phelim McAleer and Ann McElhinney, *FrackNation*. For a critique of fracking, see Walter M. Brasch, *Fracking Pennsylvania* (Carmichael, Calif.: Greeley & Stone, 2013).
14. Helman, "George Mitchell"; Katie Tubb, "Thank You, George Mitchell, for Fracking," *Foundry*, July 31, 2013.
15. Jennifer Steinhauer, "Democrats Joining G.O.P. on Pipeline," *New York Times*, April 19, 2012; Juliet Eilperin, "Is Keystone Pipeline Losing Democratic Support?," *Washington Post*, May 24, 2013; Joseph Weber, "Obama Comments on Keystone Spark Ire, More Concern about Project's Future," Fox News, July 29, 2013, www.foxnews.com/politics/2013/07/29/obama-comments-on-keystone -sparks-ire-more-concern-about-project's-future.
16. C. J. Ciaramella, "Bankrupt Solar Company with Fed Backing Has Cozy Ties to Obama Admin," *Daily Caller*, September 1, 2011.
17. Ibid.; Matthew Daly, "George Kaiser, Obama Donor, Discussed Solyndra Loan with White House, Emails Show," *Huffington Post*, November 9, 2011.
18. Ciaramella, "Bankrupt Solar Company."
19. Carol D. Leonnig and Joe Stephens, "White House Got Heads Up on Solyndra's Pending Layoff Announcements," *Washington Post*, January 13, 2012.
20. Carol D. Leonnig, "Obama-Backed Car Battery Company Files for Bankruptcy Protection," *Washington Post*, January 26, 2012; Leonnig, "Battery Firm Backed

by Federal Stimulus Money Files for Bankruptcy," *Washington Post*, October 17, 2012.
21. Timothy Carney, "Lobbying Blitz to Save Tax Credits for Wind Energy," *Washington Examiner*, December 28, 2012.
22. Carney, *Obamanomics*, 193–215.
23. Timothy P. Carney, "Green Stimulus Profiteer Comes under IRS Scrutiny," *Washington Examiner*, October 12, 2012; "Inspirations with Elon Musk," at www.oninnovation.com/videos/detail.aspx?video=1259&title=Inspirations; Todd Halvorson, "Elon Musk Unveiled," at www.spacex.com/media.php?page=36.
24. Carney, "Green Stimulus Profiteer."
25. Timothy P. Carney, "Sen. Max Baucus, Master of Revolving Door, Heads for the Exit," *Washington Examiner*, April 24, 2013.
26. Ibid.; Carney, "Max Baucus Rewards Ex-Staffers with Tax Breaks for Their Clients," *Washington Examiner*, January 4, 2013.
27. Carney, "Sen. Max Baucus"; Carney, "Max Baucus Rewards."
28. *Wall Street Journal*, "No Need to Panic About Global Warming," October 11, 2013.

CONCLUSION

1. Stephen E. Ambrose, *Nothing Like It in the World* (New York: Simon & Schuster, 2000), 23.
2. Walter Isaacson, *Steve Jobs* (New York: Simon & Schuster, 2011), 329.
3. *Los Angeles Times*, March 15, 1951.
4. We develop this argument in Larry Schweikart Jr. and Burton W. Folsom Jr., "Obama's False History of Public Investment," *Wall Street Journal*, August 6, 2013.
5. The president lamented in 2011, "So how can we now sit back and let China build the best railroads? And let Europe build the best highways? And have Singapore build a nicer airport?" President Obama's assumption is that industries will step in once government-initiated infrastructure is in place. There is no historical example that we know of where the sequence worked like that.
6. Burton Folsom Jr. and Anita Folsom, *FDR Goes to War* (New York: Simon & Schuster, 2011), 146–53.
7. Jonah Goldberg, "The Goldberg File," October 17, 2013.

Index

About the Authors

BURTON W. FOLSOM JR. is the Charles Kline Professor of History and Management at Hillsdale College, and the author of *New Deal or Raw Deal?*, *The Myth of the Robber Barons*, and *FDR Goes to War*, written with his wife, Anita. He has written for the *Wall Street Journal*, *American Spectator*, *National Review*, and *Human Events*. He writes for his blog at BurtFolsom.com.

ANITA FOLSOM is the director of the annual Free Market Forum at Hillsdale College. She pursued a career in both politics and the teaching of history. She is coauthor of *FDR Goes to War* with her husband, Burton, and she has also written for the *Wall Street Journal*, *American Spectator*, *Human Events Online*, and the *Detroit News*. She has appeared on television interviews with Neil Cavuto, Glenn Beck, and also ReasonTV. She and her husband have been featured on BookTV.